MW01620878

Neo Rauch

LUND HUMPHRIES | CONTEMPORARY PAINTERS

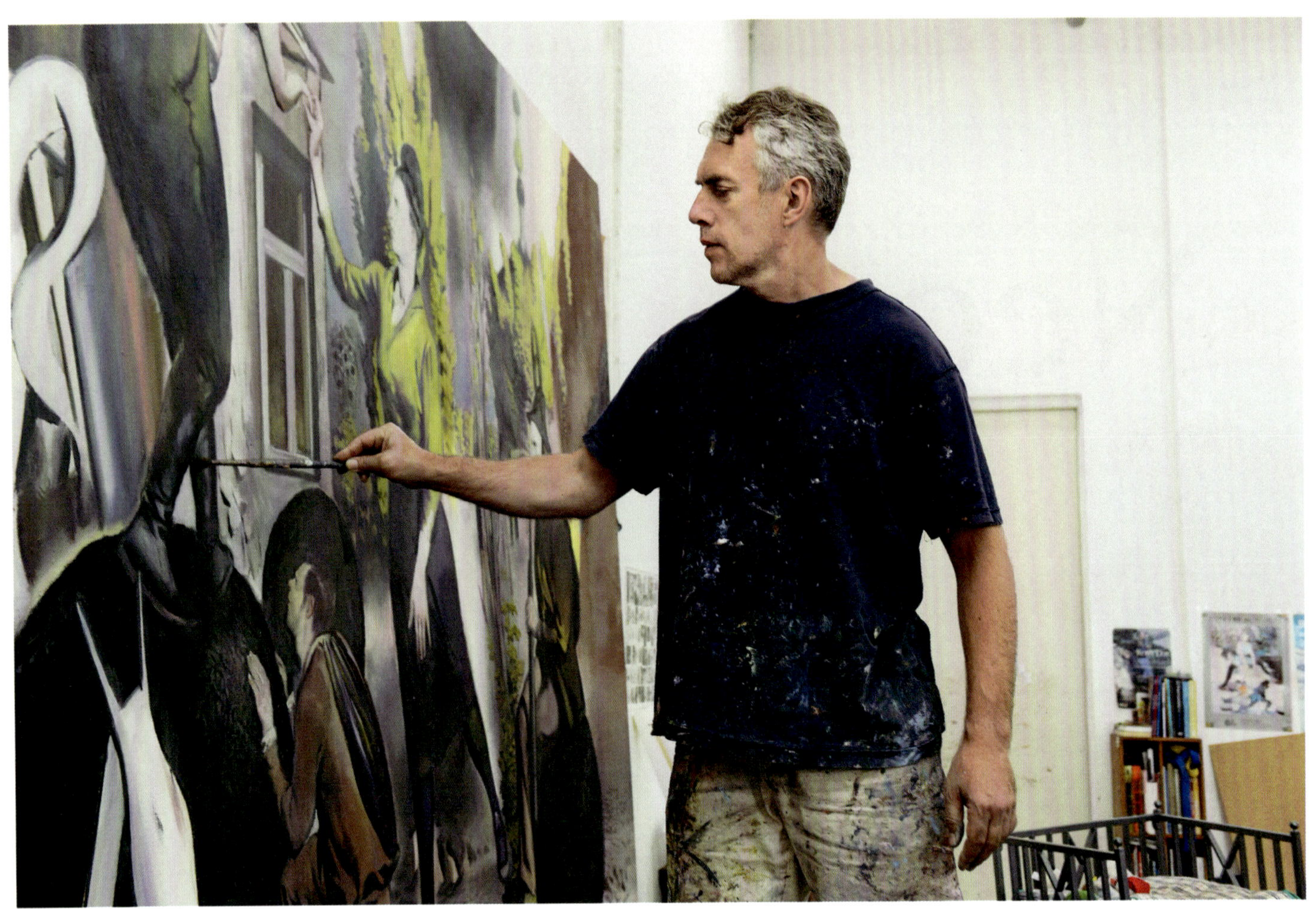

Michael Glover

Neo Rauch

LUND HUMPHRIES | CONTEMPORARY PAINTERS

Contemporary Painters Series
Series Editor: Barry Schwabsky

The Contemporary Painters Series is a new, curated series of accessible, authoritative and highly illustrated monographs on the world's leading living painters, which locates painting as a vibrant and vital part of contemporary art.

The series is edited by American art critic Barry Schwabsky, supported by an international advisory board with a specialist interest in contemporary painting. It aims to redefine 'painting' in the contemporary context as work which is done within the conventions and history of painting, but which may incorporate other materials or techniques.

Also available in the series:
Etel Adnan by Kaelen Wilson-Goldie
Lois Dodd by Faye Hirsch
Philip Taaffe by John Yau
Thomas Nozkowski by John Yau
Verne Dawson by John Hutchinson

Contents

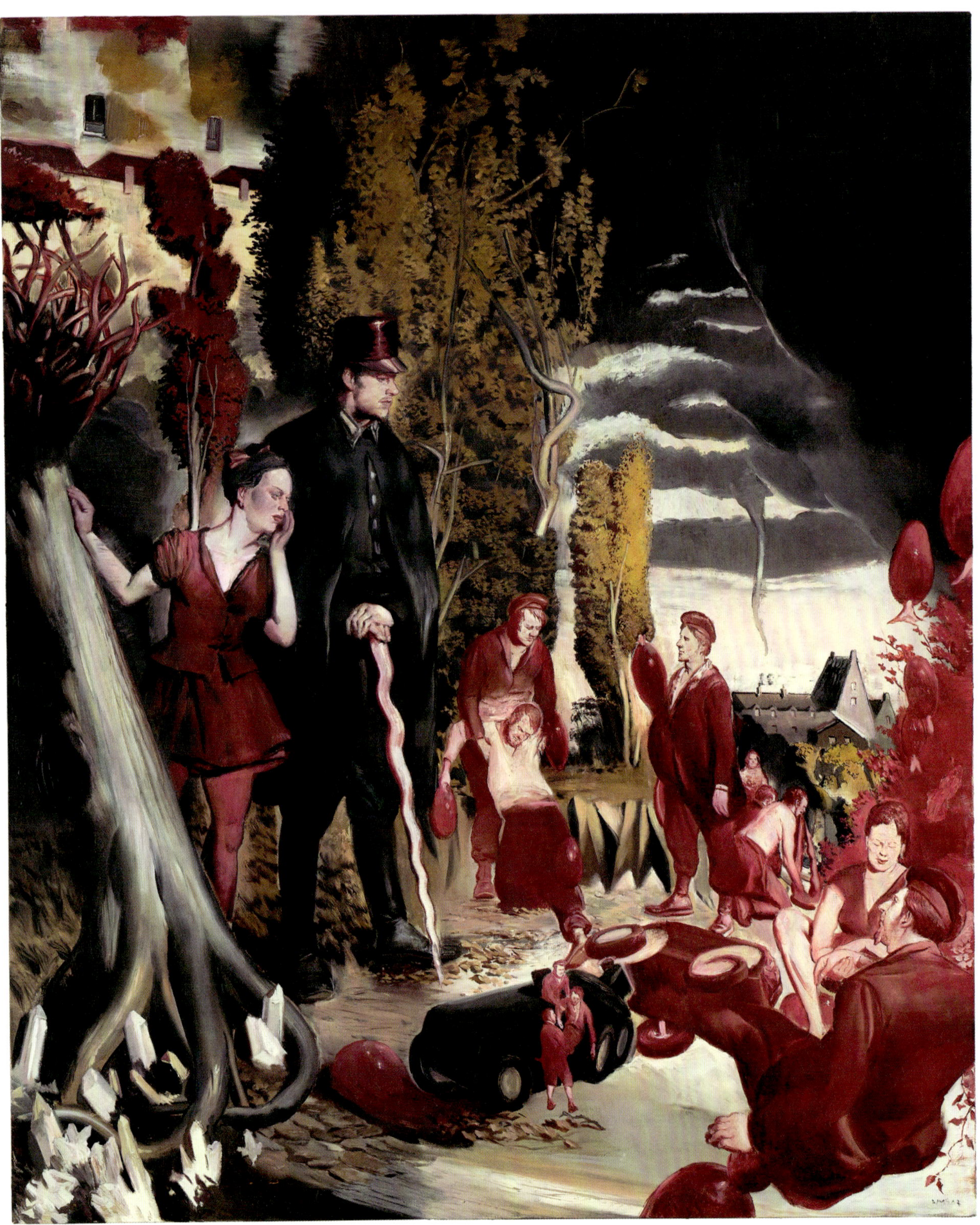

1. Blutsbrüder 2017

Oil on canvas
300 × 250 cm (118¼ × 98½ in)
Collection of Michael Wilkinson, New Orleans

Foreword

Among the consequences of the fall of the German Democratic Republic (GDR) and the reunification of Germany as a member of the Western coalition, one of the least expected was the emergence of an unfamiliar approach to painting. At first, the so-called New Leipzig school was viewed suspiciously: Hadn't East Germany hobbled its artistic culture by isolating itself from the consequential developments of the postwar years, and even from the prewar advent of Abstraction? Weren't these young painters, who had been trained under the old regime – not simply as producers of Socialist Realist propaganda, as many Westerners seemed to think, but nonetheless according to the canons of traditional figuration – merely serving up a rehash of outmoded styles?

Perhaps some of them were mere *pasticheurs*, but time has a way of sifting the wheat from the chaff, and often it doesn't take long at all. Neo Rauch soon became recognised as not just a leading light among the new talents out of Leipzig's Hochschule für Grafik und Buchkunst – along with Tilo Baumgärtel, Christoph Ruckhäberle, and Rauch's wife, Rosa Loy, among others – but also as one of the most interesting and idiosyncratic painters working anywhere today: an artist who has managed to make something new out of seemingly outmoded elements.

In Rauch's work, everything that looks strange feels strangely familiar. That familiarity only makes it all the more uncanny. If this perplexing imagery carries conviction, maybe that's because to this painter it comes naturally. 'Painting is to me a second skin', Rauch once said, and 'everything I want to express has to come through this skin'. Moreover, as Michael Glover explains, Rauch's work remains rooted in its specific German and Saxon soil; as the artist himself put it, 'You have to stay close to where you came into the world, in order to draw on the energy that was around you when you were being born . . . Where you were born, that is where the telluric currents flow.'

All the more reason, then, for those of us who have been affected by Rauch's art without knowing much about the 'telluric currents' that surge through it to be grateful to Glover for mapping them out for us, and for showing us how Rauch's work helps us along in the art of interpreting it by constantly returning, as Glover says, 'to the subject of the painter and his task: what his role is to be; how he stands in relation to the works that he makes; how much he is at the behest of forces just beyond his control'. The painting itself begins the task of interpretation; however spontaneous or intuitive its making may be, it has a critical component. As Glover's fellow poet Barrett Watten has observed, 'Rauch dismantles social allegories that cannot be totalized or interpreted within a stable framework.' Rather than try to fit the artist's work into a single interpretive structure, Glover points out the many currents that animate it.

Barry Schwabsky

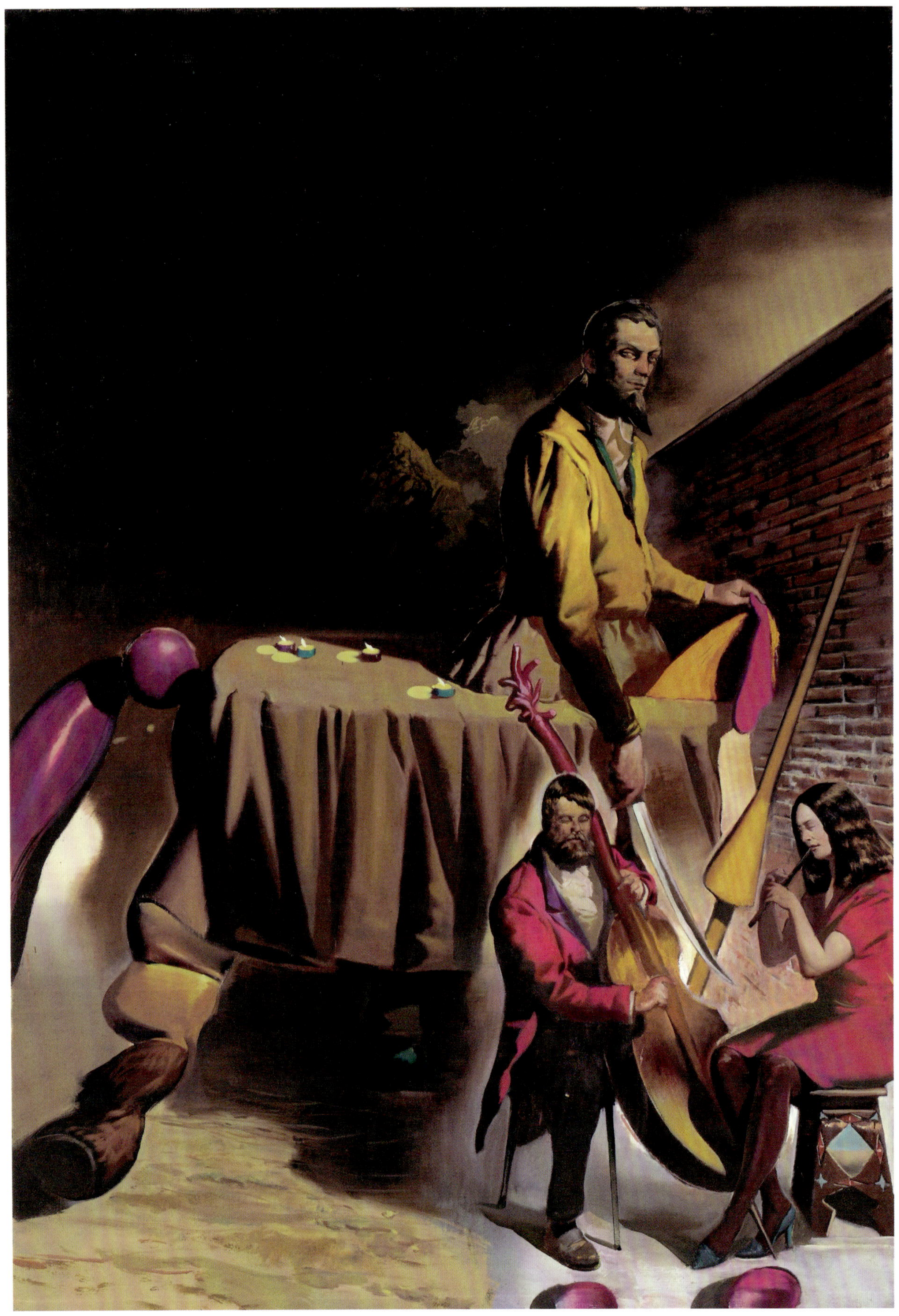

1 In the Studio

To be admitted to an artist's studio is a privilege, and one not to be proffered or accepted lightly. Neo Rauch admits few to his cave of making, his *sanctum sanctorum*, in the old cotton mill at Leipzig, a space that he has occupied for almost a quarter of a century. Nor does he speak too readily about his work, except in fairly general terms. In fact, he does not like interviews. This is understandable. He wishes to protect his sources, his image-bank, you might say. He does not want to talk himself out. His method of creating a painting is highly unusual. There are those who begin with the life model. There are others who do many, many preparatory drawings before setting paint to canvas – especially the kind of artist who needs to organise and then populate vast spaces, such as, say, Peter Paul Rubens. Where would Rubens have been without his oil sketches?

Neo Rauch's paintings, which are sometimes almost as large as a Rubens altarpiece, are also heavily populated sites of great commotion and complexity. His works are often crowded with activity – built structures coming into being; human forms in flight or fight; areas of strangely amorphous shapes, semi-abstract, as if self-generating. And all this is tightly orchestrated. But not beforehand. Never beforehand. There is almost no evidence – as would have been the case in the studio of Peter Paul Rubens – of anterior preparation with Neo Rauch. Nor are there studio assistants. These are paintings conceived and made by a single hand, products of his own deft wrist.

He attacks the blank canvas directly, with little preconception or preparation. A mental image, a sense of adventure and perhaps a few lines on a scrap of paper are all that are required. There is no underdrawing, and no serious preparatory drawing. He does not yet know what exactly is going to emerge. Only as he paints does it all become a little clearer to him what is coming into being. The canvas fills and fills, and then, at a certain point, the painting begins to possess the confidence to take over from him, and at that point he becomes a kind of choreographer, a theatre director, an administrator,[1] at the bidding of the painting itself. He lets go of it, having recognised that it has taken on a life of its own, that it is now in control of the situation, as he once explained to an interviewer. 'A painting is a living organism which grabs what it needs. From a certain moment of working on a painting, it will take over and paint itself through me.'[2] And that living organism is full of characters (or 'creatures', as he is also fondly inclined to call them) which, finally, dictate their own destinies to their creator. They can be a source of torment, on and off the canvas. They are capable of accosting him at nights. They keep him awake. They can be overbearing – especially if they have not yet found their final forms.

2. Reiter 2010

Oil on canvas
300 × 210 cm (118¼ × 82¾ in)
Collectie de Heus-Zomer

The canvas itself is a kind of field of energy. Its pulsing nodal points radiate excitement, directing or guiding the obedient hand. Rauch speaks of painting casting a spell. Of its triumphing over the horrors of the world, of its warding off – or perhaps balancing the polar opposites of – good and evil helping to bring the world itself into a balanced state – as if art were to be construed as a kind of sanctuary or haven. 'If you want to deliver yourself up to the art and can, then it can reconcile you even with the horrors of the world', he once said. Does not this sound more than a touch mystical – or even magical? Is this some god breathing through him? It sounds more than a little like it, which is itself a bit of a paradox because Neo Rauch would describe himself as an atheist, albeit one who is subject to pantheistic spasms.[3] Some indeterminate, god-like impulses may perhaps be at work somewhere then. He would perhaps acknowledge that possibility.

Rauch's paintings, he tells us, occasionally begin in dreams,[4] and if this is the case he is perhaps claiming a loose kind of kinship with classic Surrealism. And you can indeed see something of a Delvaux, a Magritte, a Buñuel, an Ernst, a Dalí or even a de Chirico in many of the works, fleetingly coming and going – how, for example, his characters can soften and bend and even wisp away puts you in mind of Dalí immediately. Consider, for example, the table legs and the double bass in *Reiter* (Rider, fig.2), that extraordinarily macabre and unsettling painting of 2010. The legs of the table appear to be walking; the upper half of the double bass is surely metamorphosing into a tree. The giddy, self-contradictory perspectives of de Chirico feel half-present in the way that Rauch often constructs contradictory perspectives within the formal constraints of a canvas – the strangely haunting emptiness of a doubled face by Magritte lurks somewhere in the shadows from time to time – or in the zestful, illogical impulses, those scene-by-scene clashes of plot line, to be found in Buñuel's film *Phantom of Liberty*.

In short, the works testify to a release of exuberant irrationality, but his practice as a painter also amounts to a kind of letting go into worlds which possess clear reference points of all kinds, from the art-historical to the historical and the theatrical. Who can deny the ghostly presence of Caspar David Friedrich, for example, in Neo Rauch's flights of romantic grandiosity: in that mood, so often evoked, of beings teetering on the brink? Or that of Giotto and Tintoretto in his fleeing, floating human forms? So the mix is rich and strange. All ages have melded into one. These are paintings of many periods and not quite any. They have an ancient modernity about them – or the freshness of renewed antiquity. They are palimpsests, consisting of strange layerings. And all this goes on in the everyday world of a studio with wooden filing cabinets; aluminium ladders; white walls; paint-bespattered floors; books by the dozen; a globe that spins; and, oh yes, a clock on a wall. From time to time, even Smylla the dog, a little pug, might wander in, and nudge at a food bowl pleadingly. In short, all necessary human and canine clutter is here.

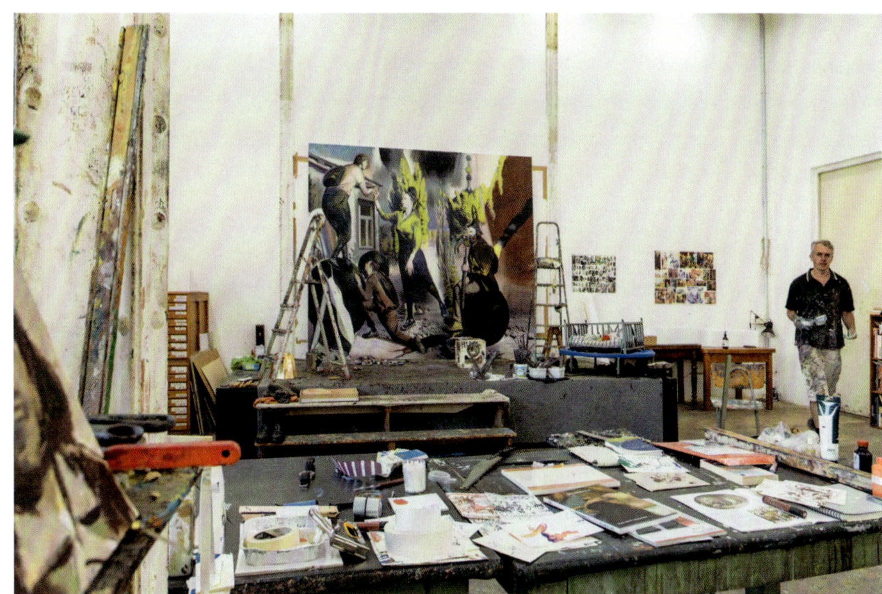

3. Neo Rauch in his studio.

Does the painter habitually walk into that studio invisible – as he did at the beginning of a recent documentary[5] – hidden behind the blank canvas that he himself is obliged to carry in through the door and then heave up into position above his long painter's dais? Faithful to day-to-day reality or not, that opening scene was a marvellously comic image of the self-sufficiency of the maker. There was no sign of any dutiful, scuttling assistant. And what, today, is to be done here exactly, the painter must then ask? In that documentary, he mutters something about making a fool of himself. Could that conceivably be the outcome then? There is always that risk because his paintings are acts of great personal hazarding, from first to last. How does he attack that blank surface? Let us watch him at work.

Neo Rauch himself, standing side on to the canvas in his enormous, monstrously clumsy-looking black gloves (how can a pair of clumsy black gloves be compatible with the fineness of what is slowly emerging?), clutches a multiplicity of brushes of varying thicknesses in his left hand as he applies the paint with his right. He is a lean-faced, taut, guarded, handsome, softly spoken man with greying sideburns who never rushes at a phrase, and never moves his face unnecessarily. He does not raise his voice. He does not gesticulate. He is not his own impresario. When he talks, he holds his face almost immobile as if he is more a listener to his own words than their speaker. He speaks cleverly, intricately, slowly, in considered bursts, but the words, when they come, are always an astute encirclement, carefully ruminated upon, even a form of scene-setting if you like – somewhat reminiscent of the way in which Francis Bacon responded to the relentlessly persistent questioning of David Sylvester.

You feel that Rauch does not want his pictures to be explicated until they are reduced to mere husks of themselves. Nor does he have much faith in the importance or the relevance of such explication. He believes that their impact should be an immediate one, and he wants the person untutored in art or art-historical matters to enjoy them in all their fullness just as readily – to feel that same racing of the pulse – as he who brings an entire library of art-historical knowledge to bear upon them. He does not want or invite prior knowledge from the onlooker. Perhaps the opposite, in fact: a fresh, almost naive shock of bewildered pleasure would be better.

Surprisingly, watching him paint is not quite what you would expect either. The application of the paint is not at all Wagnerian – in spite of the fact that *Lohengrin* is a particular favourite of his. There are no drum rolls, no flourishes of any kind. There is no posturing, no artist's smock. On the contrary, he is dressed in a black T-shirt and black trousers. After all, he arrived a little while ago on a bicycle – and now he has just struggled into the studio carrying his own blank canvas.

Rauch's approach to the actual painting of his works seems fairly studiedly matter-of-fact too, and even modestly understated, as if he is merely assembling, little by little, the pieces of an enormous puzzle, which emerge from the scrub and the scurry of his brushstrokes. And those brushstrokes themselves – from the quick and almost febrile scrubbings and infillings to a finicky fineness – often look workaday, and sometimes even hesitant, as if he is teaching himself to paint all over again. Is this because he is perpetually on the brink of waiting for something to emerge? The paint into which he dips his brush might be sitting in a paint pot's shallow, plastic lid – there are few things more matter-of-fact, few things less worthy of reverence or contemplation, than a disposable plastic lid. He works, back and forth, with the brush, sometimes quite furiously – up, down, from side to side – as if he is doing nothing other than filling in empty space with practised haste and efficiency and professional application – just like any diligent workman going about his everyday business. Yes, there is an everydayness about his general approach. This is serious work to be done. Sometimes he will climb down from his raised platform in front of the painting, sit himself down in his tubular steel chair with the saggy black seat and just look at what he has done, in silence. And then look some more. Pausing to take stock, to consider issues of balance, form, colour, etc. Does that heel require greater definition? Sometimes his wife, the painter Rosa Loy, will stand beside the canvas and make suggestions of her own. Is that the top of the head? Or is it a cap? Sometimes his long-time friend and dealer Gerd 'Judy' Lybke of EIGEN+ART will join in the discussion. What of the new intensity of a particular colour? Has that made a difference? No comment about the work is out of bounds.

Sometimes Rauch will sit down alone to make a new drawing, but this is never an underdrawing. It is something quite separate – as is the enigmatic world of his painting. And it is a world which, as he continues to work and age and mature, becomes more and more difficult to conjure into being because he is forever seeking out paths which

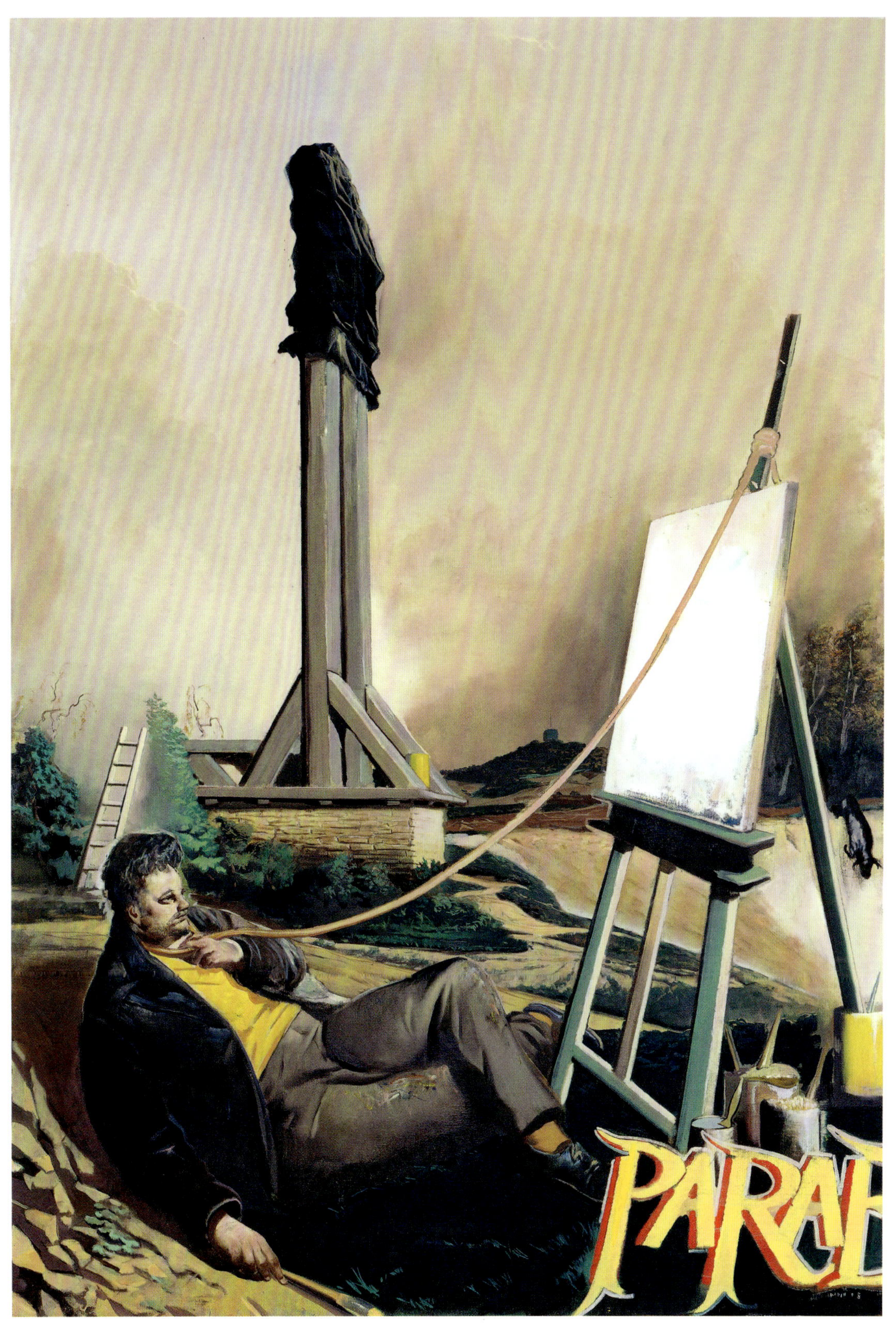

4. Parabel 2008

Oil on canvas
300 × 210 cm (118¼ × 82¾ in)
Private collection

he has not trodden before, virgin forest you could say . . . You never quite know where – across the broad, tall, virginal plain of the white-primed canvas – he will choose to make a mark at any particular moment, where he will find that particular source of energy. It could be at a wholly unpredictable height. He might stroke in a brow, an eye. Yes, a face, or a part of a face, may be coming into being. What size are the paintings to be? It all depends. Many of the paintings of recent years have been huge, polyphonic. 'The paintings announce their own spatial requirements', he once said,[6] with a slightly deceptive and almost offhand modesty, as if making could almost be reduced to a rather neat-sounding formula. He knows it never can, that he is always at its mercy in the end. And, in the background of the studio, music washes around: music of all sorts, from all periods. Like a child, he is seeking, always, something new, the joy of an unexpected, unprecedented discovery.

*

Neo Rauch was born in 1960, almost a year before the Berlin Wall went up. Due to the tragedy of his parents' early death – they died at the ages of 19 and 21 when a train derailed just outside Leipzig station – Neo, at just four weeks old, became a ward of the East German state. Brought up by his maternal grandparents, he grew up in a small town called Aschersleben, in west Saxony-Anhalt, central Germany, within sight of the Harz Mountains. On a good day, the boy Neo could catch a glimpse of their tallest peak. And it is to this small town in Saxony-Anhalt, a little over one hour by train to the north of Leipzig, with the remnants of its medieval walls, 15th-century towers – each one individually named – and grander, later architectural accretions, from the 16th century to the Jugendstil splendour and panache of the Villa Richard Bestehorn on Bestehornstrasse, that we should go if we are to find the young Rauch. His grandfather was a *Buchhalter* (bookkeeper), a man of numbers, and his beloved grandmother (she was just 39 years old when he went to live with them) a *Hausfrau*. Her grandson habitually called her 'mother', although he always knew otherwise. She died in 2009.

Aschersleben, with its population of 25,000, is smaller now than when Neo Rauch was a boy there in the 1960s, attending elementary school and, later, the Gymnasium Stephaneum. The smokestacks of heavy industry no longer pollute its old centre. And yet many of the buildings that he would have known then (including the pitiless *Plattenbauten* that sit on the hillside just beyond the centre where he once lived – those concrete, flat-roofed apartment blocks which speak so loudly of Communist control) and many of the lost places that we see in his paintings, repeatedly washed in on the tides of memory – a clock tower here, a Baroque gable end there – exist, still. Look at the tumbling gable end, several times replicated as it falls, in a painting called *Vorführung* (Performance, 2006, fig.6), for example. That gable end is in Aschersleben.

Aschersleben is no longer the place that Neo Rauch knew so intimately as a child and a growing man, and which his paintings often recall, sometimes quite glancingly.

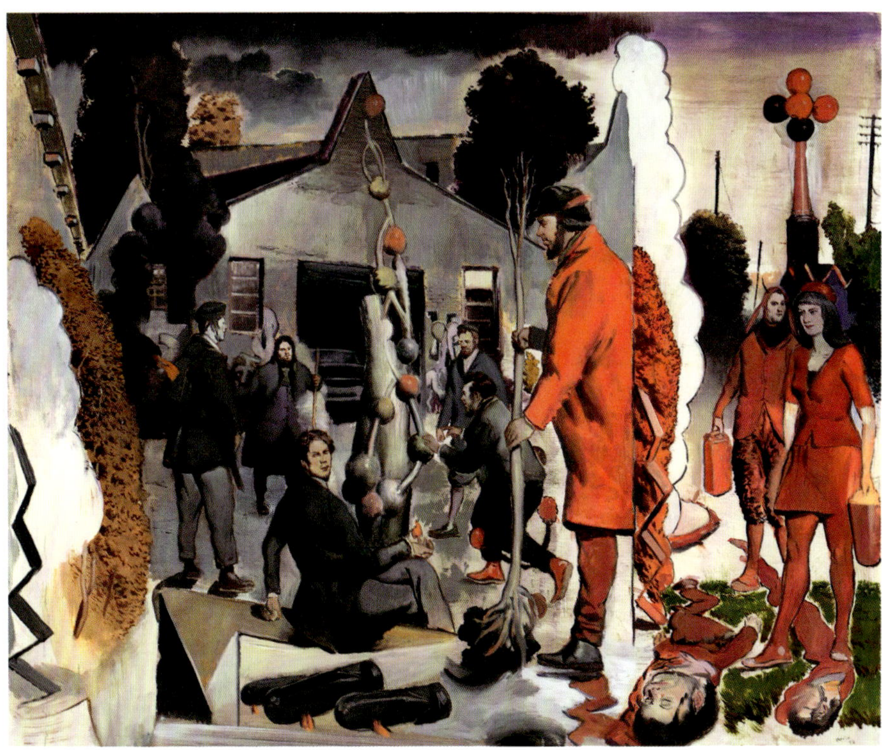

5. Der Stammbaum 2017

Oil on paper
168.3 × 206.7 cm (66¼ × 81½ in)
Private collection

Then, it was 'one big blob of grey', 'a grey town with grey people, *triste* . . .'[7] Now it is prosperous again, and those once dilapidated villas shine anew in the sun. From there, Rauch went on to art college in the great metropolis of Leipzig. It was his road to the big world, his portal onto the future, albeit a shabby one in those days. 'She was a dirty old lady in the 1980s. She had seen better times.'[8] And yet the Hochschule offered him something completely precious: the freedom to paint. 'In the rest of the world, they had to make videos.'[9]

A recent painting of 2017 called *Der Stammbaum* (Family Tree, fig.5) seems to summon up the bewildering instabilities of the very idea of family as a fixed and dependable unit. All human life seems to be coming and going in this scene, with its medley of lived moments. Who exactly are these people – some ancient, others less so – who stand around; look back as if about to depart; arrive with strange, sustaining gifts? One uproots a tree, as if wrenching up the one natural thing which might root us. This gesture puts us in mind of a statement by Nietzsche, which seems poignantly apposite: 'the contentment of the tree in its roots, the happiness of knowing that one is not wholly accidental but grown out of a past as its heir, flower and fruit, and that one's existence is thus excused and, indeed, justified.'[10] And then there are the flattened images of dwarfish creatures, so easily trampled underfoot; the 'bomblets', so carelessly strewn around, so indicative of

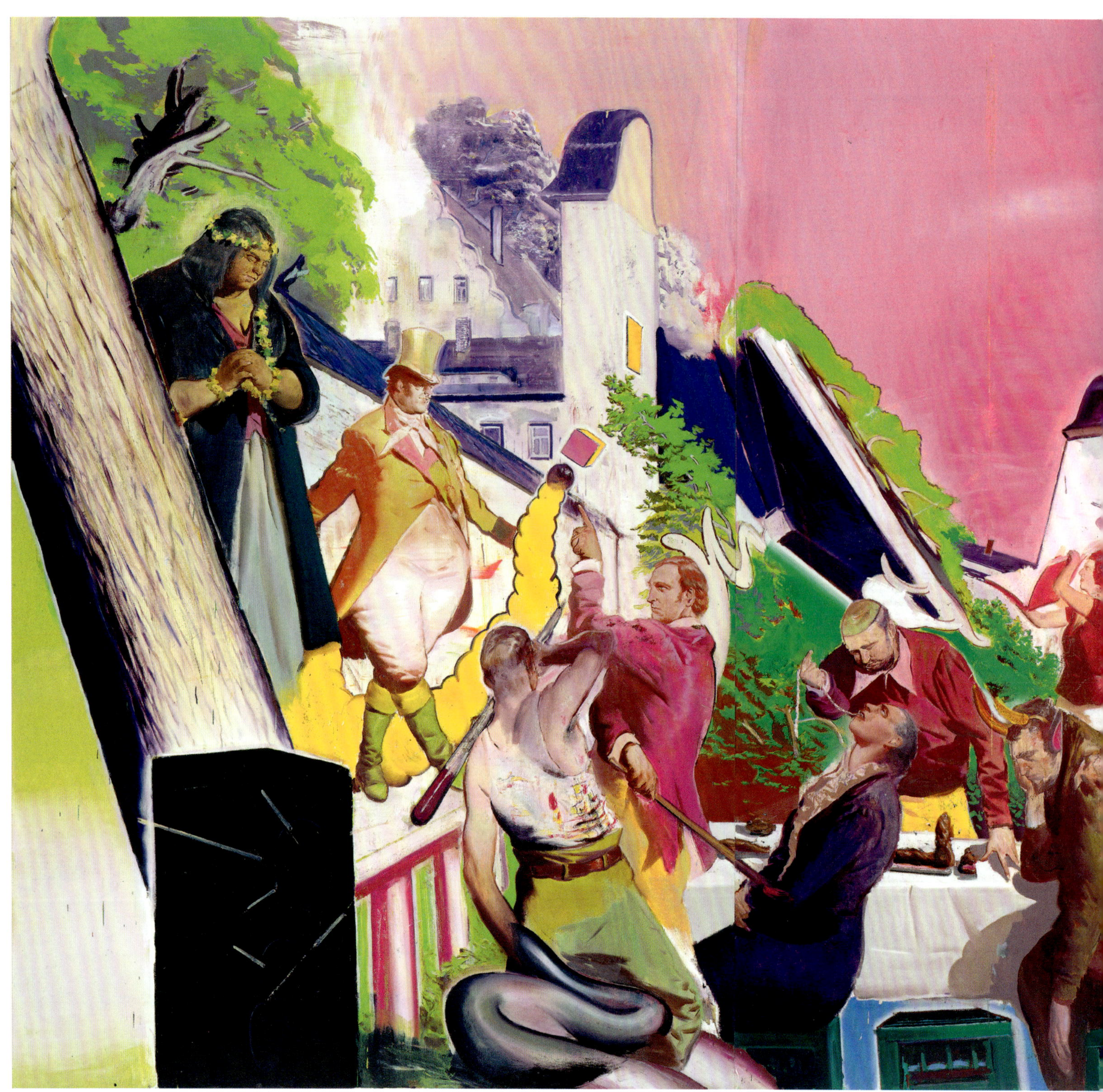

6. Vorführung 2006

Oil on canvas
300 × 420 cm (118¼ × 165½ in)
Rubell Family Collection

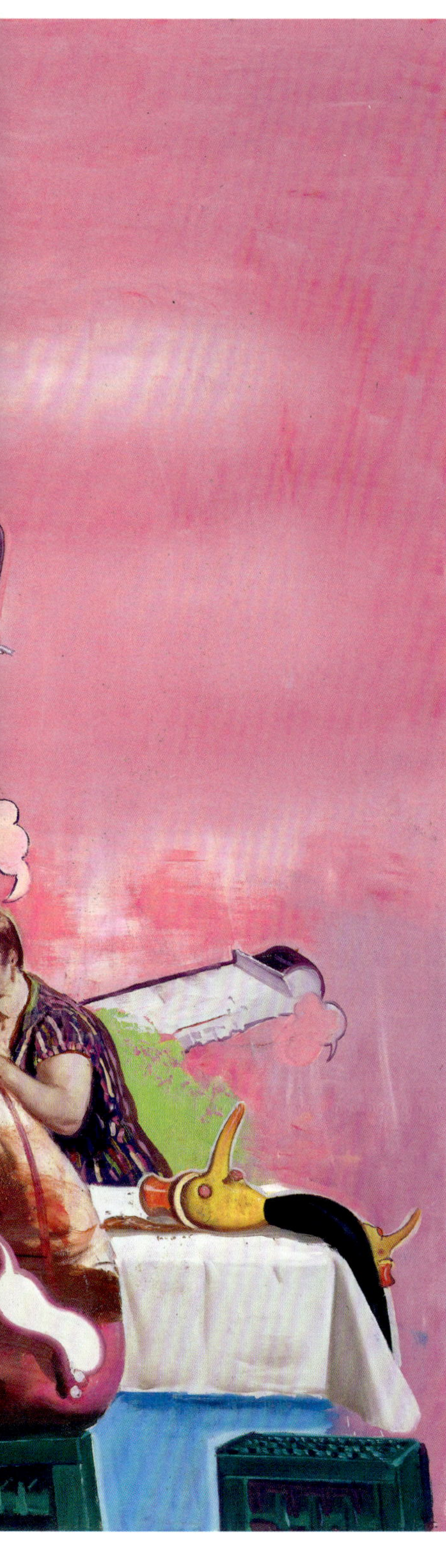

easy destruction; and these curious globular upgrowths. Is this a fanciful reimagining of the mapping of the human genome?

And it was here, in Aschersleben – where this painting currently hangs in the old printworks that, in 2012, became the Grafikstiftung Neo Rauch, a gift to the town from the painter, a foundation which exists to exhibit his own (and others') graphic work – that this child of the 1960s became utterly absorbed in his drawing and his painting. He made his first drawing at the age of two. And the subject? A woodpecker stuck on a tree trunk. 'I just loved to draw. I didn't stop. It was my way of seizing control of the world, of discovering the strange things behind reality, the strange worlds that existed behind those drawings.'[11] At the age of ten, he attended an art club run by the academic painter Heinrich Rademacher. Such were the precocious talents of his young pupil that Rademacher would soon be wondering whether there was anything more that he could teach him.

Neo Rauch's grandparents never adopted him. They dealt with the terrible fact of the death of his young parents with great tact and sensitivity, he has said. They also made sure that photographs of his parents were in the house, on full view, so that Rauch grew up with these images. This meant so much to him: 'They were like older siblings.'[12] A photograph of his mother also hangs high on his studio in the Spinnerie, a little like a precious, personal icon. 'Sometimes I turn in desperation to her, when my flow of ideas dries up. I send a pleading sigh in her direction. Sometimes it is heard . . .'.[13]

He went on to become a student at the Leipzig Academy of Graphic Arts, the very art school at which his father, Hanno, had also enrolled, studying under the direction of Arno Rink from 1981 to 1986 and later working as a master student with the school's director, Bernhard Heisig, from 1986 to 1990. He then went on to become a teacher himself, and then a full professor, continuing in that role until 2009.

Given that Leipzig was in the GDR, the Hochschule was anachronistic in its way, almost a time capsule. At a time when much of the West had fallen violently in love with abstract painting, and was soon to fall in love all over again with what was once called 'the new media' – video and installation art – this art academy taught, shockingly, figurative painting. What is more, the school was rigorously pedagogical in its methods. It taught the full range of academic disciplines. Neo Rauch once described how Arno Rink, who died in September of 2017, painted. It was truly awe-inspiring for the young student: 'The fact that Arno Rink could paint a droplet of water on a pumpkin in such a way that you felt you could reach out and wipe it off – that, for me, was the same thing as truly great art'[14] (fig.7).

Did the fact that Leipzig was in the GDR and embraced figurative painting mean that it had time for nothing but Socialist Realism? Not at all. On the contrary, that 'unifying concept'[15] (Rauch's words) had died long ago – perhaps in the 1950s. Rauch regards himself as fortunate: he was born just a little too late to have to suffer from the oppressive notion that art must function as a weapon in the social struggle, that a painter is obliged to wear his class allegiances on his sleeve. Now he speaks with

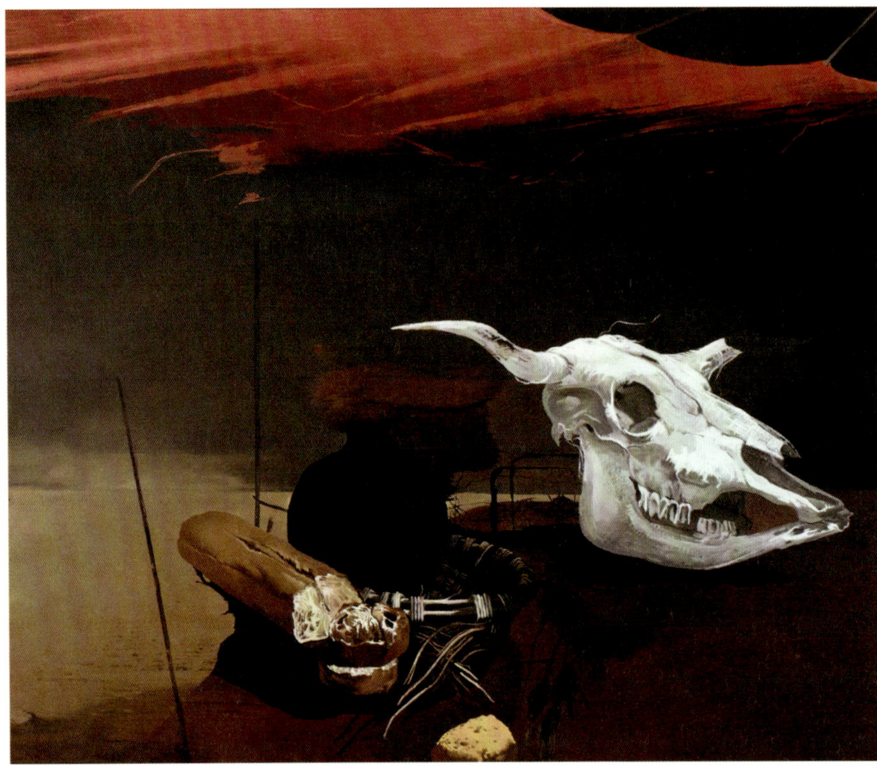

7. Arno Rink
Spanisches Stilleben (Spanish Still Life) 1983

oil on board
130 × 160 cm (51¼ × 63 in)
Museum der bildenden Künste, Zeipzig

horror of political art, as if, from his own perspective at least, it is a poisoned brew. The 'household deities' of the Hochschule when Rauch was a student there were Max Beckmann (another painter from Leipzig), Otto Dix, Lovis Corinth, Oskar Kokoschka, Salvador Dalí, Karl Hofer and Matthias Grünewald. What is more, the school was a remarkable island of independent-spiritedness in a society whose values were rotten to the core. The school brooked no political indoctrination of any kind – thanks to its principal, the rigorous 'gatekeeper' Bernhard Heisig. 'It was the opposite of enforced modernisation in the West, it was the old-fashioned way of painting,'[16] Rauch said in 2016. In short, the school encouraged robust individualism to flourish. And so it did. This is not to say that the work of Neo Rauch is not touched by the spirit of Socialist Realism. It ghosts in and out, in his early, middle and later work.

Two great events took place at the end of the 1980s which had a profound influence on Neo Rauch as both human being and painter. In 1989, the Berlin Wall fell. In 1990, his son Leonard was born. The arrival of a son meant that he could embrace child-play once again without apology or explanation,[17] in the nursery and the studio. The fall of the Wall meant that Rauch could travel, and see for himself the art of Italy – the marvels of Giotto in the frescoes of Padua and Assisi, for example, or the extravagant, fleeing figures of Tintoretto at the High Altar of the Madonna del'Orto in Canareggio, Venice. He would no longer need to depend upon printed images, but could now go to see for himself. (Could his horror of the idea of painting from printed images have something to do with this emotionally constricting dependence, for so long, upon the mediation of poor-quality, black-and-white images of great paintings, and of his thirst to see the real thing?) Other great masters made their powerful mark on him too: Piero della Francesca, Velázquez, Balthus. Those frescoes by Giotto gave him 'a call to order . . . [They] guided me away from the confusion of semi-abstract doodles.'[18] Neo Rauch understood very well what it was to fall under the spell of Abstraction. He had already done a master's degree in West German Abstract Painting of the 1950s.

In part, this monograph is the story of the flourishing of a particular kind of German and Saxon rootedness. Neo Rauch has never lived abroad. He did not escape from East to West Germany like Georg Baselitz or Gerhard Richter or Sigmar Polke before him in response to some siren's ever-elusive song of freedom. Unlike Anselm Kiefer or Sean Scully, he does not have studios in more than one country. He has never responded to the glitzy allure of internationalism, city-hopping from place to place. He has tilled his home turf, you might say, from first to last. This rootedness is not a negative thing. He is not stuck in a rut. He travels – but he also returns, always. There is a simple reason for this: he does not want to be regarded as the foreigner. He never wishes to feel that at some point in his life, he will be obliged to leave the places that he holds so dear – Leipzig itself, where he was educated, or Aschersleben. Unlike Heinrich Heine, he is not obliged to live in exile in Paris, forever pining for the lost homeland of childhood. He wishes to be someone who is always familiar, confidently familiar, both to himself and to others. What is more, he cannot imagine working anywhere else. He could live elsewhere – but it would mean the end of work. 'A certain energy is present here in this place of my birth. You have to stay close to where you came into the world, in order to draw on the energy that was around you when you were being born . . . Where you were born, that is where the telluric currents flow.'[19]

As a painter, Rauch's method of making is – to a degree, at least – rooted in tradition. He abhors the idea of painting images of images, and he never works from photographs. What is more, he continues to subject himself to the discipline of painting – he does not shift mediums or take long breaks. When he stops painting, his reason for being gradually begins to slip away from him. Life descends into uselessness, and he loses his sense of himself. He needs to have what he continues to create reflected back at him, perpetually. His paintings are a form of self-completion, and when he stops he is very much aware of the fact that the lights continue to blaze in other studios. That does not seem quite right to him. And so it goes on.

But that is to get ahead of ourselves. Let us consider the earliest works in this book, which date from the first years of German reunification, that defining moment at which the German Democratic Republic became part of the Federal Republic of Germany and a reunited nation was born. That was in 1990. We are therefore beginning this monograph at the point when Neo Rauch is 30 years old, and approaching the years of his maturity. The early works of his experimental youth, when he was striving to become a painter in the modern idiom, will not be fully revealed until 2020, when a large exhibition will open at the Museum der bildenden Künste in Leipzig.

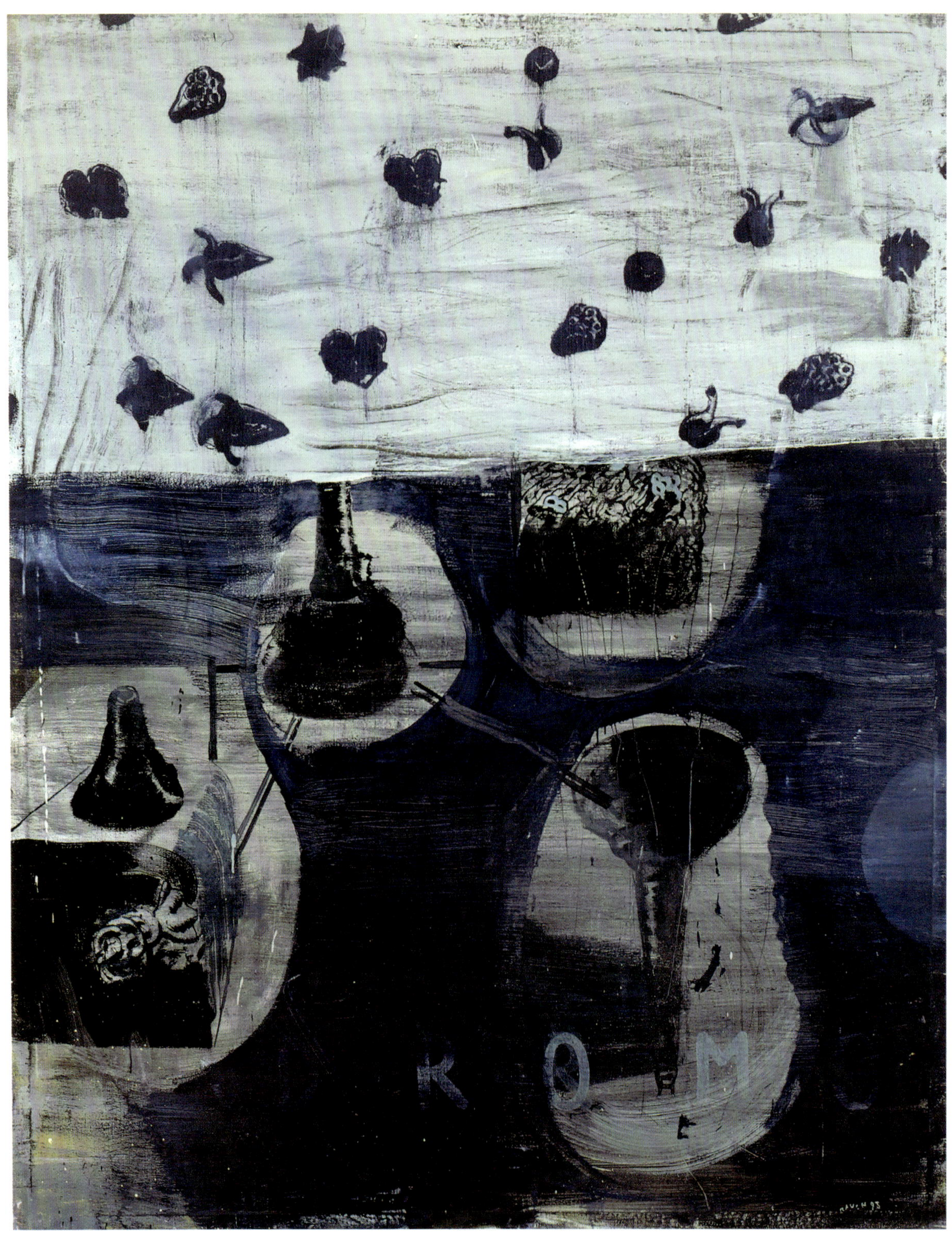

8. Dromos 1993

Oil on canvas
250 × 198.5 cm (98½ × 78¼ in)
Private collection

2 Emerging from the GDR

The paintings of the first half of the 1990s such as *Dromos* (1993) (fig.8), *Taufe* (Baptism, 1994) (fig.9) and *Die Große Störung* (The Great Disturbance, 1995) (fig.10) are much cooler and more graphic in impulse and execution than the works of Neo Rauch's maturity. Colour is often used very sparingly, but there is a reason for this. Rauch removed colour quite deliberately in those years so that he could concentrate on form. His earliest works had used colour too thickly, in his opinion. They inclined towards kitsch. From 1993 onwards, he drew back: 'I used only black and white and a little bit of brown, and that was my rescue.'[1] There were other reasons too, which will emerge as we examine the works themselves. Those reasons can, however, be summarised thus: he was a man who had lived all his life in the GDR.

The Greek word *Dromos*, the title of a key painting of 1993, means an avenue that leads to a temple or a tomb, an approach to a sacred space. What is the significance of this arresting choice of word? Neo Rauch is moving in the direction of the works that he is to make in the 1990s. That movement, however, is both tentative and unsure. He has arrived at the end of his apprenticeship as a painter, but nothing is yet quite clear. Now it is his task to discover how to create the content of a pictorial space. It is an act of groping ahead, through a tantalising murk of blueness or unclarity – or, at the very least, partial indefinition. He is on the brink of breaking through to a new conception of painting. But what exactly is it to be? Line and tone seem to be seeking each other out, exploring the possibility of a relationship.

The painting *Dromos* is a nocturne in grey, black and indigo. The motifs seem to propose themselves as the beginnings of solutions, as if they are rising into being as shapes, types, forms. They float across two painted realms of blueness which abut each other, creating a division between sea and sky. The idea of water is evoked by dragging, sideways brushstrokes. What exactly are these shapes? Is this nothing but abstract mark-making? Not at all. Some of these shapes, set against pale cartouches, look hard, metallic, part-industrial – up-spinning coils of metal, perhaps in motion, which taper at top or base. The same shape is also inverted – as if greater understanding may come by turning the world upside down. They look somewhat practical, utile, as if they might be components of a machine. On the other hand, they might also be sacred – some of them evoke the shape of a Buddhist shrine, one of those stupas to be seen in the Yellow Mountains of China. The title of the painting is both coming into view and being lost to view – simultaneously, as if it hesitates to propose itself, as if it would prefer to hide. It has been incorporated into the painting itself. It is a part of its identity. The painting seems to possess an aura of menace, as if war is being waged, as if these might be

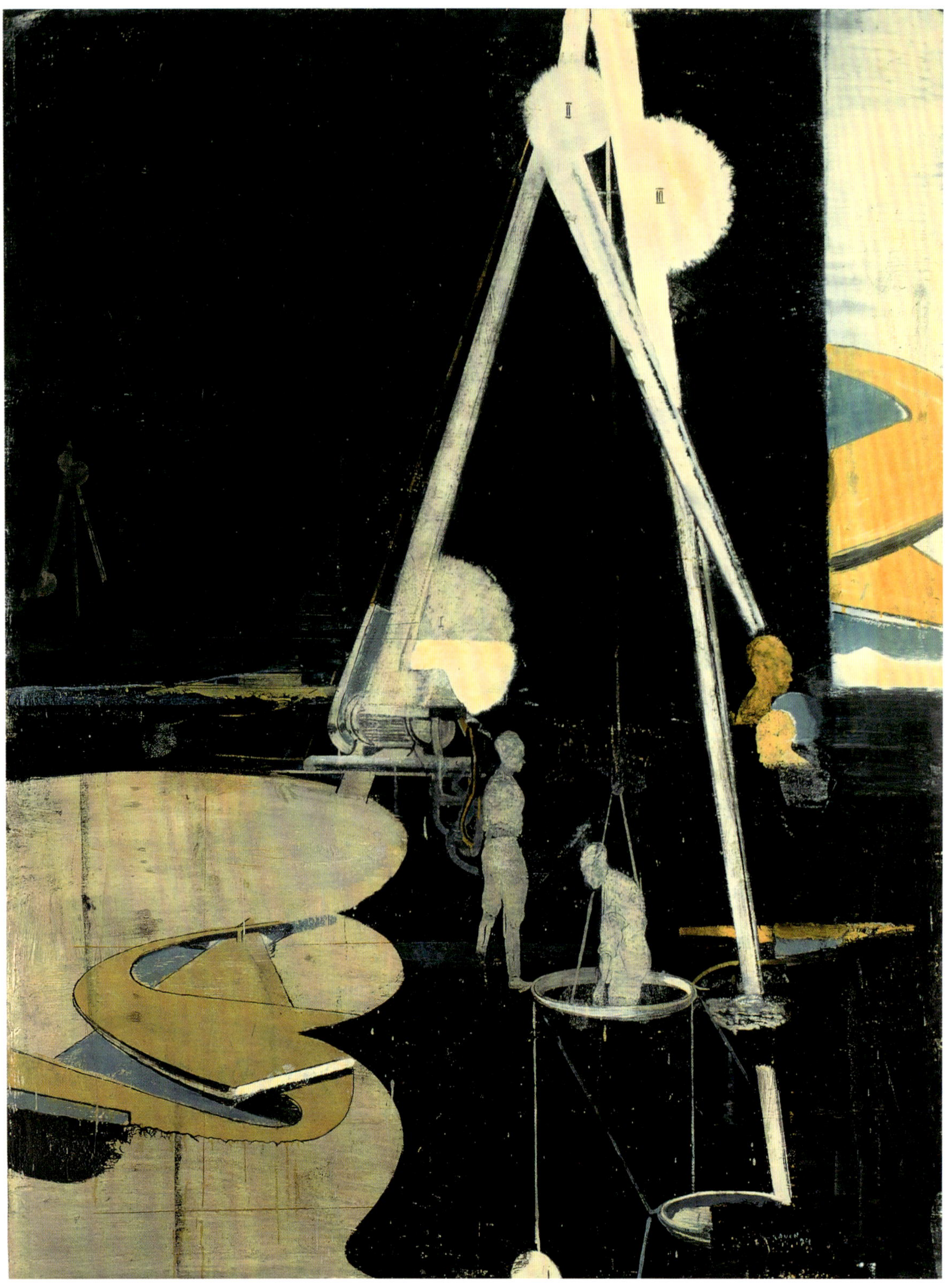

9. Taufe 1994

Oil on canvas
250 × 190 cm (98½ × 75 in)
Private collection

battleships moving through enemy waters, as if what is floating through the air may be dangerous fragments of ordnance. The entire scene seems to be slowly floating down through the air, as if it is here for the briefest of brief moments, and then gone again. Furthermore, the painter seems rather reluctant to define or to confront whatever is coming into being. There is little real depth here, a relatively shallow graphic surface, nothing into which we might sink. In short, the painting feels more like a proposal than an outcome.

To narrow that colour range was a quite deliberate strategy, the creation of a new way of considering how a painting might be brought into being. The use of such a constricted range of colour in *Die Große Störung* (fig.10) enables us to see through to the painting's construction – its architecture, perhaps – that much more clearly. Its form is laid as bare as a skeleton stripped of its flesh. It is as if we are staring down into a maze of perspectival complexity. The lines, such is the way that they fall in their spillikin-like criss-crossings, look almost industrial in their heft, their weight, as if they are props or girders to hold this painted assemblage in place. The painting feels like a free-flowing meditation upon the nature of work itself – how it gets done, who does it, what might be its constituent parts, what might be the products of all this labour. There are blank-faced factories, long, featureless buildings, stretching away into the distance far beneath us. There are also men in profile, with faces either obliterated or part-obliterated, bending over, as patient in their load-bearing as machines would be. Our own view down into the painting feels almost aerial, as if we are examining a landscape of human making from a great height. It feels like a giddy construction site. Are rivers being dredged? Is mining going on? Are those yellow loopings autobahns in the making? The colour range shifts from black to grey to yellow to blue – but all these colours feel a little washed out, a little restrained. There is no intensity of colour here. They are the sort of tones we might readily associate with products of utility, anaemic product packaging – washing powder, for example. And yet there is something else here too: an interruption which seems to disturb, and even work against, a too-easy reading of this painting as a reflection of certain circumstances which prevailed in the GDR. This curious something takes the form of a bewigged figure with his back to us (top right) who appears to be exercising his fingers at a keyboard. Has the shadow of the great Johann Sebastian Bach (sometime choirmaster at Thomaskirche in Leipzig) come to dwell here too in order to remind us that the worlds conjured by even the young Neo Rauch are never exactly simple, that the promise of the spirit of the Enlightenment hovers somewhere nearby?

As often with Rauch's paintings, the title is at ambiguous play with what we are seeing in front of us. The physical *disturbance* of the painting's title is world-engulfing – the entire painting consists of it. This is the disturbance of work, how humanity pitilessly makes and remakes the terrain that has been gifted to it by covering it and recovering it in buildings, roads, everything which serves to obliterate its natural contours. The tonal coolness – if not the coldness – of the painting suggests that this

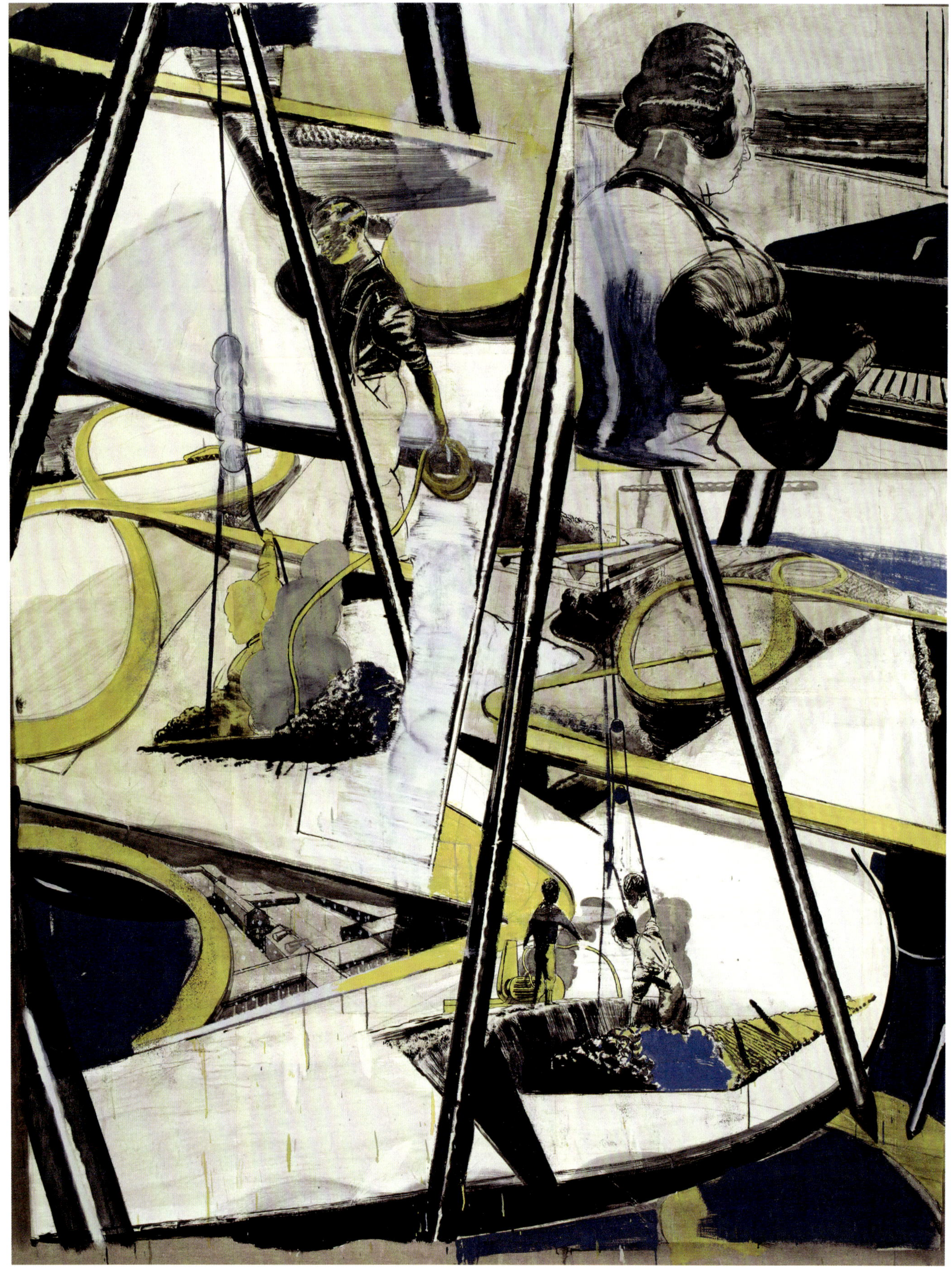

may be nothing to be proud of. It merely happens, all this human-driven mechanisation. A Honecker – or, elsewhere, a Stalin – has made it happen. And those workers who make it happen are anonymous and ant-like and drone-like. They work to serve.

The title, however, can also be construed in quite a different way. Perhaps it is a reflection upon the way that this painting has been made. Perhaps it is urging us to reflect upon the way in which the painter has fractured, fissured, scrambled the painted surface in a quite bewildering fashion – near is far, far is near . . .

The figure of the male worker appears and reappears throughout the paintings of this decade. He is never stagey. He is unassuming. He does not look back at us. He does not crave our attention. He exists side-on, an embodiment and an extension of the work that he does. *Sucher* (Seeker, 1997) (fig.11) brings together the twin themes of work and painting. It holds up the idea of the painter and his task, and juxtaposes that with another kind of work. We have a single man engaged in a routine which to the onlooker is inscrutable. What is this man seeking exactly, with his hovering metal detector? He is dressed in the uniform of the National People's Army – Neo Rauch served as an officer in that army. This time, the painted surface consists of a few planes of understated colour in conjunction with each other. There are no clean lines here. These planes of colour are ragged, provisional. They draw our attention to the idea of work in progress, unfinished work. There are curious breakings out – that shaft of orange paint streaking down on the diagonal looks like a lightning bolt. This painterly effect – the sudden intrusion of amorphous shapes, often in alarmingly assertive colours, into the painting's narrative – will become increasingly familiar to us as the years pass. The painting is telling a story of sorts, but it is an enigmatic and constrained one. It possesses few markers of narrative meaning. In fact, there are so few that if the figurative elements were removed altogether, this could be an abstract painting.

The man is turned away. His seeking will never be our seeking. What is the relationship between the toil of the painter and the toil of the anonymous seeker? Are they similar? The work that he is doing is routine, unexceptional – as its results may be. Or they may be exceptional. The seeker may find something extraordinary. The easel is preparing to be of use to a painter. Those paint cans may have readied themselves for the task ahead. Except that they look like common-or-garden cans of household paint. What is wrong with that though? How would the paint used by a fine artist differ from household paint? Is his task so far removed from everyday life?

Is this walking man the painter? It seems unlikely, such is his indifference to the fact of the canvas's presence so close to him. And is the easel here really an easel, propped as it is in this ill-defined landscape? It looks too tall for a mere man to use it with ease. It is certainly too tall for the seeker to use it with ease, even were he to wish to do so, which is by no means certain. These shifts of scale cause unease. They throw up unanswerable questions – here and throughout the oeuvre of Neo Rauch, as we will be discovering. Perhaps it is not so much an easel as easel-like scaffolding, then – or even a billboard. Perhaps the idea of the painter and his painting is a little too much at odds with the rest

10. Die Große Störung 1995

Oil on paper on canvas
273 × 210 cm (107½ × 82¾ in)
Staatliche Kunstsammlungen, Dresden

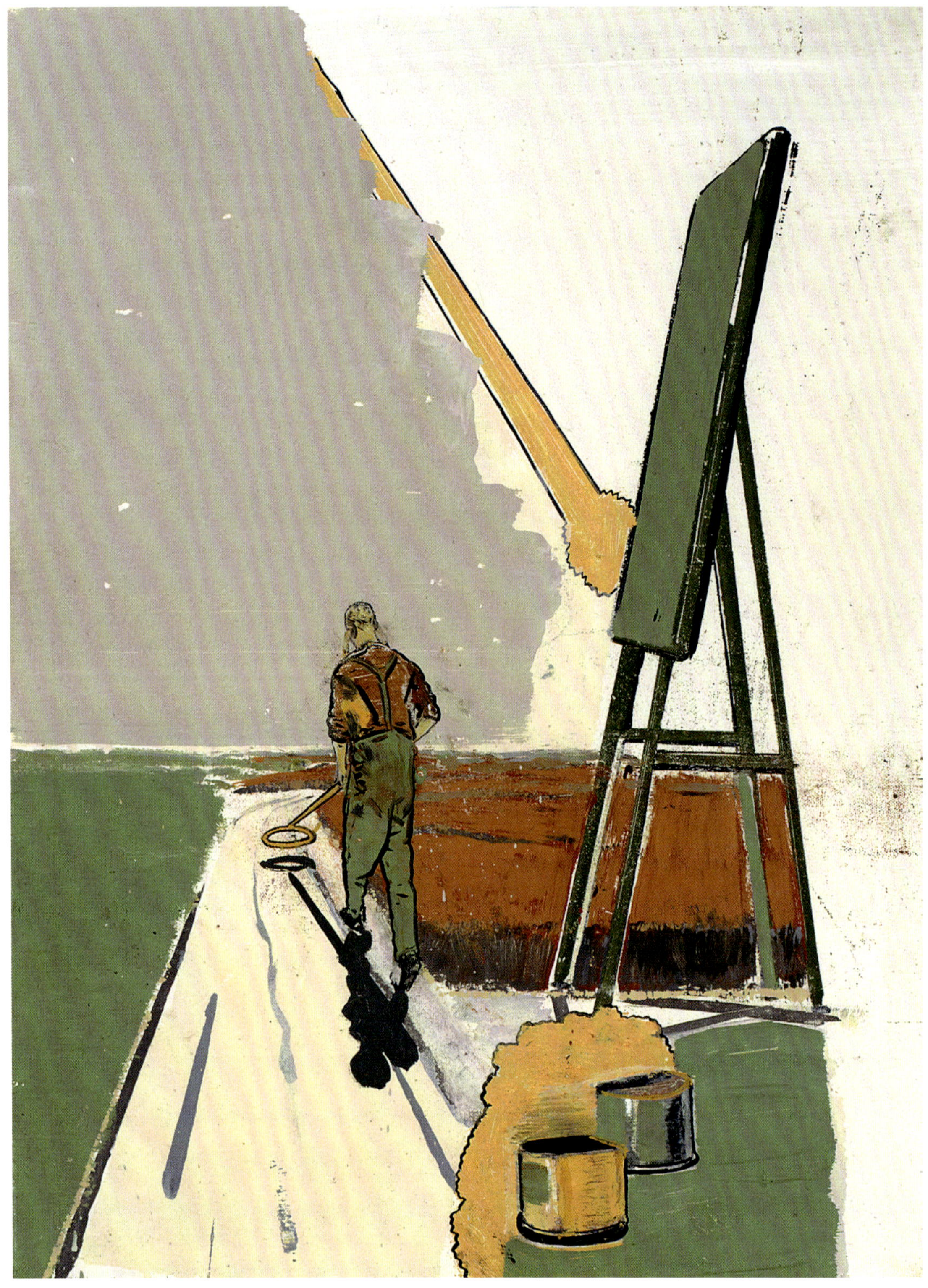

11. Sucher 1997

Oil on canvas
60 × 45 cm (23¾ × 17¾ in)
Sammlung Ruth

of what is going on here. If that is the point, we are faced with the possibility that this is in fact a reflection upon the preoccupations of the painter Neo Rauch himself, the painter of this painting rather than the painter of the painting on the canvas which is yet to come into being. The fact that it does not yet exist seems question-begging. What is to be the role of the painter in this new world of a reunified Germany? How much of the past is to be of use to him? And how will Neo Rauch create his own future? How will he see his role, his task? How will he shape his own vision of himself as an artist? Or will the paintings themselves tell him when he does, finally, come to paint them? Will they dictate to him what manner of painter he will come to be?

The fact is that the painting at which we are staring has absorbed – or perhaps realised – the figure of the man with the metal detector. He is part of the painting's subject matter. But the canvas itself, the one propped on that easel, is unpainted. It is a blank-faced and intimidating challenge to its artist – as Neo Rauch himself will always find a blank canvas. And who would not be thus intimidated? What is more, the easel is not set within a space which could ever be defined as a studio. It is too indeterminate to be a studio. In fact, it looks like an unfinished fragment of landscape in which a man with a metal detector is going about his humdrum business. The easel with its propped canvas is a part of all of this, as are those pots of paint. Does the painter know how to respond to the challenges of the situation in which he may have placed himself? Perhaps he is absent altogether. Perhaps this is a portrait of the state of mind of Neo Rauch, a young painter from the GDR who is now faced with the burden of the fact that an entire world of possibilities is open to him. There is no barrier between East and West. He can become what he chooses to be. And that predicament is an agonisingly difficult one. The worker with his metal detector is part of the world that he knows. But to what extent can he be fully accepted as the subject matter of a modern painting?

How little or how much of the GDR – its colours, its architecture, its workers, its soldiers in their uniforms, its totalitarian rigidities, its signage, its landscapes (often scarred by heavy industry), its cast of mind, the discredited orthodoxies of Socialist Realism – actually gets into these early paintings? A great deal, it has to be said. The more important questions are these, though: What is the attitude of the painter towards such matters? To what extent is he able and actively wishing to embrace them and embody them imaginatively? Or does he keep them at arm's length? Are they merely specimens or types of something? Are they images of which he must rid himself before he reaches the epicentre of his own fundamental concerns? Are they, in short, merely a means to an end? After all, Neo Rauch lived for the first 30 years of his life in the GDR. He was a participant: he saw it, he felt it and he was also a witness to its final collapse. How oppressive was it to a young artist, though? How constraining did he find it? It is perfectly possible to overstate the case. To call the GDR nothing but oppressive is at best a half-truth, comments Dr Alfred Weidinger, director of Leipzig's Museum der bildenden Künste. 'In fact, everything was possible here when Neo Rauch was at college. There was TV, a book fair twice a year. Books could be exchanged through the black market . . . Artists were by no means ignorant of what was going on in the wider world.'[2]

Built structures float through such paintings as *Energiebild* (Energy-picture/scene, 1997) (fig.12), but they feel not so much solid as disembodied, reconstituted in the mind and the memory of the curious onlooker, as if they are dissolving into semi-abstract counters even as we look at them, as if the painting is both dreaming of a world that exists and striving, simultaneously, to reduce it to a play of abstract forms.

Other paintings such as *Das Haus* (The House, 1996) (fig.13) hold various painterly impulses, ones that might even be at odds with each other, in a strangely troubling balance. In this painting, there is a combination of abstraction, a small fragment of a very precisely rendered world of actuality, and what inclines towards a species of mythical dreamscape. The title trumpets its theme: the house. A building is under construction. We see through its skeletal form – will it ever be substantial enough to be described as a house? – to a worker with his wheelbarrow. Another is heaving a plank. They are in the process of creating the building that we are staring at. What kind of playful and insubstantial building is this though, with those slats of coloured wood?

The painting's title seems to suggest that this house should be our focus of attention. And yet it is not because it is too shrunken and small and insubstantial, too marginalised by the fact that it is set to one side, at the painting's foot, and too overwhelmed by what else is happening in this painting – not least, by that regular downstreaking of vertical black and white lines. Is this an abstract interruption into a figurative painting? It feels less so because there is a smeary yellow road here which leads back towards a strange landscape: part trees, part tree-like rocks. That landscape, stretching away from us, inclines us to believe that these vertical lines might after all be evidence of something elemental – a tremendous downpour of rain, for example. Something is being squeezed out. Is this the impulse towards abstract painting? Something is striving to get in, though it feels comically powerless to do so. Is that the narrative impulse in general? Or is it a scene of a building in the making that might have been very familiar? The whole issue is left unresolved.

Nachtarbeit (Night Work, 1997) (fig.14) is yet another act of eavesdropping upon the nature of work and what exactly it consists of. The way in which the scene is presented is a surprise – there is a sudden eruption into an unexpected reality. It is as if the canvas has been torn, broken into, violently fisted through, in order to create a shocking revelation of the kind of activity that goes on while the rest of us sleep. For all that, the scene itself is surprisingly uneventful, mind-numbingly low-key. Nothing heroic is happening here. Once again, the colours are very restrained and almost anaemic – rusting reds, yellows which seem to be edging back into colourlessness, military greens. The areas of beige at the torn-looking bottom edge of the painting look roughly sanded away suggestive of some cheap industrial material. Planes of

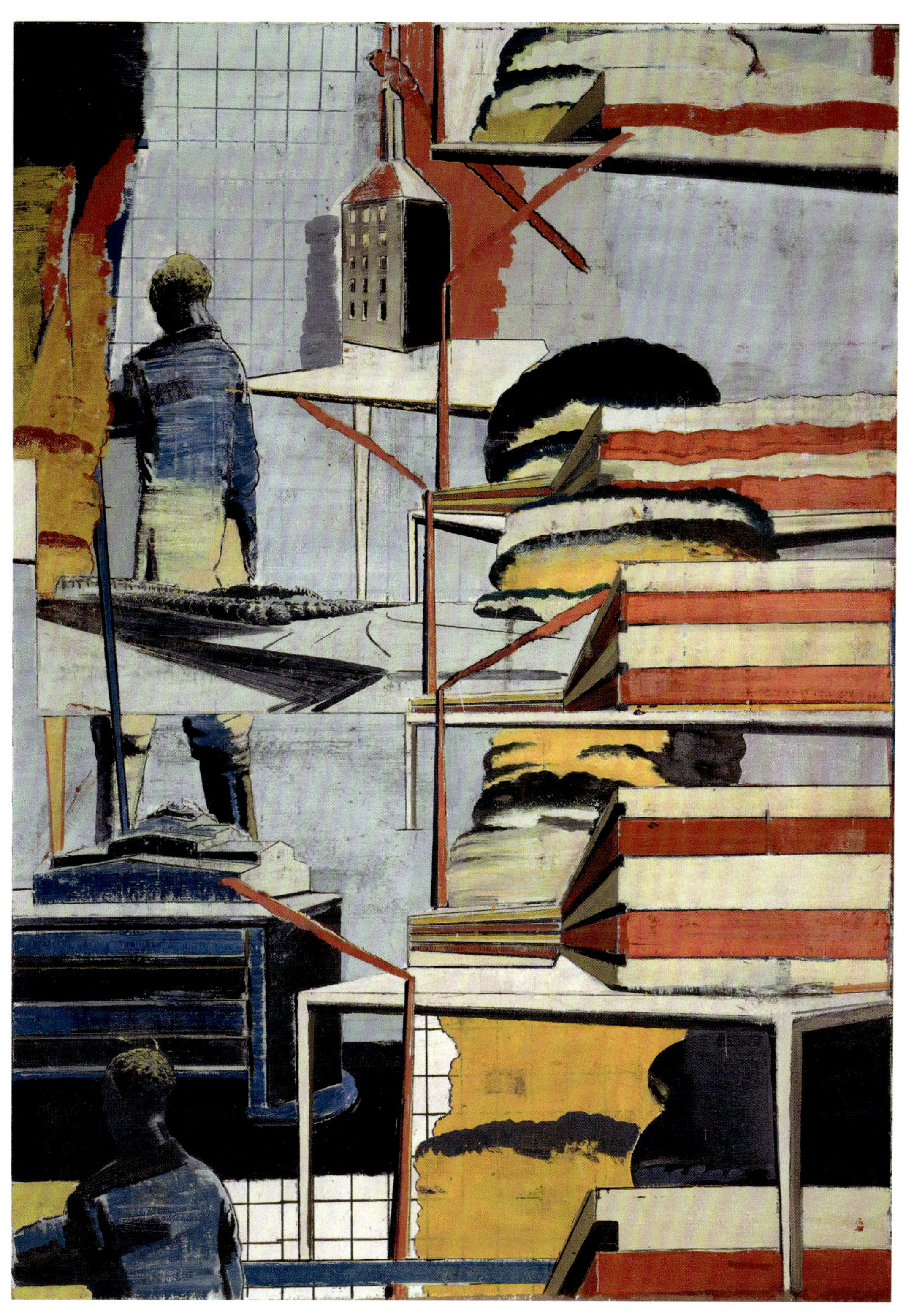

12. Energiebild 1997

Oil on canvas
260 × 200 cm (102½ × 78¾ in)
Konzentration GmbH, Berlin

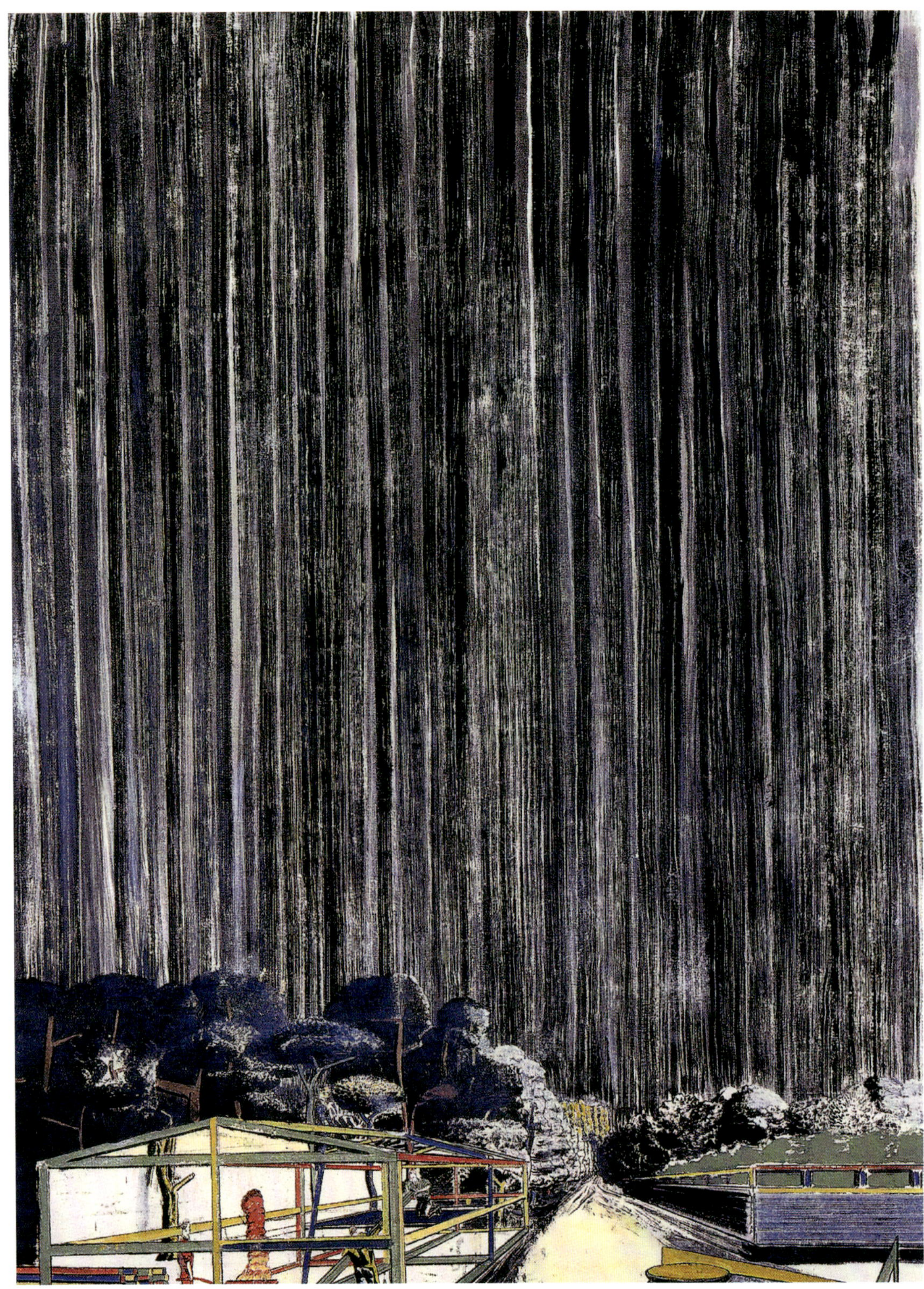

13. Das Haus 1996

Oil on canvas
196 × 137 cm (77¼ × 54 in)
Sammlung Deutsche Bank

colour recede from us, floatingly, as if gliding on air. These planes are in fact the walls and the furnishings of this factory. The very materials which are being used here create the illusion of a deep perspective that recedes and recedes into the blackness of an outside world which reveals yet another factory, perhaps akin to the one which we are seeing close up. Everything seems to be opening out. What exactly is happening though? Perhaps what looks insignificant may in fact be highly significant. On the receding tabletop over which two workers appear to be leaning or crawling (it is impossible to say for sure), there seem to be fragments of architectural schemes in the making – the tower of a church, a toy model of yet another factory. A third worker is pushing two small green vehicles. Perhaps the grandest of grand civic projects is coming into being under cover of darkness, under cover of secrecy? Or it may be something altogether less significant. Perhaps these are toys which are being made. Yet because the unfolding narrative is in part thwarted – made less stable, less certain – by the fact that the painting is once again poised between abstraction and figuration, having feet in both camps as it were, it is impossible to pin that narrative down. It is impossible to take the painting's emotional temperature: it looks and feels emotionally neutral. The workers themselves are familiar types – unassuming drones whose job it is to be busy with the task in hand. They are at the service of the work they do.

None of these early paintings could be construed as overtly political – if by that we mean that they are in the service of an ideology. None of them espouses a cause. And yet a common atmosphere pervades them. They are as if a little stained by politics. There is much settled desolation in these early works. In *Landschaft mit Sendeturm* (Landscape with Transmission Tower, 1996), an ugly, blockish, Stalinist structure settles itself in the landscape against a threatening sky, as if fresh arrived from Planet GDR. In *Leider* (The Sufferer, 1999) (fig.18), a female figure holds up a tiny male puppet above a vista of empty, rectangular rooms. A speech bubble is void of content. In *Geschäft* (Business, 1998) (fig.16), patient shoppers are queuing to buy abstracted images of a human face. In *Museum* (1996) (fig.17), we look out onto pale, desolate, drifting, unanchored, Modernist spaces. Everything feels suspended, afloat on nothing. Humans pose like sculptures.

Here is what Neo Rauch said, when challenged about the influence of Socialist Realism: 'There was most certainly a time when I was flirting with Socialist Realism . . . Much more important was the figurative painting which happened outside of the Socialist world.'[3] And in Great Britain especially, where there had been 'an unbroken tradition of figurative painting that was not connected with political intentions – Frank Auerbach, Francis Bacon, Lucian Freud . . .'[4] An intriguing reflection indeed: Auerbach and Freud had both escaped to Great Britain from Germany in the 1930s to avoid Nazi persecution. Bacon, self-taught, was Irish by birth.

Rauch scrutinises the predicament of the painter yet again in *Wahl* (Choice, Option, Alternative) of 1998 (fig.15). We are confronted by the image of the painter in his over-busy studio – that table in the bottom right-hand corner is almost overflowing

overleaf
14. Nachtarbeit 1997

Oil on canvas
200 × 320 cm (78¾ × 126 in)
Ostdeutsche Sparkassenstiftung

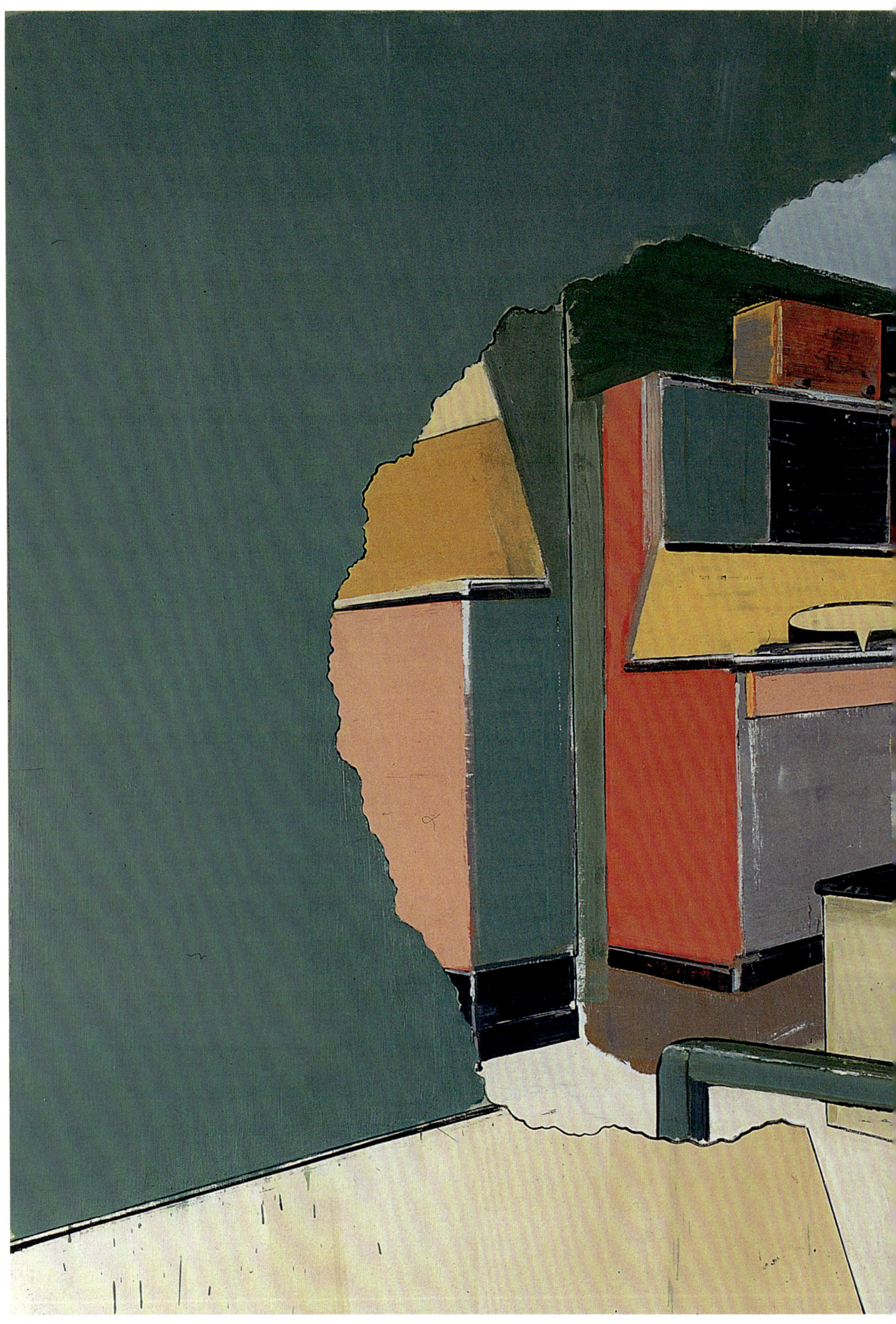

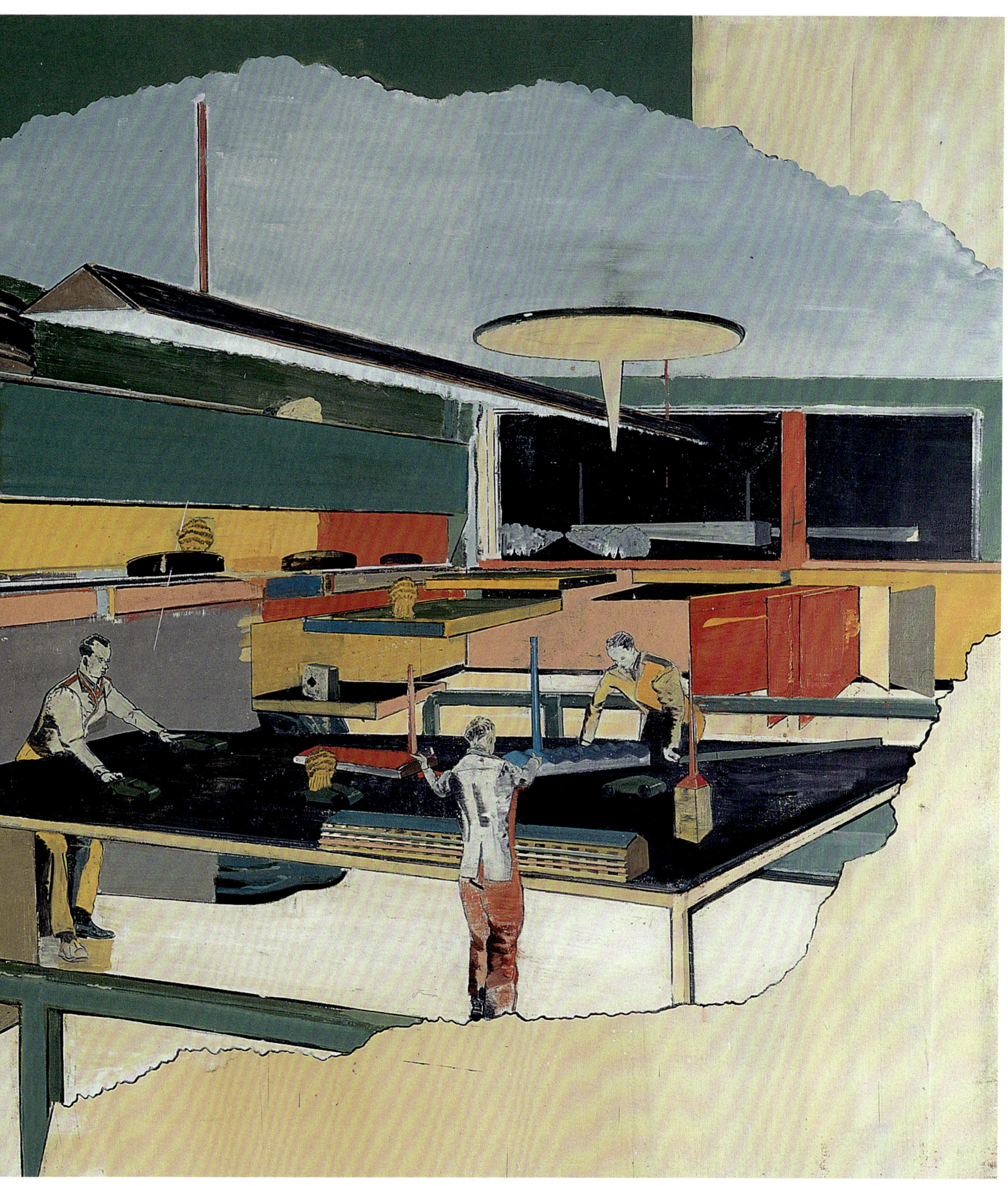

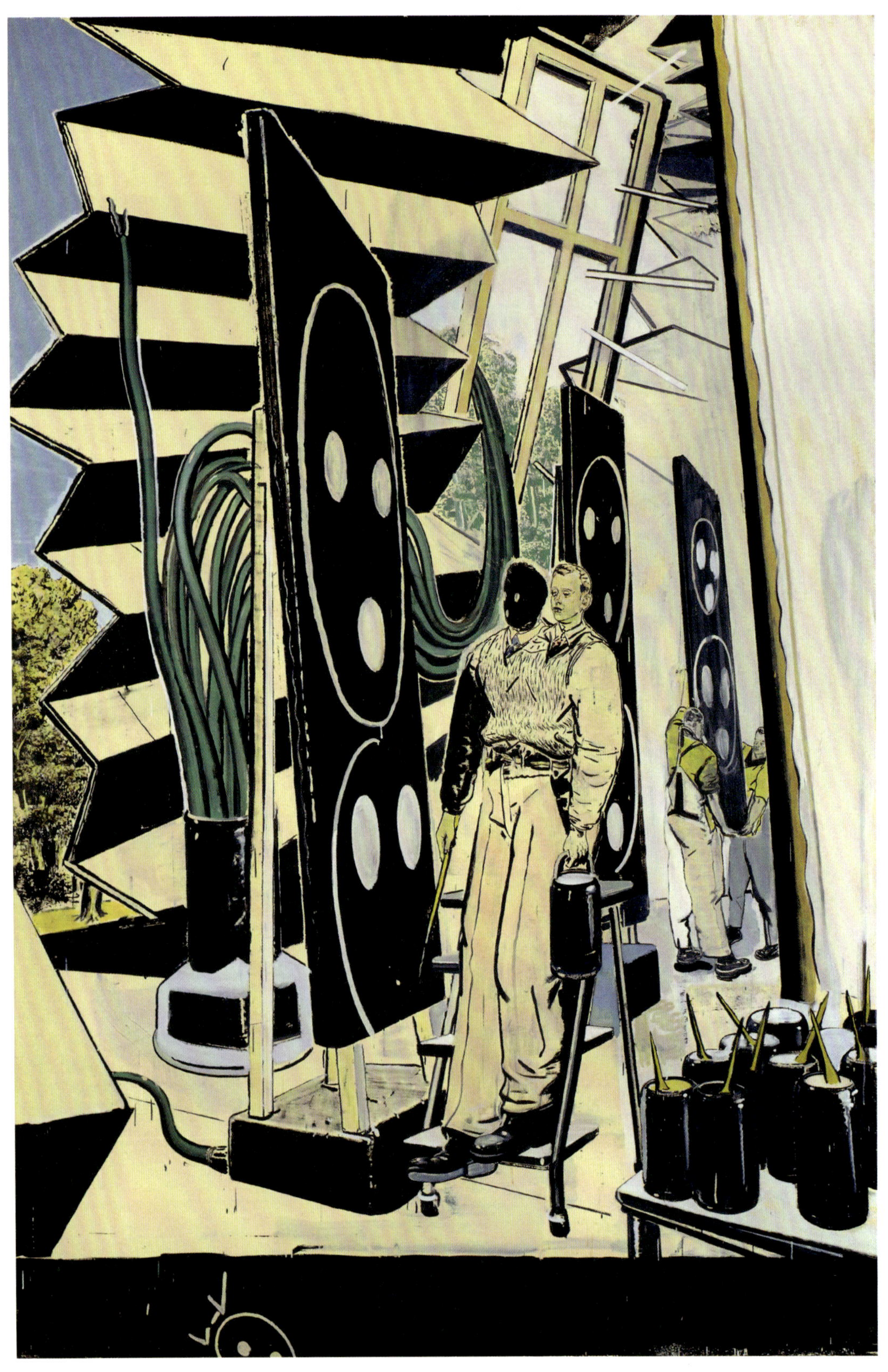

15. Wahl 1998

Oil on canvas
300 × 200 cm (118¼ × 78¾ in)
Pinakothek der Moderne, Munich, PIN.
Freunde der Pinakothek der Moderne

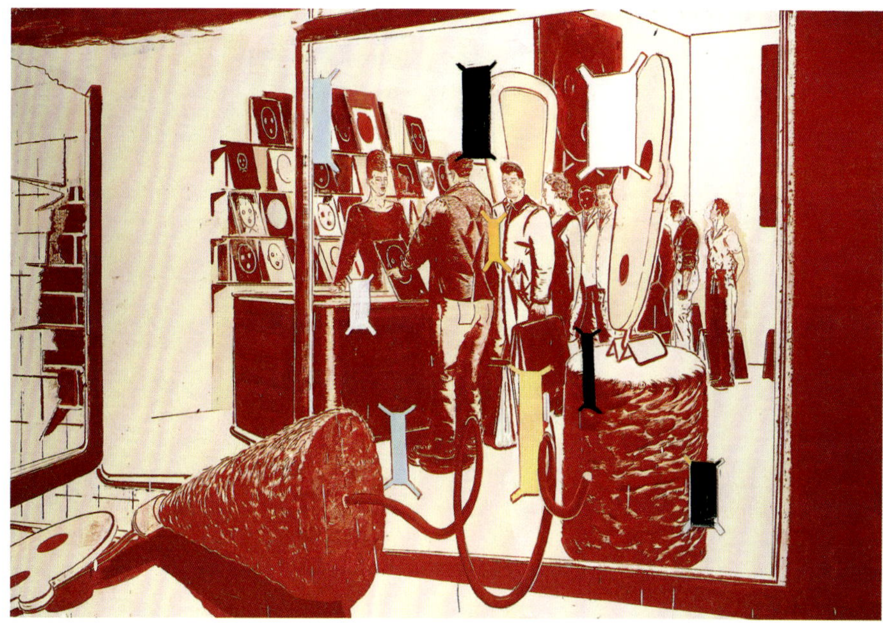

16. Geschäft 1998

Oil on canvas
200 × 300 cm (78¾ × 118¼ in)

with opened pots of black paint, each one flourishing a brush. He is about to step off the bottom-most rung of the stepladder positioned in front of his easel. In fact there is more than one easel, and the way in which his assistants are removing that third painting at the rear, together with its careful, perspectival alignment with the other two paintings, almost seems to suggest that there might be a production line of easels to be filled – just as there might be a production line of the same repeated image. The painter no longer perplexes us by his absence. He is very much present in front of us this time, attending to the matter in hand by staring at what he is painting, wielding a long, thin brush in the one hand and holding a pot of black paint in the other. Instead, he perplexes us by his presence because his upper half at least is a being who is dividing off, peeling away, into more than merely himself, into a double self, which is certainly not a doppelgänger, even as he strives to capture a bold, simple, childlike image of a double head on the canvas – one that he repeats over and over.

What is more, this simple image of a head which is being repeated appears to be a kind of part-echo of the black head (the first of the two heads, that is) of the painter. It seems to repeat – with a reductive exaggeration – the eyes and the mouth of the human head which stares back at it. Furthermore, just as the image on the easel is a combination of black and white, so the identity of the painter himself is a combination of black and white too – white head behind black head, white arm on one side of the body and black arm on the other. The white head is quite different in character from the black head. It is handsomely serene in a rather comic-book way. In spite of the fact that we feel perplexed, and the black head may feel a little perplexed too, by the image

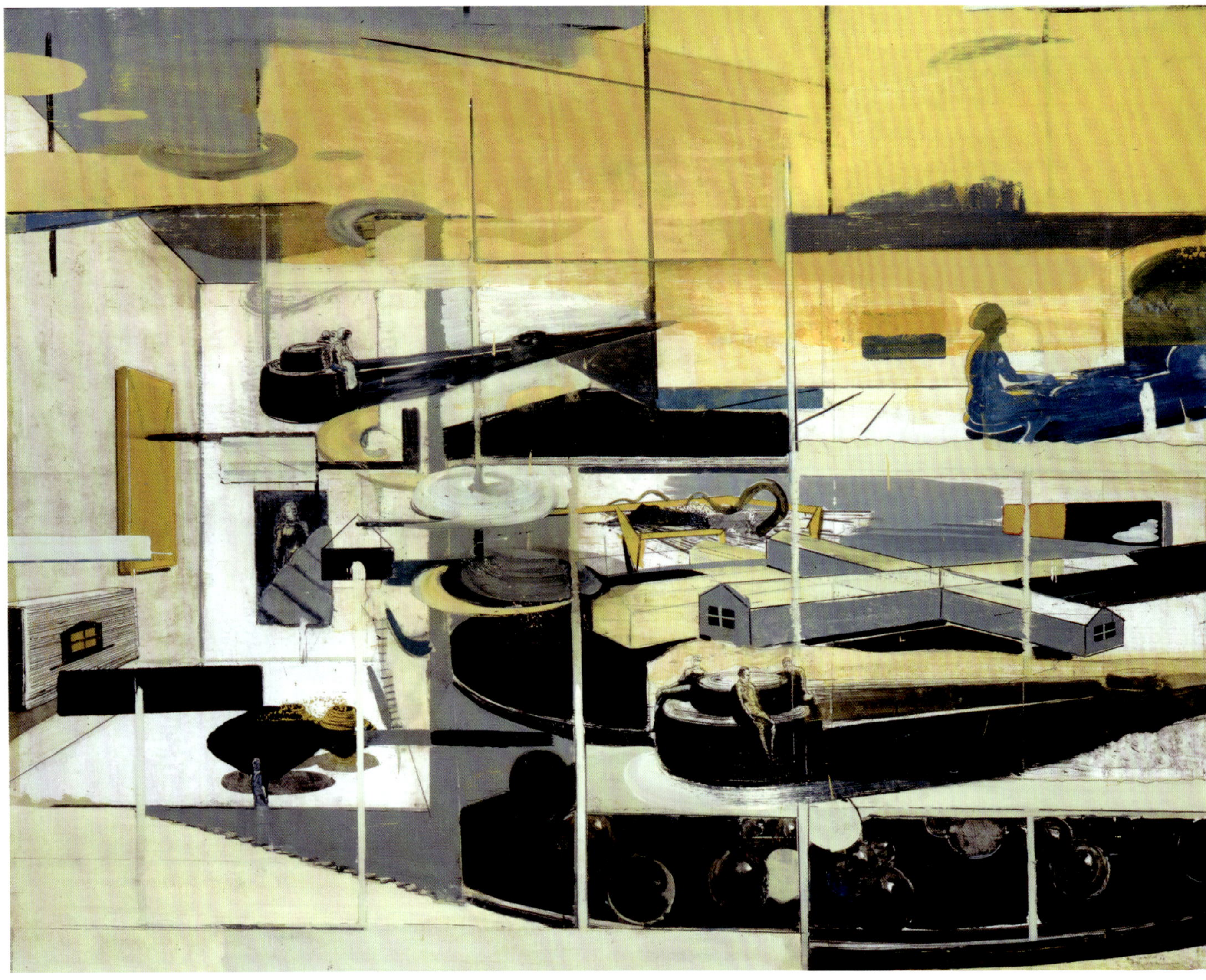

17. Museum 1996

Oil on paper on canvas
159 × 204 cm (62½ × 80½ in)
Sammlung Leipziger Volkszeitung

which is emerging from the brush, the white head seems quite set apart from such psychological challenges.

And then there is the studio environment to consider too. Everything seems to be collapsing in on itself – the shattered window is falling forwards; the staircase is concertina-ing up and away. Nature's fat, green, gliding, rope-like shoots are worming their way through most ominously. It is a calamitous scene of disorder. The centre is not quite holding, to borrow some words from the great Irish poet W.B. Yeats.[5] There is one other important matter, too, one which is perhaps a prefiguring of the future. The whole scene is being presented to us on what looks like a makeshift stage of

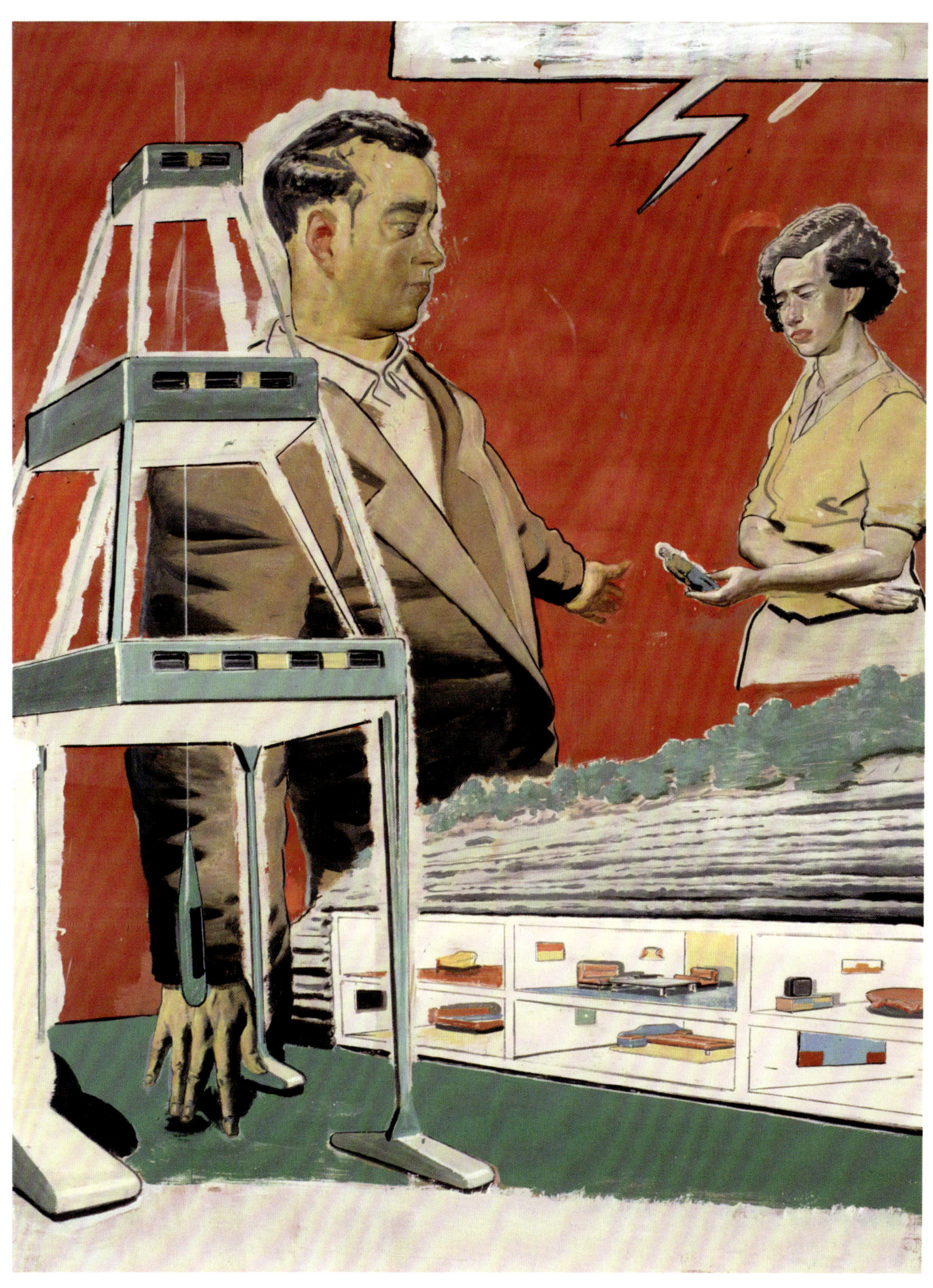

18. Leider 1999

Oil on canvas
200 × 150 cm (78¾ × 59 in)
Hort Family Collection

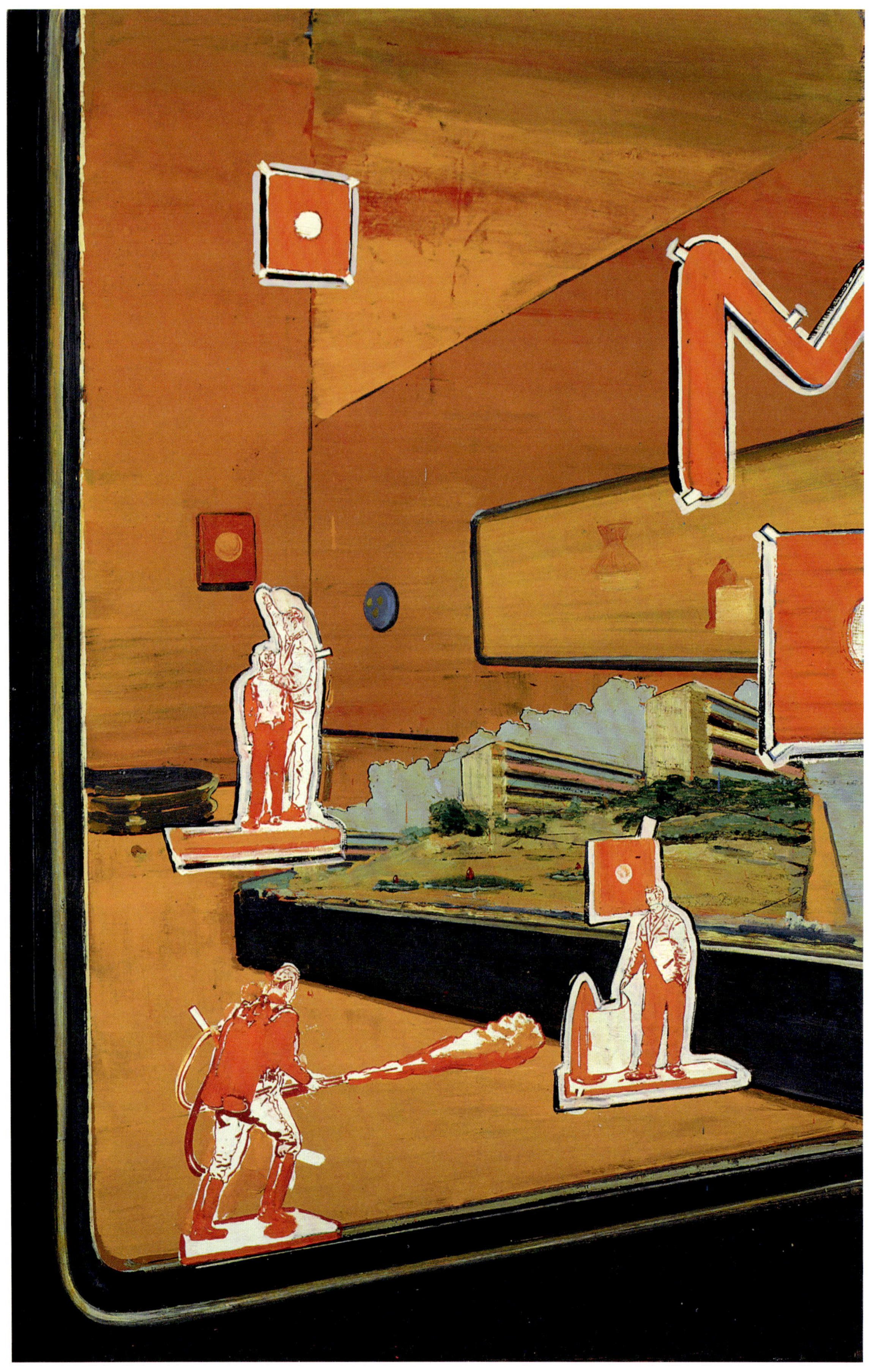

sorts – see how the area of black at the painting's foot seems to delineate a raised surface in front of it. The world of the painting is a stage, then. The painting itself is a theatrical event of sorts, the presentation of a performance. Neo Rauch is becoming a choreographer of scenes of wild theatricality. We will witness much more of this in the coming years.

Little by little, a different kind of work emerges, and that emergence begins to happen as Neo Rauch approaches the new millennium. Colour, little by little, begins to surge back in like an unstoppable sea, and with that colour comes a new sense of emotional heat. Colour is no longer felt to be the enemy of good painting. Many of those works of the early-to-mid-1990s feel like calculated, constructed things, slightly at a distance from their fabricator. The effect is as if the painter is playing with, eavesdropping or reflecting upon those elements out of which he is assembling his own subject matter and his own pictorial space even as he conjures his works into being, trying out this and that, setting down things of the surface – that which he is seeing, that which he has learnt. *Modell* (1998) (fig.19) is all about the fabrication of the painted scene. It frames a strange interior through what looks like the window of a train carriage. We see into a space peopled by cut-outs of figures – one of them is threatening the other with a flamethrower in a threat which is 'frozen', unrealisable. The letter M – the first letter of the painting's title – seems to hang suspended in the air, affixed to a window surface which must forever remain invisible. The word to which it belongs is incapable of completing itself. The painting's menace is nothing but a manufactured thing: it is mock-menace. What could be outside appears to be inside after all.

It is in these years that Rauch's paintings begin to feel as if they are being drawn up from a deeper well than hitherto. The range of colours has increased, and the colours that he is now using feel richer in tone, more visually expansive, more commanding of the space they occupy – look again, for example, at 1997's *Energiebild* (fig.12). Anonymous, automata-like workers with their backs turned away from us are engaged in fabrication of a kind – there are stackings of slats of wood, metal, paper . . . But the total visual impact is that much greater because the blues, the reds, the yellows seem to be creating a seductive impact in spite of the subject matter. It is as if colour is beginning to seize hold of the painting's narrative by becoming a force in its own right. What is more, those billowing, yellow forms seem to be shaping a new and more fantastical, phantasmagorical story altogether.

A year later, and the use of colour is bolder still in *Front* (1998) (fig.20), and the space which the painting commands, the space which the image has carved out for itself against a circumambient void of ragged blackness, feels much airier, much deeper, as a consequence of the bizarre play of its interlocking elements, some of which feel much more playful than usual – the tubular forms, for example, look like a dance of toy balloons. It is as if the use of colour, and how colour almost seems to have willed into being a tumult of shapes – part geometrical, part natural, part tubular

19. Modell 1998

Oil on MDF
160 × 105 cm (63 × 41¼ in)
Private collection, Staufen im Breisgau

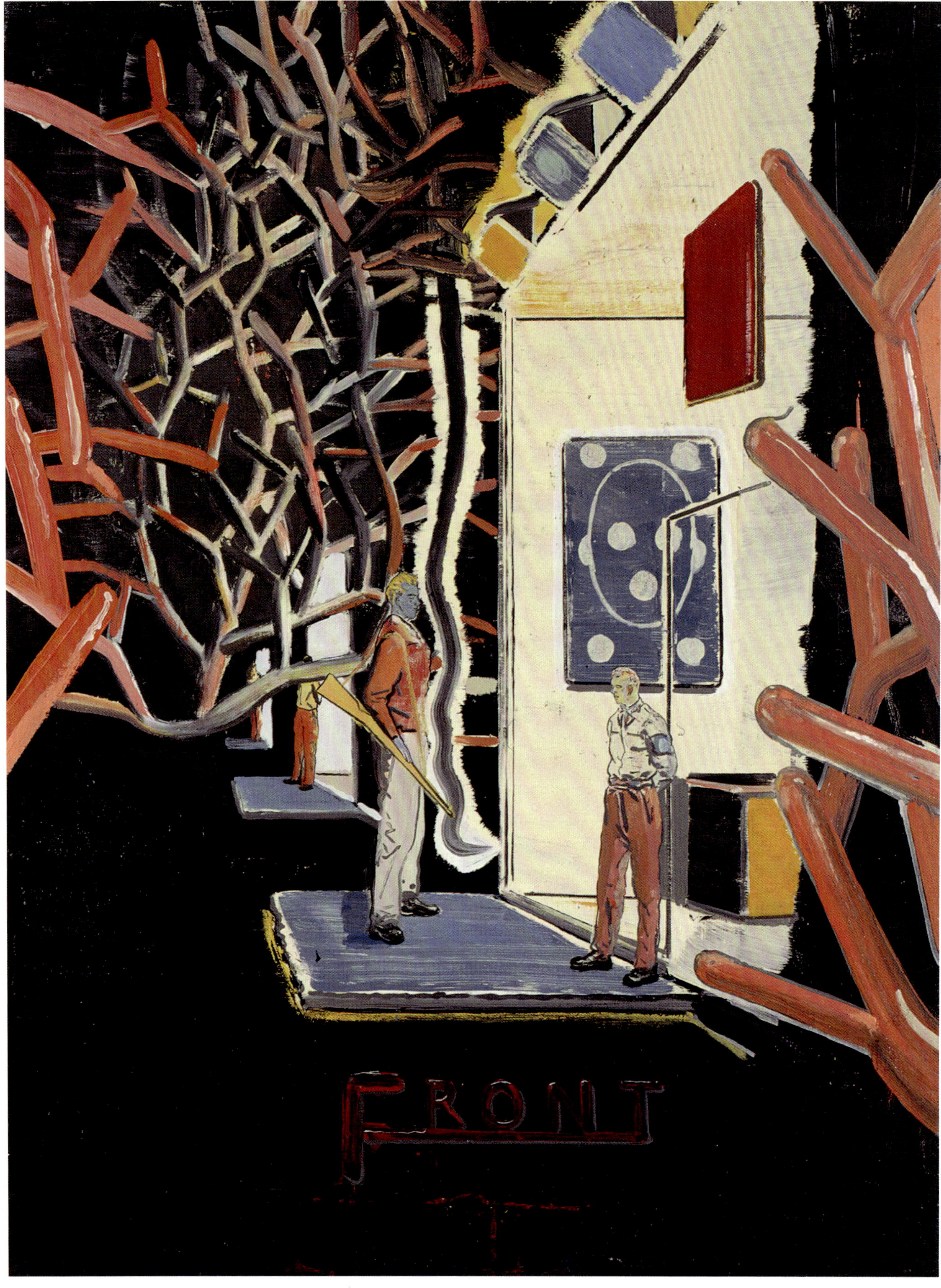
FRONT

– which edge towards recognisable things even as they also seem to strive to remain somewhat abstract, has thrown back a door upon a more expansive world.

Colour is lightening, enlivening and sharply particularising the play of surface – and this painting is very much about surfaces, how things are seen from the front. What remains unchanged from Rauch's earlier works is the stiffness, the strange inertia of the human forms. They stand as if positioned here in a very particular way. They will never be livelier than this. One – much the taller – carries a yellow gun, but its shape is crude and almost beyond credibility – more a cut-out of a yellow gun (outlined thickly in black in order to define its limits) than a real threat of any kind. The diminutive human that this colossus of a man is facing, equally resigned to his own world-weary inertia, is showing no emotion whatsoever. He stares straight ahead, unheeding. It is as if he occupies a different world altogether. Oddly, they stand on the same blue platform, which appears to be hovering against the black void beneath. The gun and the cascading, tree-limb-like shapes, together with the riddling descent of that serpentining black line with its ghostly white halo, seems to suggest that this section of the painting cleaves to the world of nature and its ever-proliferating and ever more fantastical forms. The shorter man, who stands in opposition to such a colourful incursion from the unfathomable dark beyond, exists within – in fact, he is stepping away from – the context of a human-made structure consisting of wall, floor, a desk, a painting which hovers in the air and another which is wall-bound (this is yet another example of a painting which reduces the image of the human face to a naive halo shape complete with jug ears and a sequence of nursery-wall blobs), and the bright theatre lights which are illuminating this scene. We notice, of course, that this man who steps forward onto his blue platform is one of a sequence of three men doing exactly the same thing. Only the man closest to us is confronted by an antagonist toting a gun.

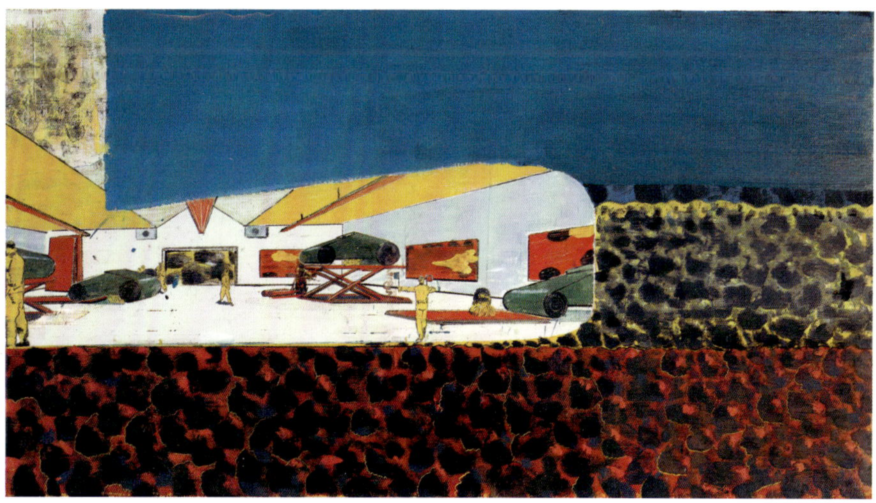

21. Der Durchblick 1997

Oil on canvas
110 × 203 cm (43¼ × 80 in)
Private collection, Hamburg

20. Front 1998

Oil on canvas
120 × 90 cm (47¼ × 35½)
Collection of Bobbi and Stephen Rosenthal, New York

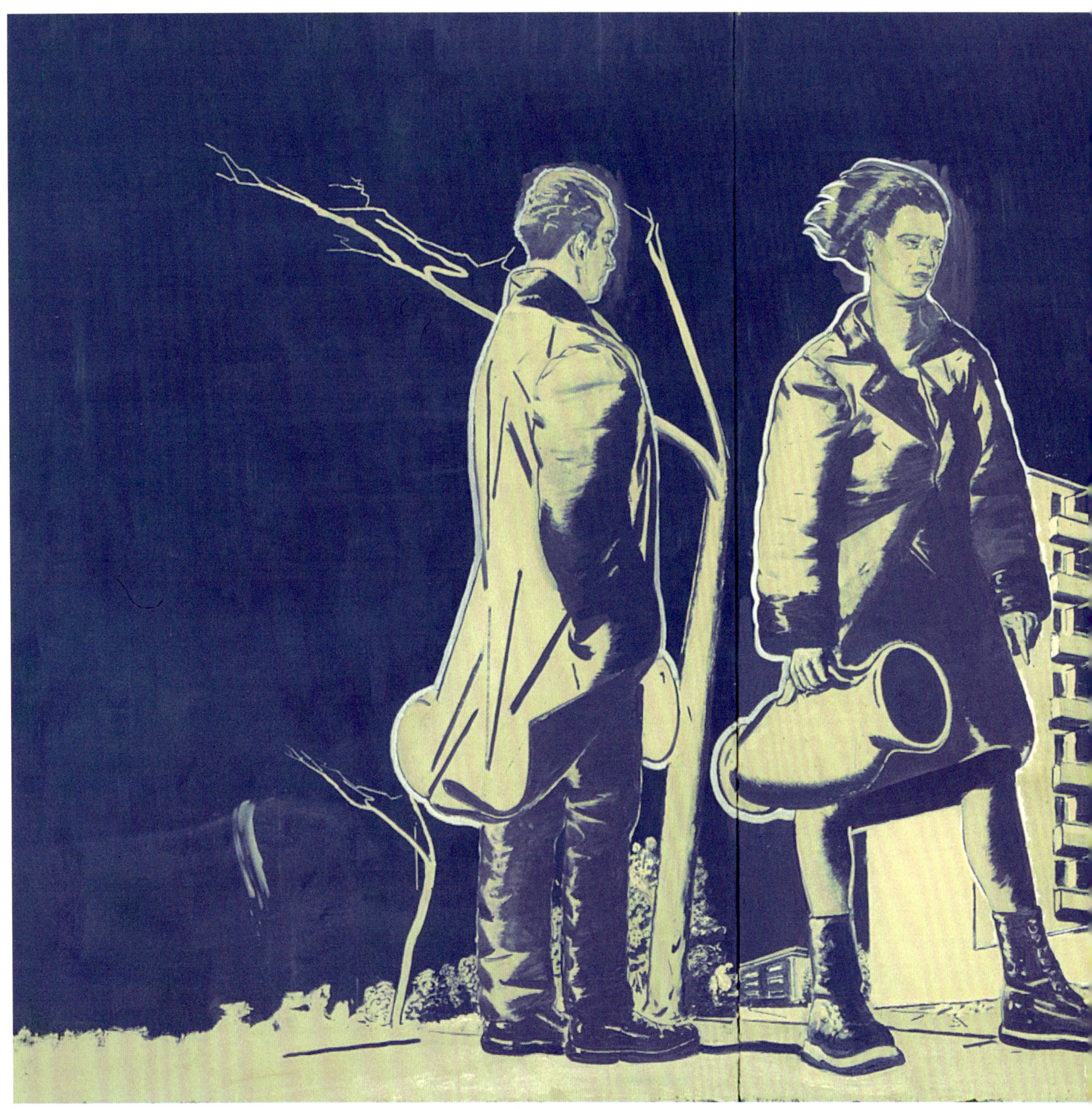

22. Quelle 1999

Oil on canvas
228 × 480 cm (90 × 189 in)
Sammlung Leipziger Volkszeitung

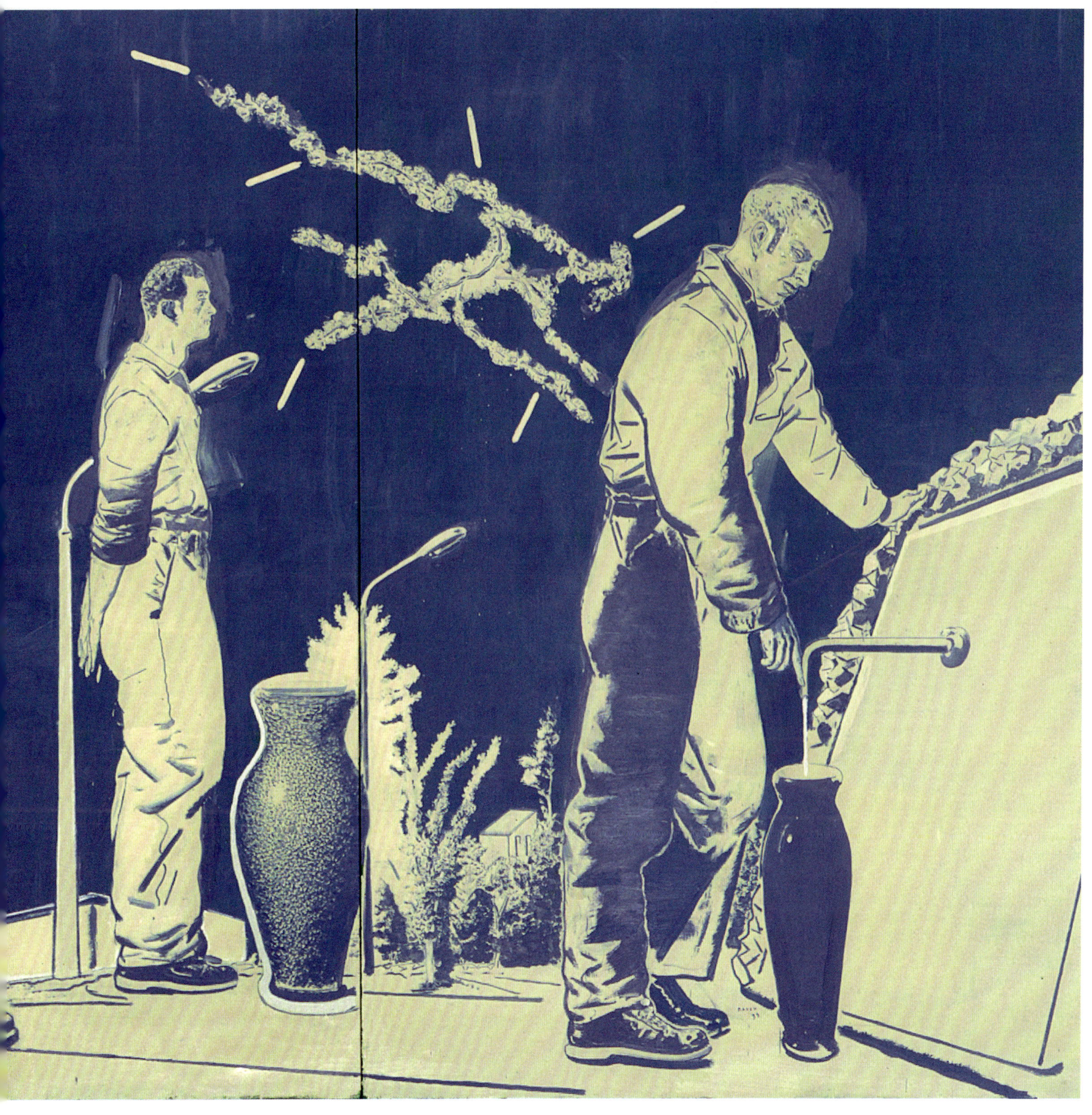

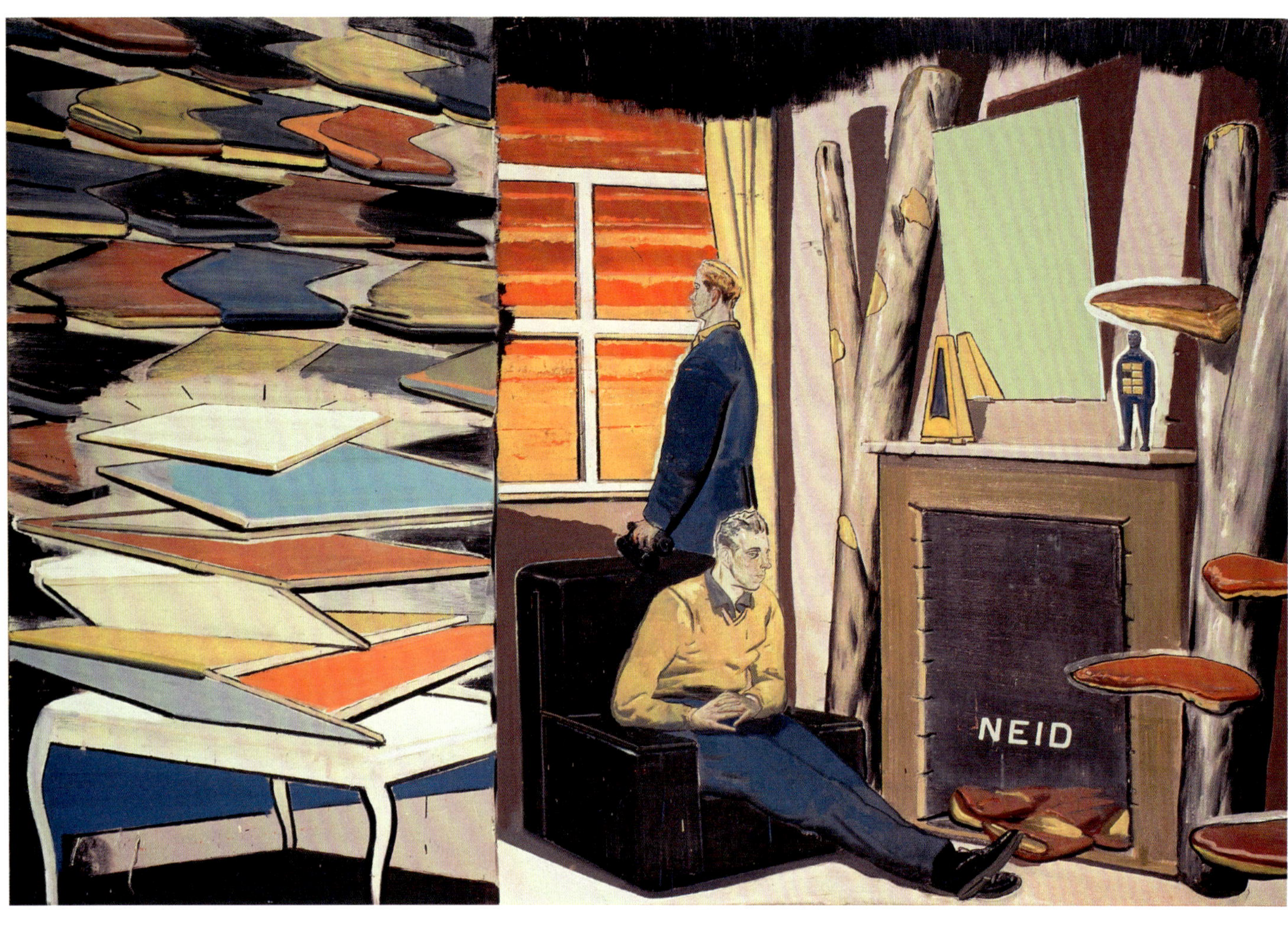

23. Neid 1999

Oil on canvas
200 × 300 cm (78¾ × 118¼ in)
Private Collection, New York

3 Towards a Fabricated Credibility

By the end of the 1990s, there are significant differences in the way that the human figure is being depicted in the work of Neo Rauch. Generally speaking, there are more of them in any particular painting. What is more, a greater flexibility, a greater mobility has entered into the way the human body is being represented. The size of the human form has grown closer to life-size. These figures are no longer anonymous ciphers, almost always turned away from us, nothing but examples of human productivity, extensions of the uniforms that they wear. They are no longer cut-outs or mere types of the human. They have thickened out; they are more credibly human.

Neid of 1999 (Envy, or Jealousy) (fig.23) demonstrates this new opening up and out. The title proposes a very human predicament, of one human being jealous of another. What is more, the seated figure facing us exists to be contemplated by the onlooker. He is no longer anonymous, or almost anonymous, but seems to idle in front of our gaze in order to be scrutinised. He is definably a civilian, dressed in casual clothes, not a soldier or a worker. An awkward relationship of some kind is being suggested between the man at the window and the seated figure. The former stares out at an angry sky. Is that an indication of the tumult within? The word 'NEID' hangs in the air, positioned low in the grate – rather chilling, unadorned, white in colour – as if it is nothing but the sum of what it tells us. The seated man stares at it, leaning slightly forward, fingers knitted, as if contemplating its significance. Perhaps the word is a description of a shared state of mind. It reminds us of those texts which often flashed up on screen before an episode in a silent film of the 1920s.

An entire dramatic scene is being proposed to us within the interior of a room with a chair, a window, a white curtain. It resembles a fragment from a play – perhaps at the moment when the curtain rises, before anyone speaks. There are other elements too, more fantastical ones – screens of floating colour which bend and fold as they rise; tree trunks stacked beside the grate; amorphous, amoeba-like floatings; and, on the mantelpiece, a metronome to mark the passing of the seconds and the minutes (its back is reflected in the green mirror – do we not habitually remark that a person is 'green with jealousy'?); and a curiously small, grey-blue robotic figure, complete with buttons down its chest, which might or might not activate some response. This entire pictorial presentation, by its sweep and its credibility, marks a shift away from Neo Rauch's characteristic painting manner of the 1990s. And it is not only the gradual incursion of vibrant, emboldened colour which has helped to bring into being this new sense of dramatic momentum

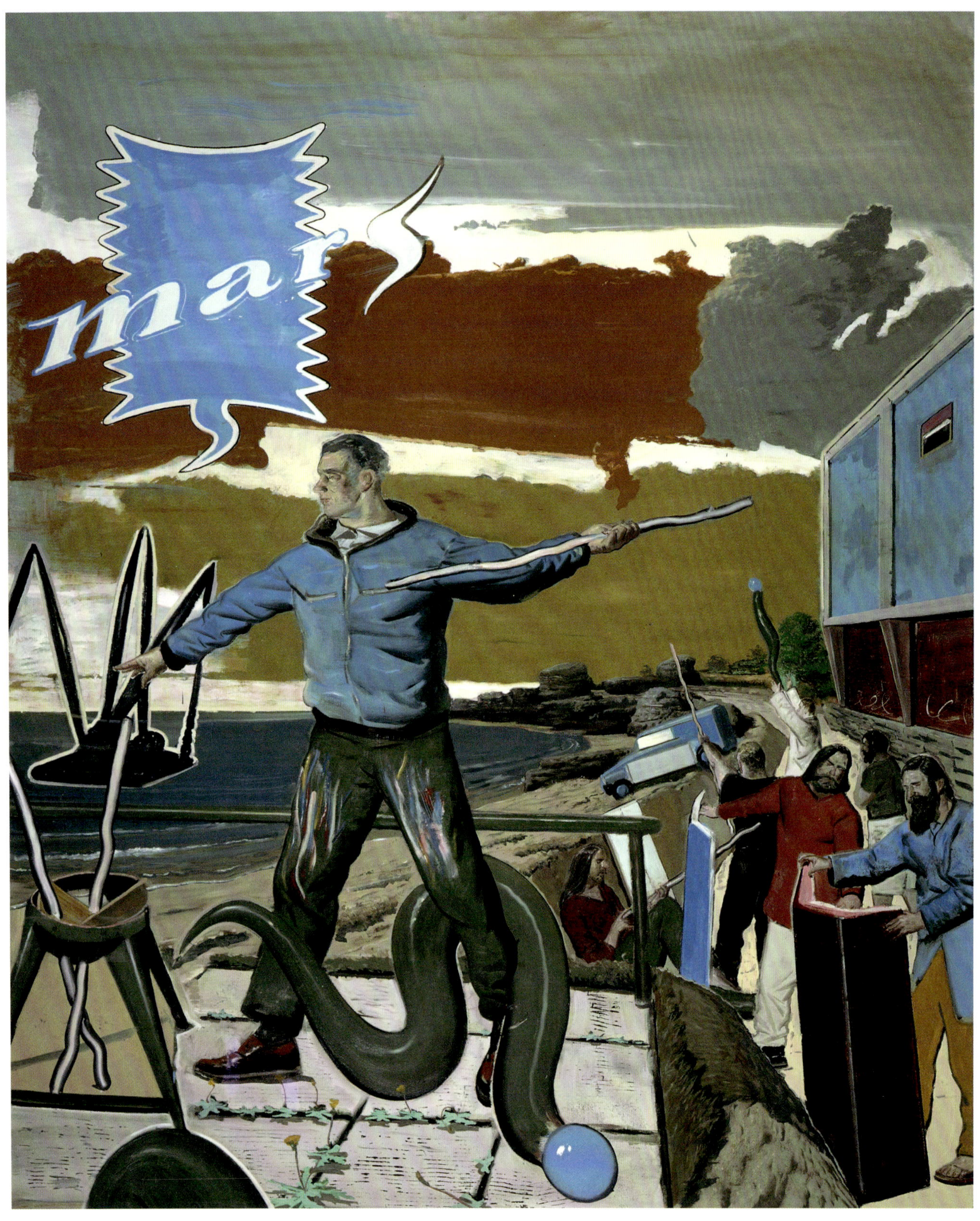

24. Mars 2002

Oil on canvas
250 × 210 cm (98½ × 82¾ in)
Private collection

but also a newly credible and dramatically scaled-up rendering of what it is to zbe human. Soon nature too, so often scarred, brutalised or wounded-looking in those early paintings, will spring back to life too, her trees and flowers particularised and beautified. She will also reveal herself to be an unfathomable source of mystery.

Neo Rauch has returned, repeatedly, to the subject of the painter and his task: what his role is to be; how he stands in relation to the works that he makes; how much he is at the behest of forces just beyond his control. How much is he in charge of that which he seems to call up from the depths of himself? And to what extent is that self-image of the painter shaped by the self-images of other, earlier painters?

Mars (2002) (fig.24) not only shows the emergence of the painter at a new level of confidence. It also presents the painter himself as a massive, dominating, world-bestriding figure – no longer in doubt about his own direction, ready to take the 'war' to his critics. We stare at a single, large tableau. The fragmentation of earlier paintings has gone. The landscape is rooted in itself, seemingly all of a piece. And there, he – the heroic figure of the painter, who uncannily seems to resemble in appearance an older, more historical version of Neo Rauch himself – stands forth as Mars, the god of war, spread-legged, in his paint-bespattered trousers. The title splashes across the canvas cinematically, as if to increase our excitement about the outcome of this decision by the painter to stand forth and anoint himself in this way. The sky boils behind it, elementally thrilling and unpredictable in its wild sweep of cloud splashings, and all realised in such furious and strangely variegated colours. Yes, the very heavens are preparing themselves for this great gesture. A god is here indeed. It is an act of great hubris, great fanfare. He is challenging, preparing to outface, the sea itself. The stance harks back to the proud self-display of Romanticism, of man facing into the void. His right hand gestures; his left arm pulls back, ready to fling the stick. What is this mysterious stick? Is there necromancy in its powers? Or is the gesture a reckless, part-comic one? What is that strange green coiling doing around his trouser leg? Is it the very paint that he will be squeezing out? Is it suggesting that it is the material itself which will decide to what use it is to be put? And will that thin wooden stake enable him to achieve his ambitions?

Surely this is a mere painter in soiled trousers. Can he really be more than this? Is the title perhaps at odds with the human reality? Various human figures stand close to him, involving themselves in this ceremony in various ways, flourishing thin, pale sticks of their own, though perhaps without the same degree of confidence. They are toying with theirs, and seem unlikely to strike out in emulation of the central figure. Who are these beings? Are they ancient or modern? Their beards lend them more than a hint of religion and prophecy, and even a measure of ancientness, though there is nothing ancient about the Modernist structure which rises behind them. Modernity also interposes itself in the presence of a van which is parked further up the sand, an object of utility which feels strangely at odds with much of the rest of this scene. The man with the longer beard appears to be grasping at the corners of a lectern of sorts – or perhaps he is holding open a great, stretched book. Could this be a sacred book, here to play a part in this ceremony?

There are other elements of the bizarre in this scene, such as the spider-like structure, perhaps part human construction and part living creature, which appears to drift on or hover over the waves, snatched from the pages of a sci-fi novel. The imperious gesture of the dominating figure of the painter suggests that it will be his task, his duty and his responsibility to hold all this together, to shape it, to make it all cohere. So many worlds – of past, present, future – are beginning to crowd in on him. There is so much work to be done. Perhaps this kind of work, all this mixing and matching, will more closely resemble the task of the sorcerer or the alchemist than that of the more habitual kind of worker in so many of the earlier paintings of Neo Rauch, with their acknowledged lists of programmatic tasks. The strangeness of it all will only intensify.

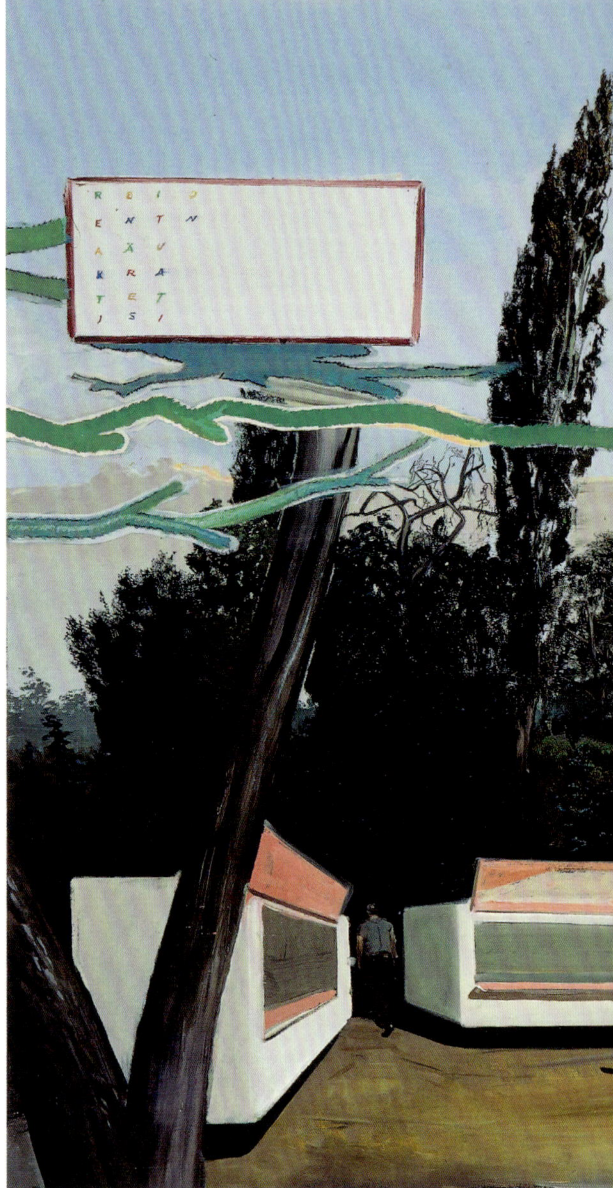

In this same year, Neo Rauch painted *Reaktionäre Situation* (fig.25), which requires no translation. That title sounds challengingly abrupt and comprehensive, and also rather severely pedagogical – unless, of course, it is tongue-in-cheek and ironic. Is this painting a reflection upon politics then? Given Neo Rauch's disapproval of political art this seems unlikely, unless he is coming to the subject glancingly. A panel, inserted into the painting itself, spells out the letters of the title one by one, with a childish clumsiness (its letters are picked out in different colours, as if on a whiteboard in a schoolroom). What exactly is reactionary about this 'reactionary situation'?

Is it the fact that it seems to cleave to the realistic presentation of the human figure in a way that would once have been applauded by the overbearing masters of public taste in the GDR in, say, the 1950s? Or does it hint at the fakeness of this evocation of the idea of the rural idyll – if this is indeed a rural idyll of sorts? We face the breadth of a sweeping landscape. We look out onto waterlogged, ploughed fields in the aftermath of harvest, hay in rectangular bundles, a distant village church (a detail reminiscent of Van Gogh), poplars bending in the wind. It may be a rural idyll then, at least in part, if there were not also certain disturbing details which might suggest otherwise – that colourful piece of toy weaponry at the painting's foot, for example. Or the way in which that structure with its propeller hangs in the air – is this a windmill or the propeller snatched from an aircraft? It seems in part to belong to the countryside, and in part to have military designs on us – those slits in the roof, for example, the very fact that it seems to be at a height designed to snoop upon us and that one of its white arms projects directly up into the clouds.

Does that ziggurat directly beneath the white arm of the propeller consist of rectangular bundles of hay (others are strewn about the field) – or is it meant to suggest a structure snatched from the Aztecs? All these possibilities hover – quite literally – in front of our gaze. What arrests us immediately is the way in which the

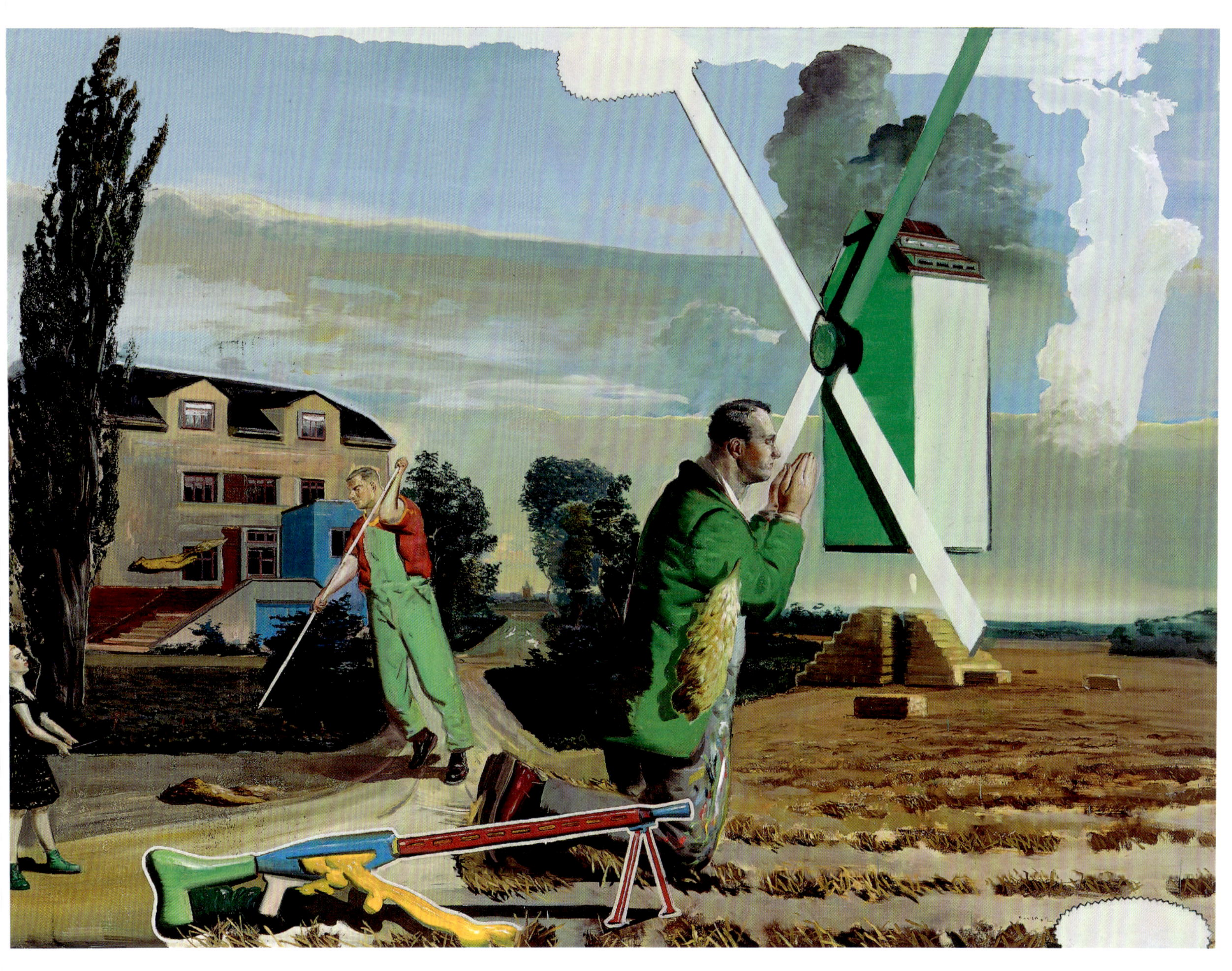

25. Reaktionäre Situation 2002

Oil on canvas
210 × 400 cm (82¾ × 157½ in)
Private collection, Berlin, Sparkassenstiftung, Ostsächsische Sparkasse Dresden

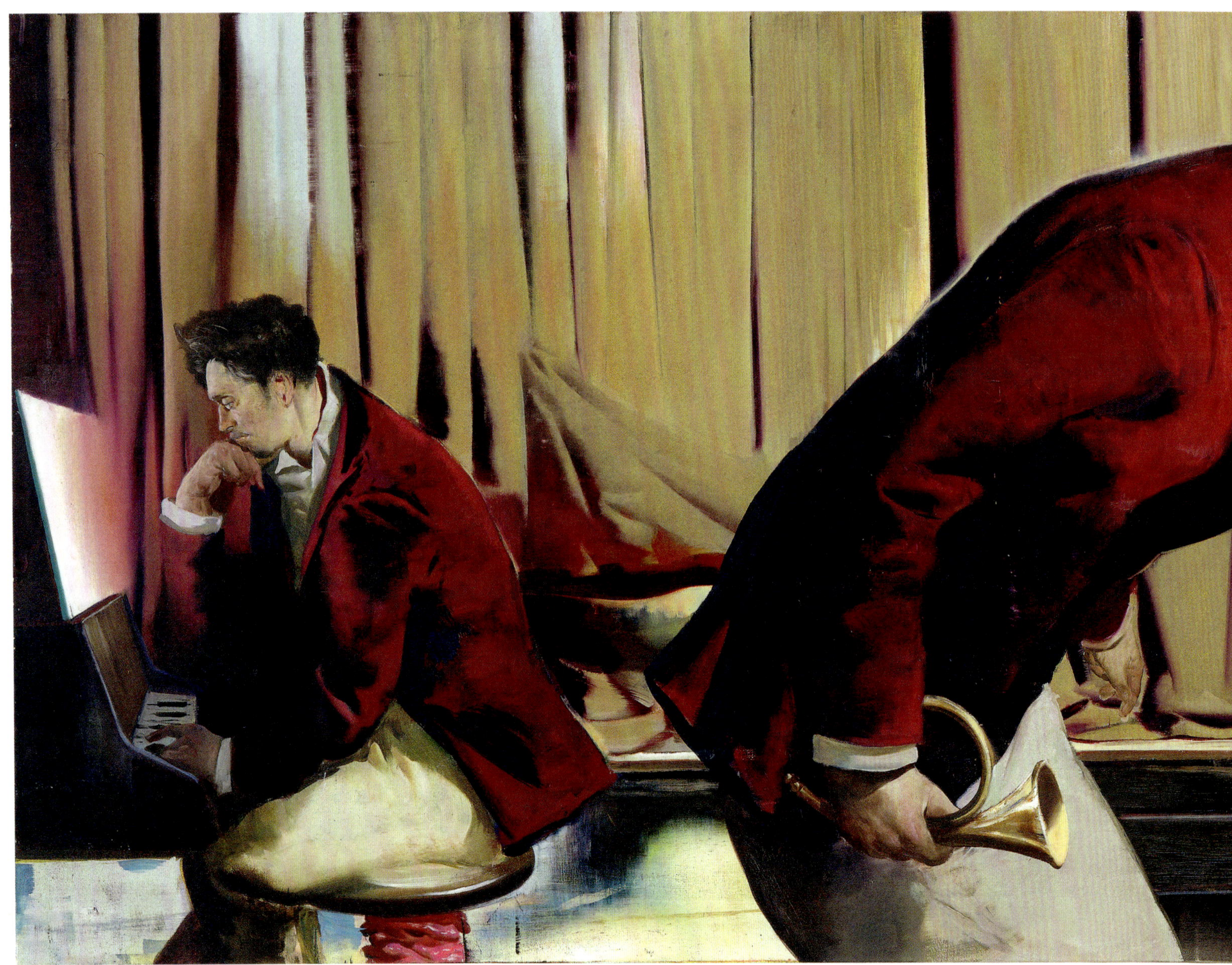

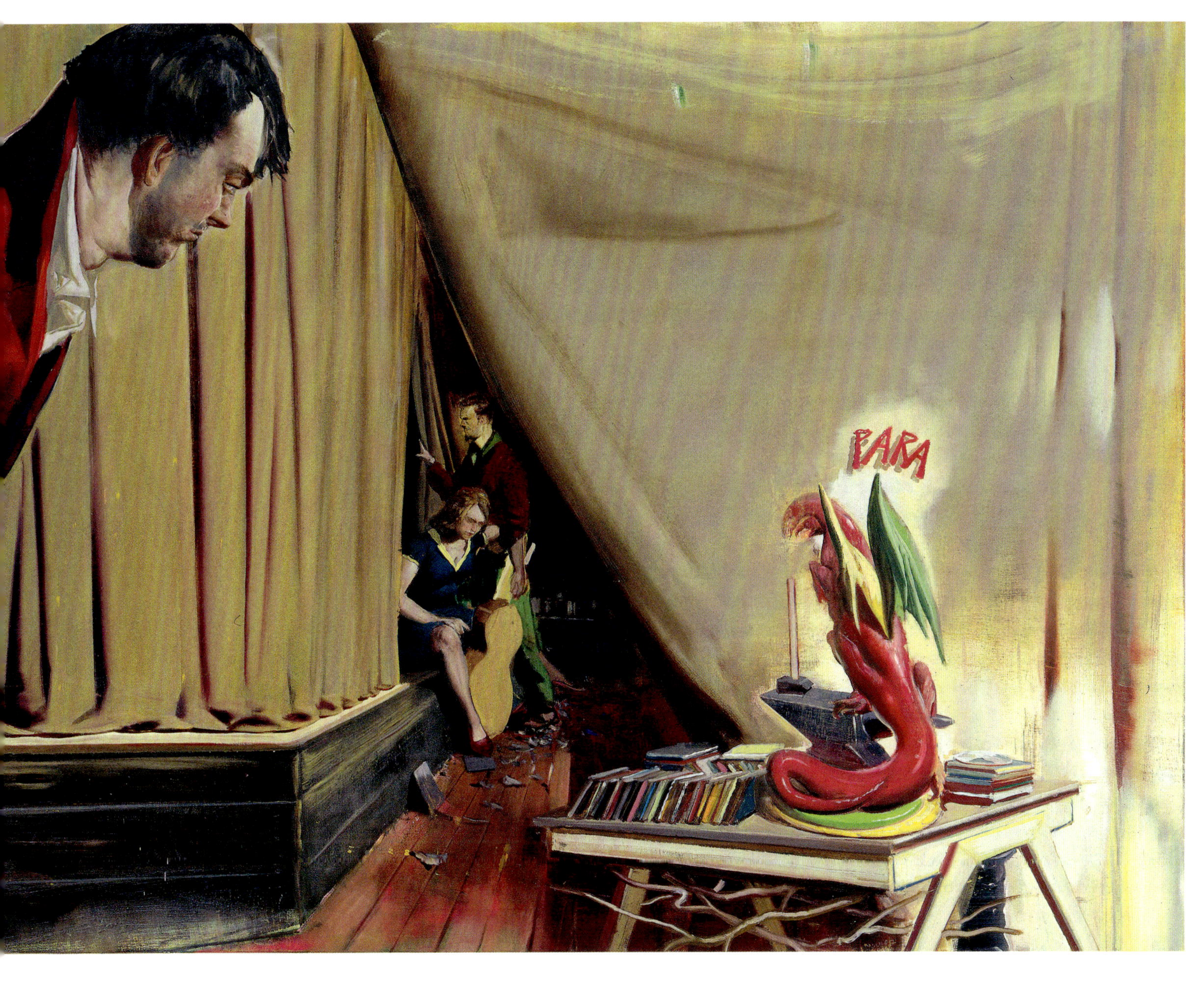

31. Para 2007

Oil on canvas
150 × 400 cm (59 × 157½ in)
Private collection, New York

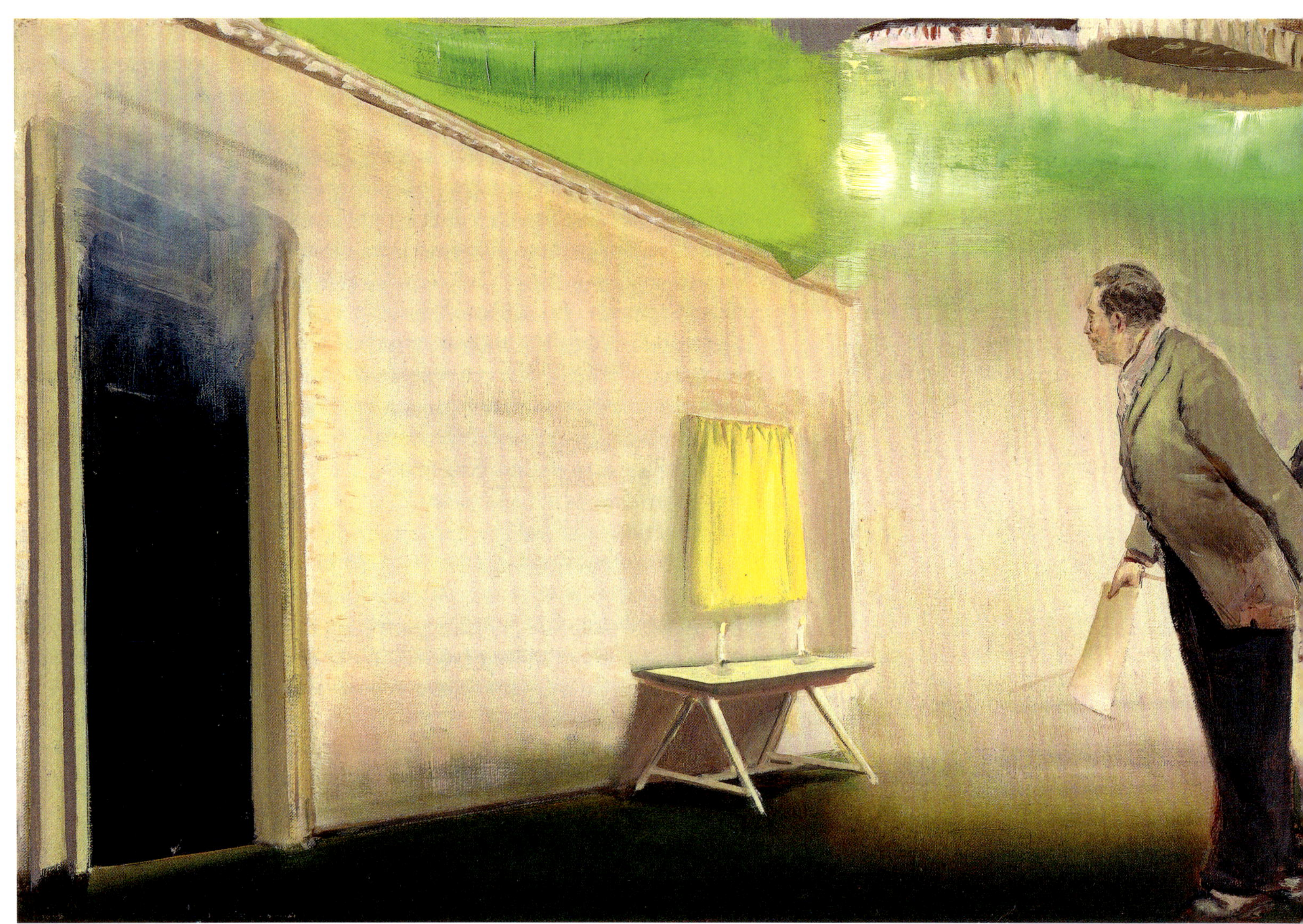

colourful; the temporal and spatial slippages intensify; the colours, ever more vitally alive, seem to live lives of ever-more unusually defiant independence; and the characters come roaring and tumbling out of their marionette's box. And yet the painter makes it all cohere – somehow. He both releases and traps, bottles, all this energy. In short, the observing eye's restlessness is ceaseless. Once upon a time, many a great painting had a principal point of focus, some place from where we could take our bearings, some axis about which everything else seemed to pivot. This is, generally speaking, not the case with the paintings of Neo Rauch. There is often no equivalent of a steady engagement with some central point of focus. There is always a muchness, and always a teeming many: the world is manifold indeed. What is more,

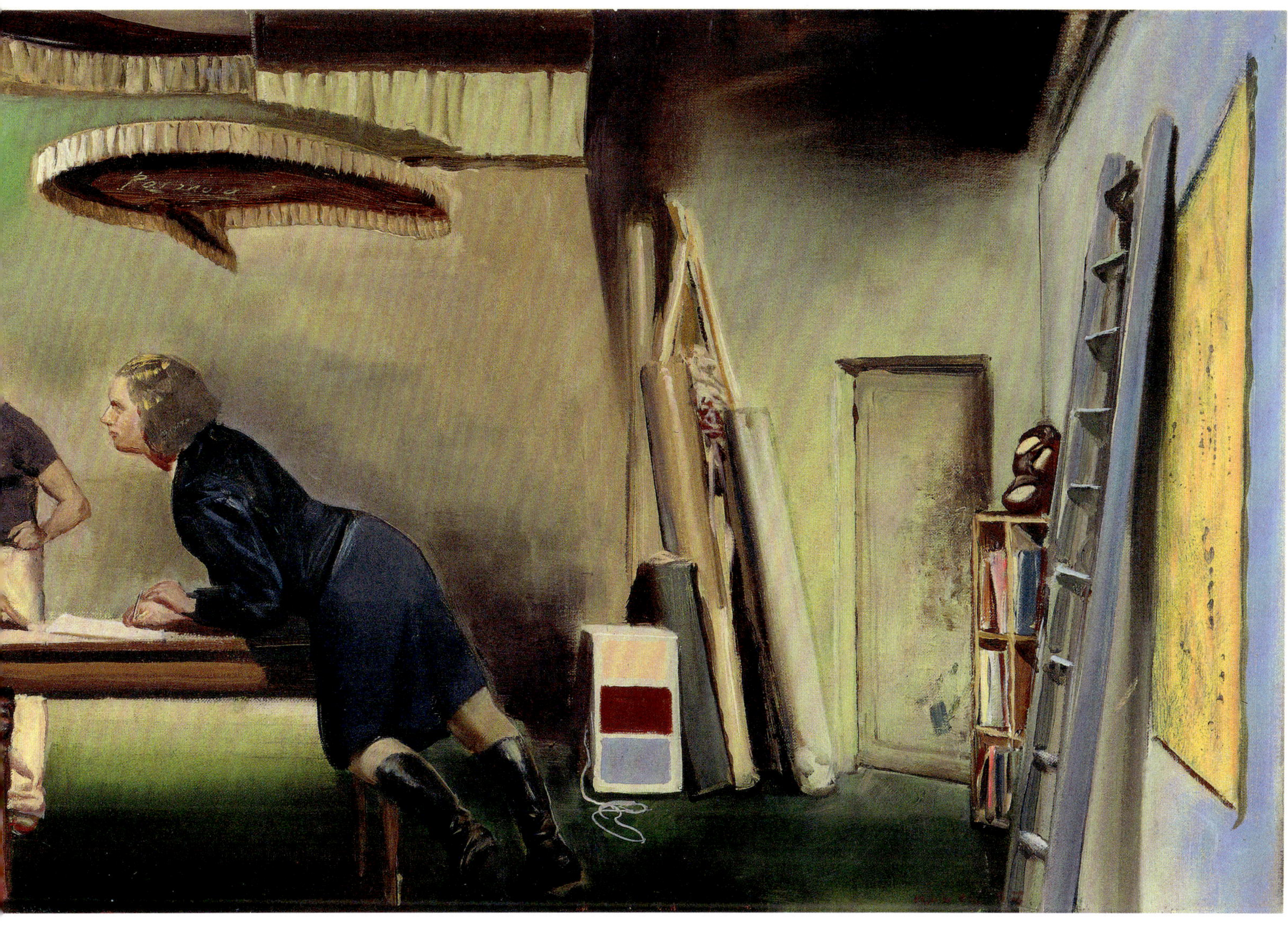

32. Paranoia 2007

Oil on canvas
50 × 150 cm (19¾ × 59 in)
Private collection, courtesy David Zwirner

we are not encouraged to seek out this point of rest so that we can then find inner consolation by saying to ourselves, 'This is it. It is from here that any fruitful interpretation must begin.' There is no such place, no such haven of peacefulness. Instead, there is often a bewildering multiplicity of starting and ending points, and each one of them is stimulatingly provisional. And this is the reason why Neo Rauch's paintings excite us so much. We bring new and ever more super-subtle notions to them whenever we look at them. The journey, and the exhilaration of that journey, always begins afresh.

Painted in 2008, the year following the show at the Metropolitan Museum, *Die Stickerin* (Woman Embroidering) (fig.33) puts us in mind of a work of the same name

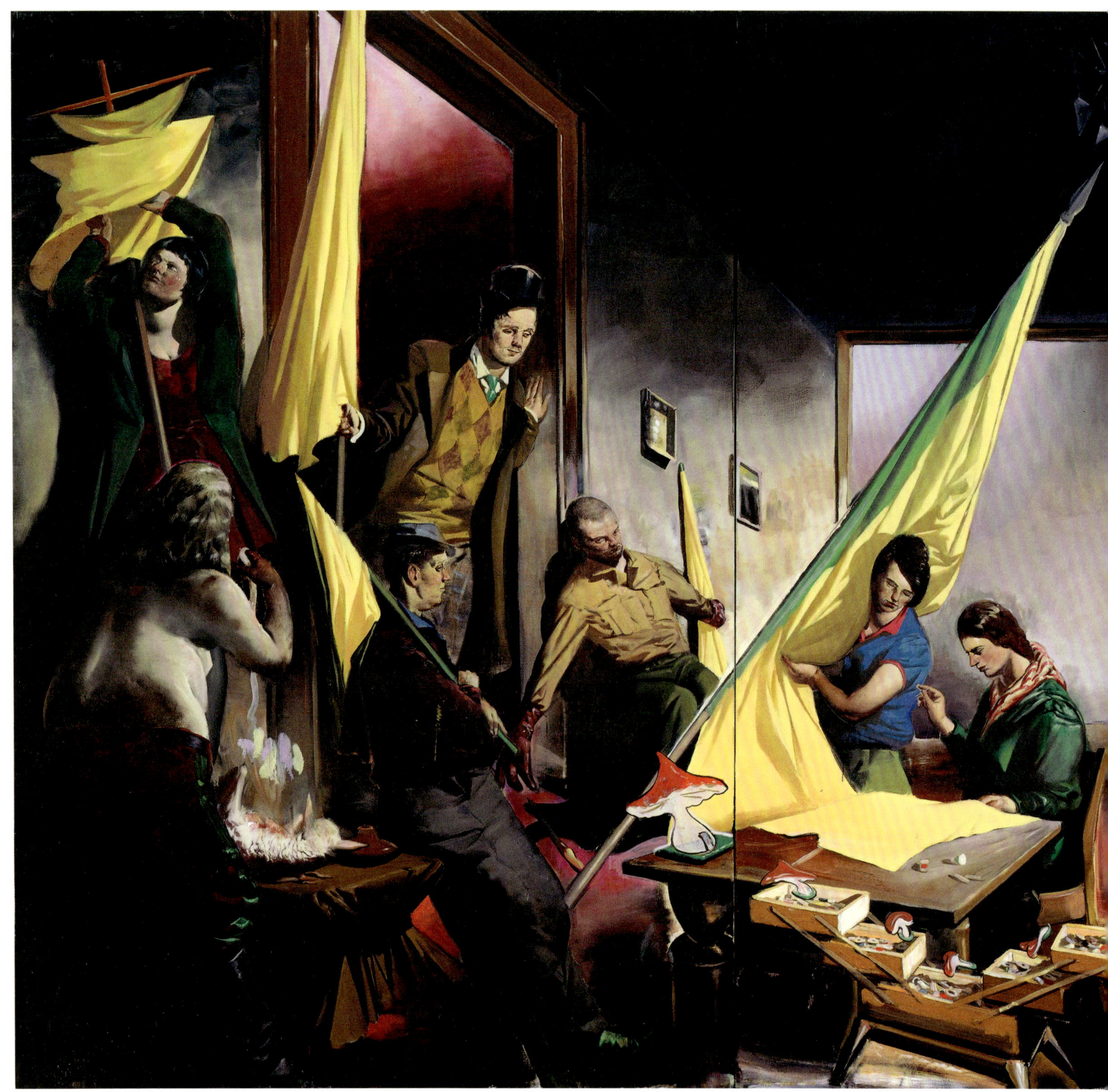

33. Die Stickerin 2008

Oil on canvas
300 × 420 cm (118¼ × 165½ in)
Broad Art Foundation, Los Angeles

William Wordsworth's 'My heart leaps up . . .', becomes father to the man. It is the child in all of us who has the innate capacity to see far.

In the work of Neo Rauch, colour sets off very particular, dramatic responses in the viewer. You feel a sense of a struggle as he tries to describe what colour means to him, how exactly he works with it:

> I often think in terms of colours first – what colours to avoid. I am always striving to reach new combinations. I try to use colours I don't like. I have to familiarise myself with unfriendly colours. I don't like a certain kind of blue – the colour of sports clothes. Or bright purple – strong aubergine perhaps. I try to use them all the same.[12]

What is his favourite colour? 'Black. But I seldom use it.'

His juxtapositions of colour take us by surprise, set our teeth on edge, unnerve us by their very audacity. They exist on the brink of jarringness. Some of his paintings are made in a single colour, whose strength and intensity vary across the sweep of the work itself.

In *Schilfkind* (Reed Child, 2010) (fig.36), the entire atmosphere – its unnerving sense of menace as we contemplate the shudder-inducing emergence through the woman's legs of that eel-like, up-squirming, penile threat from the reed bed – is created by the work's uniform moltenness. A dull gold tone imprints, impregnates, suffuses the whole. This gold is tainted, we feel. It is a wholly negative, menacing force. It reminds us of the predicament of King Midas, and of how his all-consuming lust for that precious metal led him to impotence in the end, to a life that could only ever be a non-life. Everything he touched turned to gold. There was no life for him beyond its cold bedazzlement. His very food turned to gold when he touched it.

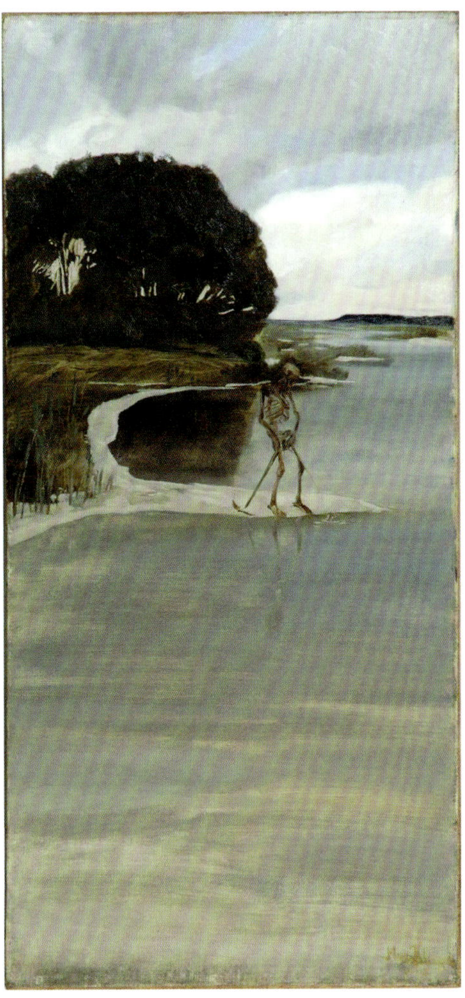

37. Max Klinger
Der Tod am Wasser (Death by the Water) c.1880

Oil on canvas
95 × 45 cm (37½ × 17¾ in)
Museum der bildenden Künste, Leipzig

And in this painting, worse even than the threat which seems to be rising up from the reed bed, is the terrible, looming presence of that boggle-eyed, puppet-headed mannequin of a child, the orchestrator of this scene, idly dangling her salamander. Consider the dramatic colour that Rauch has chosen to use for the gloved hands and the necktie of the man who strives to push her away. It reminds us of similar, dramatic interpositions of shocking and jarring colours in works by Max Klinger, a Leipzig artist of an earlier generation.

Klinger and Rauch often have much in common: the way that they combine the erotic, the religious and the shiveringly macabre (see fig.37). The man who makes that gesture of refusal in *Reed Child* has the look of a biblical illustration from the 19th or early 20th century. On this particular occasion, it is Franz von Stuck's use of purple in *The Crucifixion of Christ* (1913) (fig.38) which springs to mind as a shadowy, influential predecessor. In short, *Schilfkind* feels like a scene straight out of folklore or *Struwwelpeter* or Grimm – as old as it is new, as simple as it is impenetrably strange – the kind of stuff ripe to be seized on, with such hand-wringing glee, by the depth psychologist.

Two of Neo Rauch's finest and largest paintings of recent years are on display at G2, a foundation established in a former processing plant in the centre of Leipzig to show off works from the Hildebrand Collection of contemporary art from the city.[13] Both paintings are first glimpsed at the end of a corridor, at a distance of about 50 metres, and they announce themselves at this distance, with great fanfare, as battles of colour. *Das Treffen* (The Meeting or The Date, 2013) (fig.39) is, you could argue, a contest between the power of two primary colours, blue and red, swatches of which you can see mysteriously hanging or floating in front of the drawn-back curtain on the right. Seen at some distance, this painting is reminiscent of a great Venetian altarpiece – a work by Titian perhaps. Schematically, it looks and feels traditional. The composition is pyramidal. Figures are forced into certain positions in order to achieve a balanced arrangement. There are kneeling ones whose positions remind us of the ghosts of supplicating donors. Rauch's signature is on the face of the canvas, in the shadow – a very common habit of Renaissance painters. (It is unusual for an artist to sign his paintings on their face these days.) See how the white-painted mullions of the window (a window so enormous, we come to realise, that it almost beggars description) remind us of a crucifix. That window also creates a particular feeling of space. As usual with Rauch, this is a painting which beckons us to interpret it in very specific ways and then pushes us back by the sheer forces of unreason which seem to have been marshalled here to repel us.

The painting is both real and unreal simultaneously. The central preoccupation of four of its five figures is the clash, on a tabletop, between two giant, uprearing stag beetles, one blue and the other red, tricked out in the provocative strip of rival soccer teams. There is a landscape beyond the window, part rural and part light-industrial. Figures and objects seem to have winged in from various epochs and various sources, from comics to children's books. The entire painting, which proposes itself as story-telling and then snatches that possibility away again, seems to have an ambiguity of response, a frustration of raised expectation, at its very heart. Its size, and even its pyramidal composition, raises our hopes as to its significance; its subject matter perhaps gives the lie to that supposition, and pulls the painting back in the direction of bathos.

The onlookers, entirely emotionless, are gravely intent upon this tabletop contest. They defy our wish to relate to them. Meanwhile, a kneeling figure in a hat with pointed ears pushes some toy-like, martial vehicles about the floor which, upon closer examination, seem to be unworkable, inept, comic versions of themselves. Other parts of the painting look like fragments of abstract sculpture. Nothing quite adds up. We are thrown back upon ourselves: what should one expect of a painting anyway? What is more, the effect of the painting on us changes as we draw back from it – and we can walk back a considerable distance. When we stand close, we regard the figures as close to human size: our size. The further back we go, the smaller and more puppet-like the figures seem to become in the context of this enormous window. Perhaps, then, it is a

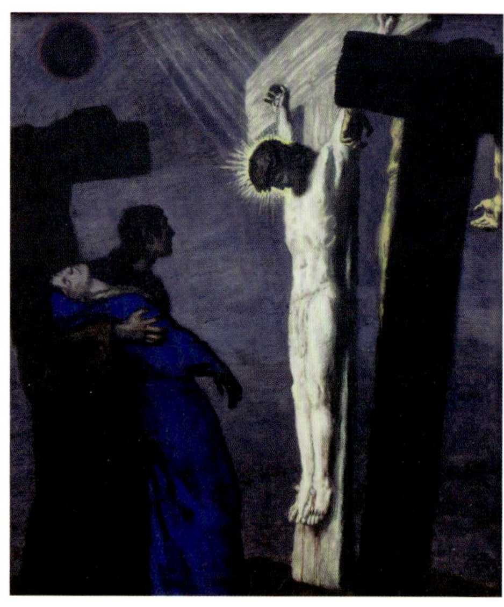

38. Franz von Stuck
The Crucifixion of Christ 1913

Tempera on canvas
190 × 165 cm (74¾ × 65 in)
Museum der bildenden Künste, Leipzig

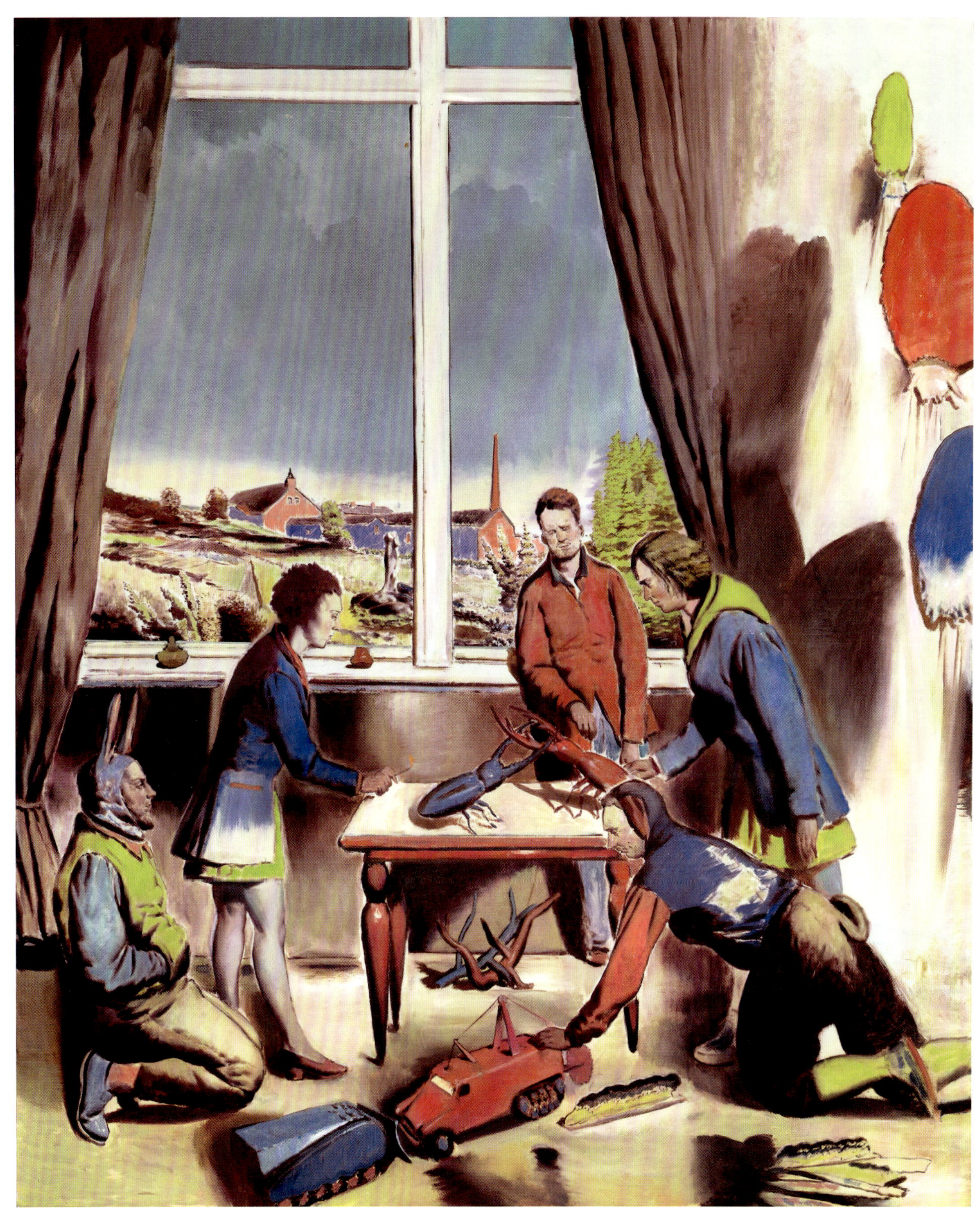

39. Das Treffen 2013

Oil on canvas
300 × 250 cm (118¼ × 98½ in)
Sammlung Hildebrand, Leipzig

painting about one's shifting feeling of space. Or perhaps it is a painting about the clash of primary colours. In short, its relationship to what we might loosely and crudely describe as reality of any kind – even the provisional, illusionistic reality of a painting – is a complicated one indeed.

At the far end of another corridor at G2, you will see *Fremde* (Stranger, 2016) (fig.40). The title puzzles us, by its lack of a definite article. That lack has opened up the possible range of the word's meanings in German: one stranger, or more than one stranger – or, perhaps, even a specifically female stranger. *Die Fremde* can also mean a place outside your knowledge or a place where you have never been, or where you feel uncomfortable. Is the stranger of the painting's title this sexually ambiguous being at its centre, a figure which at a distance appears to glow preternaturally, to draw all eyes to her – or to him? The painting's two halves – whose moods almost seem to be at odds with each other – are divided by a wall. To the left is sombreness and militarism (those threatening, tubular, bullet- or cannon-like forms held beneath the arms of the man in his *sturmhaube* [balaclava] and camouflage-coloured coat), and, to the right of the wall, near-overwhelming bursts of pinkish red – the colour of the costuming of the sexually ambivalent being herself (who is offering us mysterious, crystalline objects from a tray), and the roof of the house to her right. The two spaces are held together by a diagonal which runs from that tube beneath the left arm of the man, through the right forearm of the seller of mysteries, and up into the overhanging eaves of the house. Without this diagonal, the painting would run the risk of not cohering.

The shrillness of this red shouts at us from metres away. It causes the being's predicament – standing as she is, frontally posed, reminiscent of some rendering of Christ, finger raised as if in blessing or exoneration, in the midst of a consuming pyre – to be our central concern. Is she a willing sacrifice? Is this a scene alluding to heresy, witchcraft? Is she emerging from the flames? Or is this a hallucination on the part of the onlooker to the right of her?

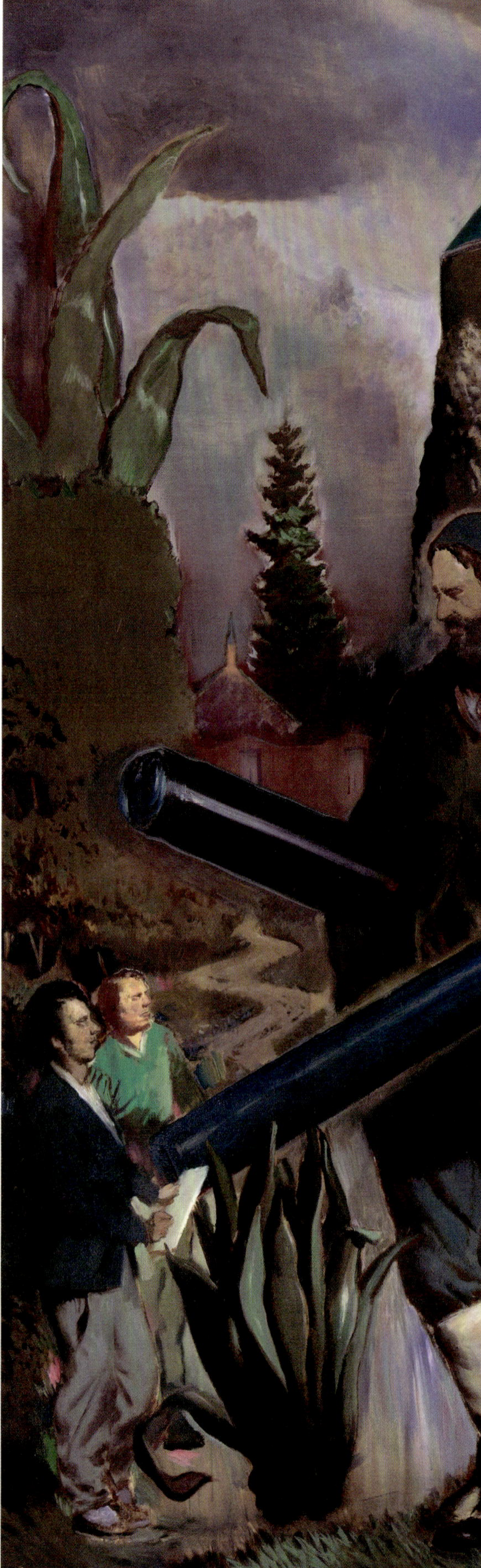

40. Fremde 2016

Oil on canvas
250 × 300 cm (98½ × 118¼ in)
Sammlung Hildebrand, Leipzig

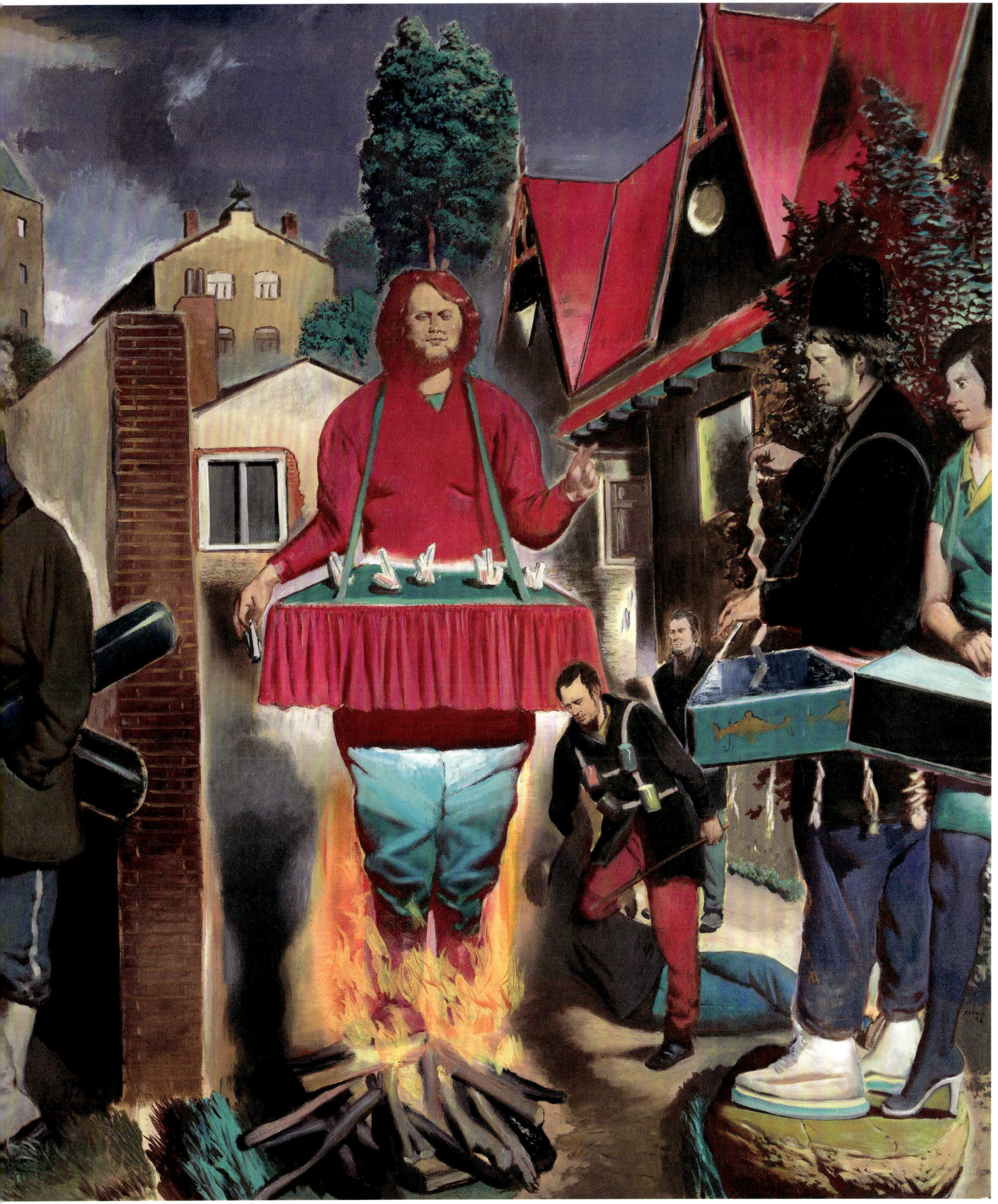

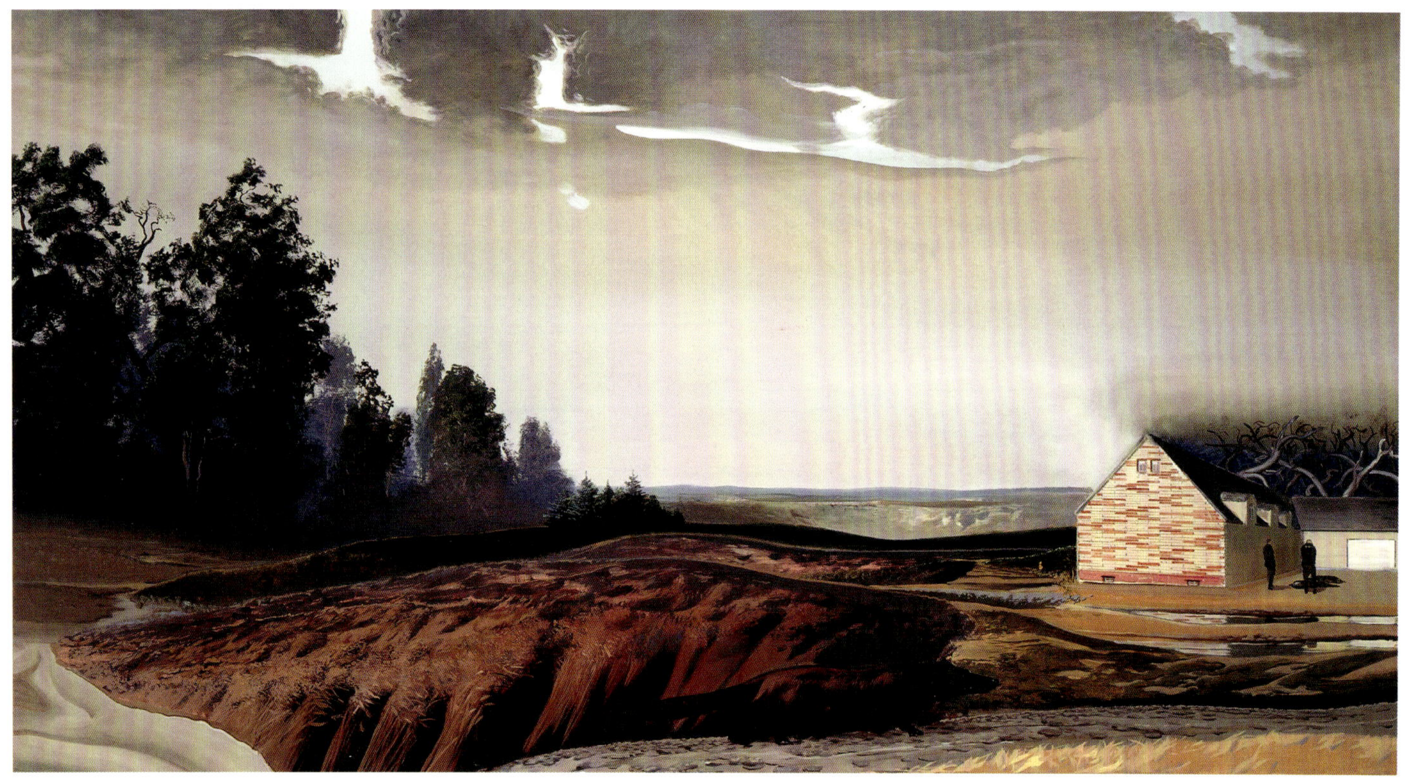

41. Waldmann 2003

Oil on canvas
160 × 300 cm (63 × 118¼ in)
Collection Family Scharpff

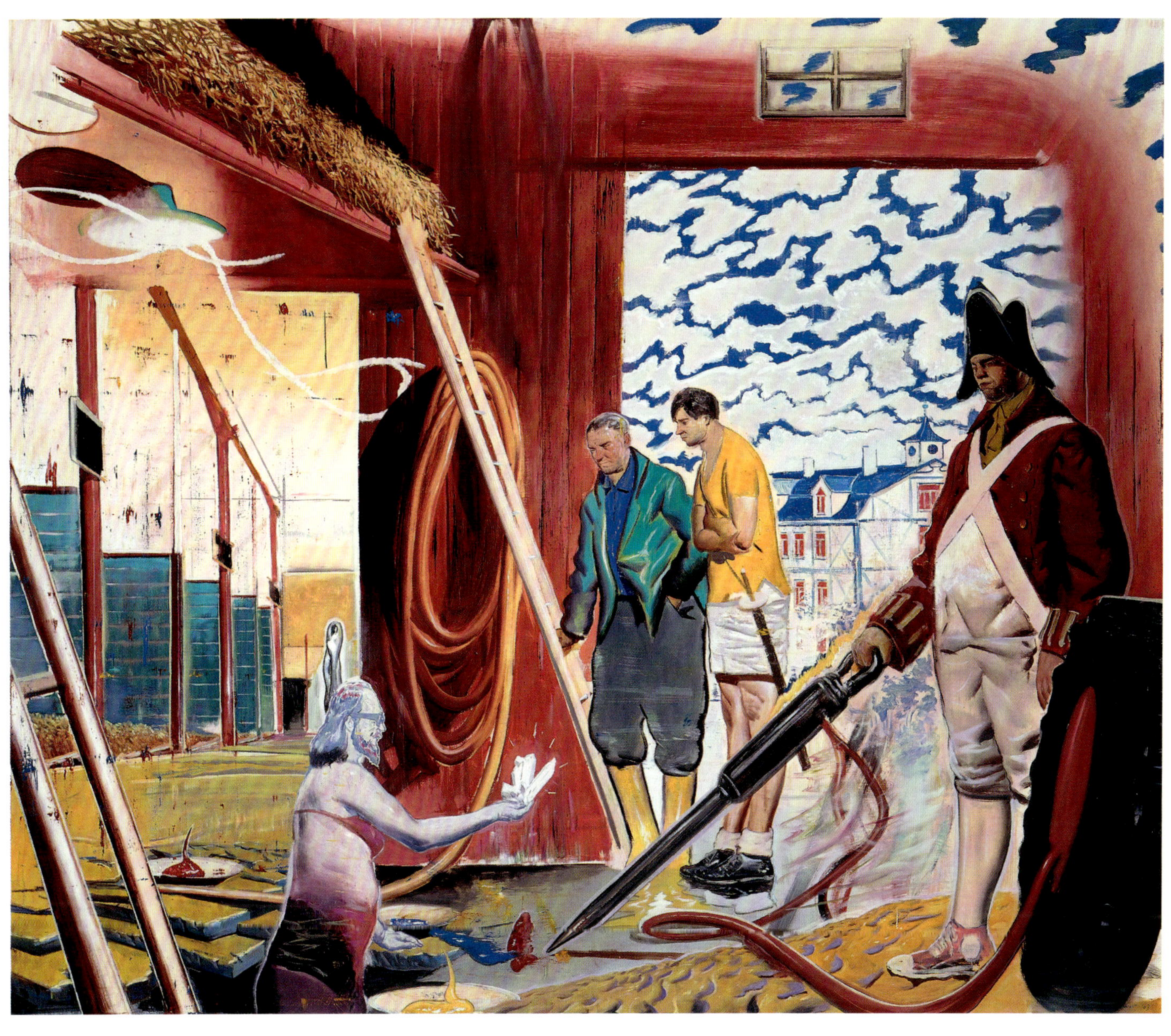

42. Scheune 2003

Oil on canvas
200 × 250 cm (78¾ × 98½ in)
Hall Collection

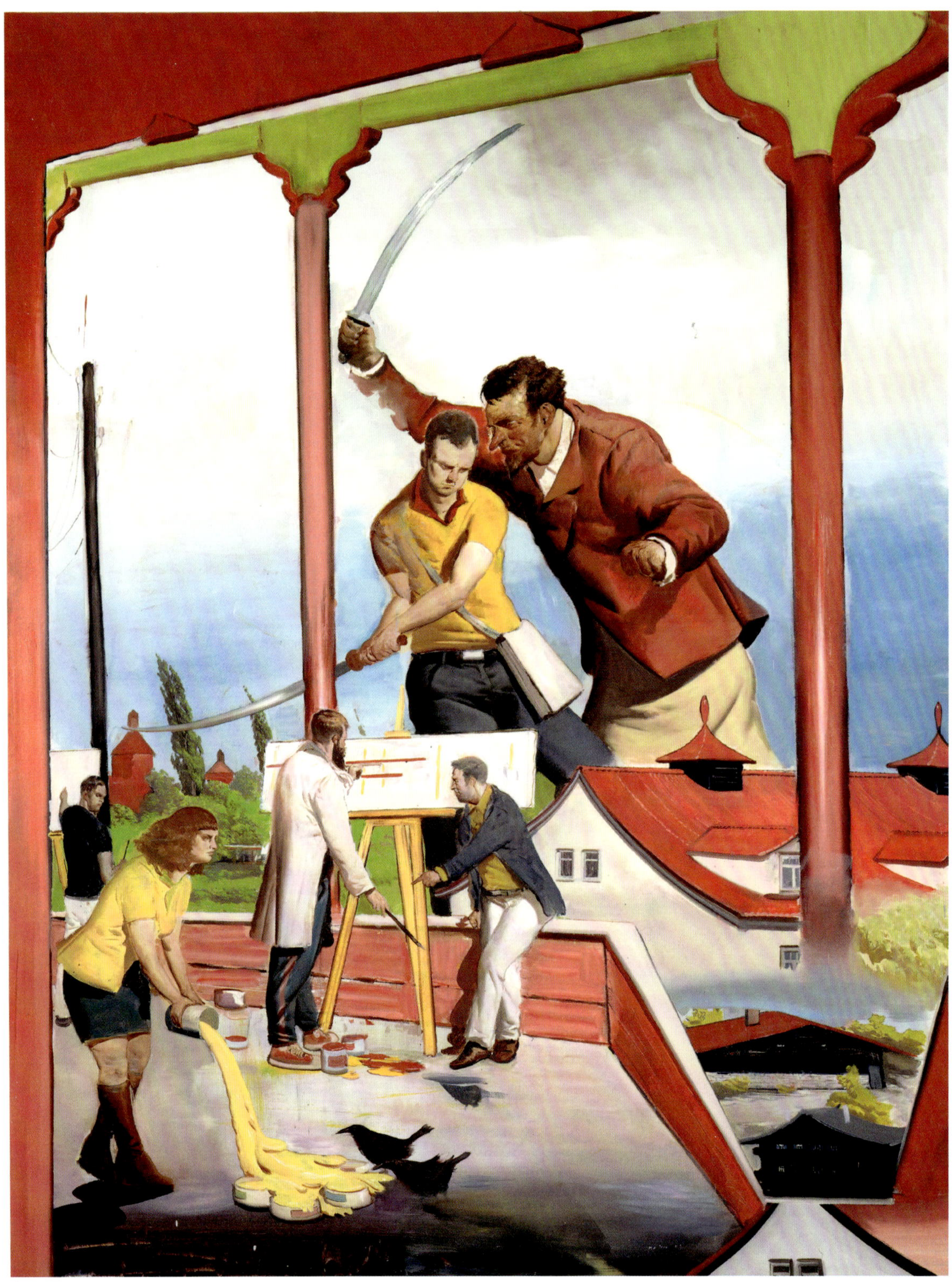

43. Abstraktion 2005

Oil on canvas
270 × 210 cm (106½ × 82¾ in)
Private collection

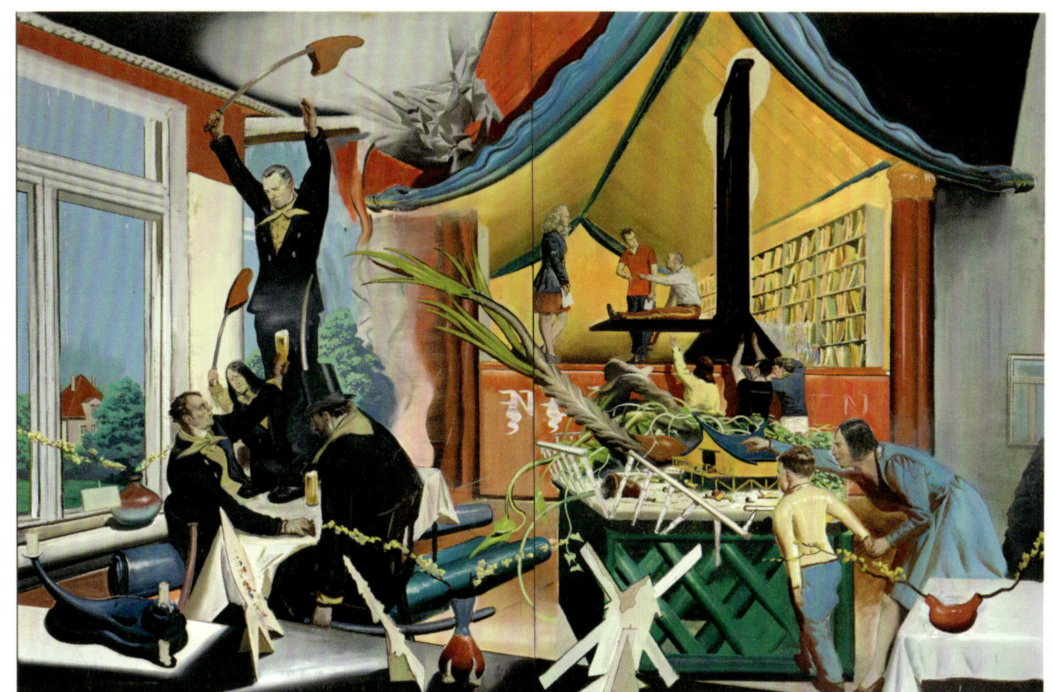

44. Neue Rollen 2005

Oil on canvas, diptych
270 × 420 cm (106½ × 165½ in)
Museum of Modern Art, New York.
Promised gift of David Teiger, 2007

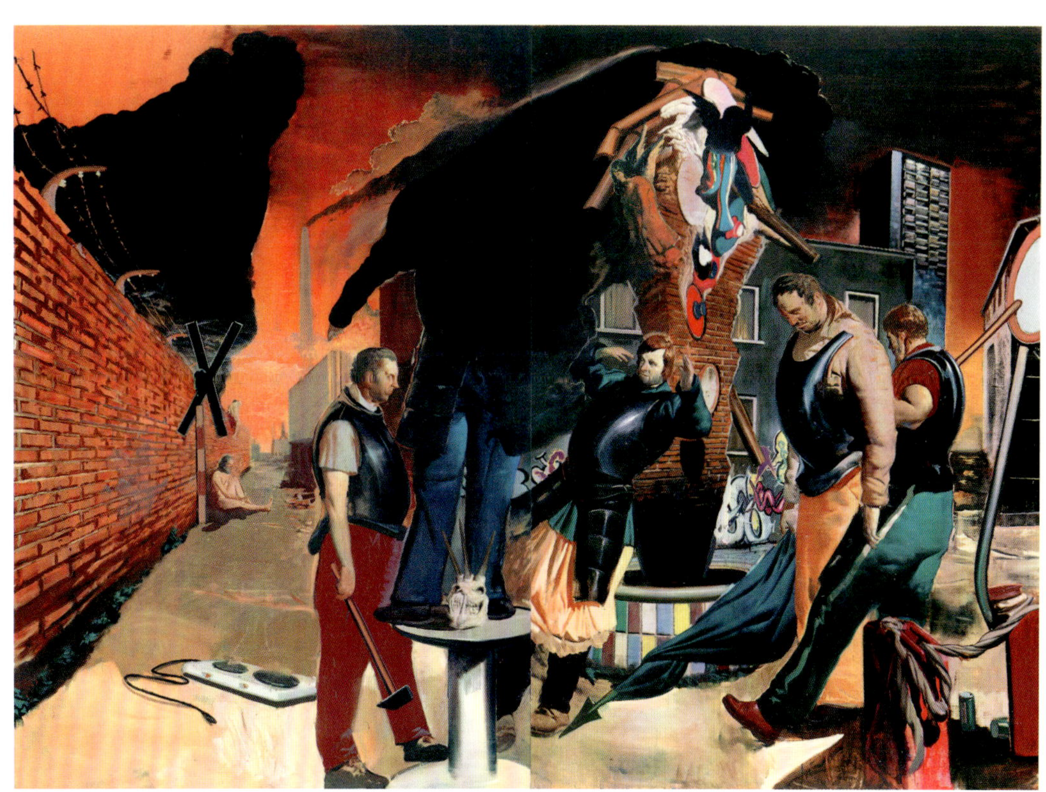

45. Die Lage 2006

Oil on canvas
300 × 420 cm (118¼ × 165½ in)

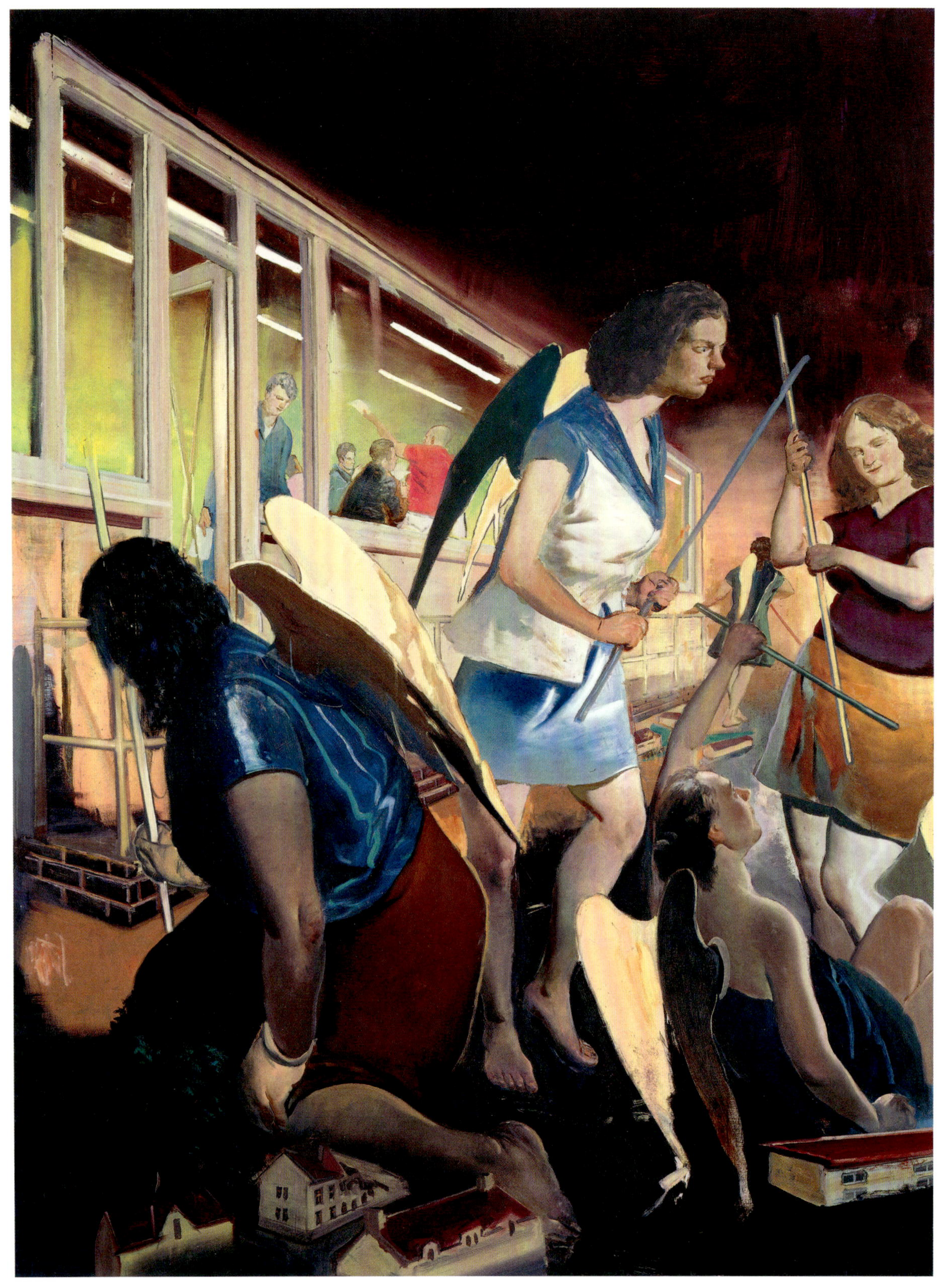

46. Theorie 2006

Oil on canvas
250 × 190cm (98½ × 74¾ in)
Sammlung Queenie, Munich

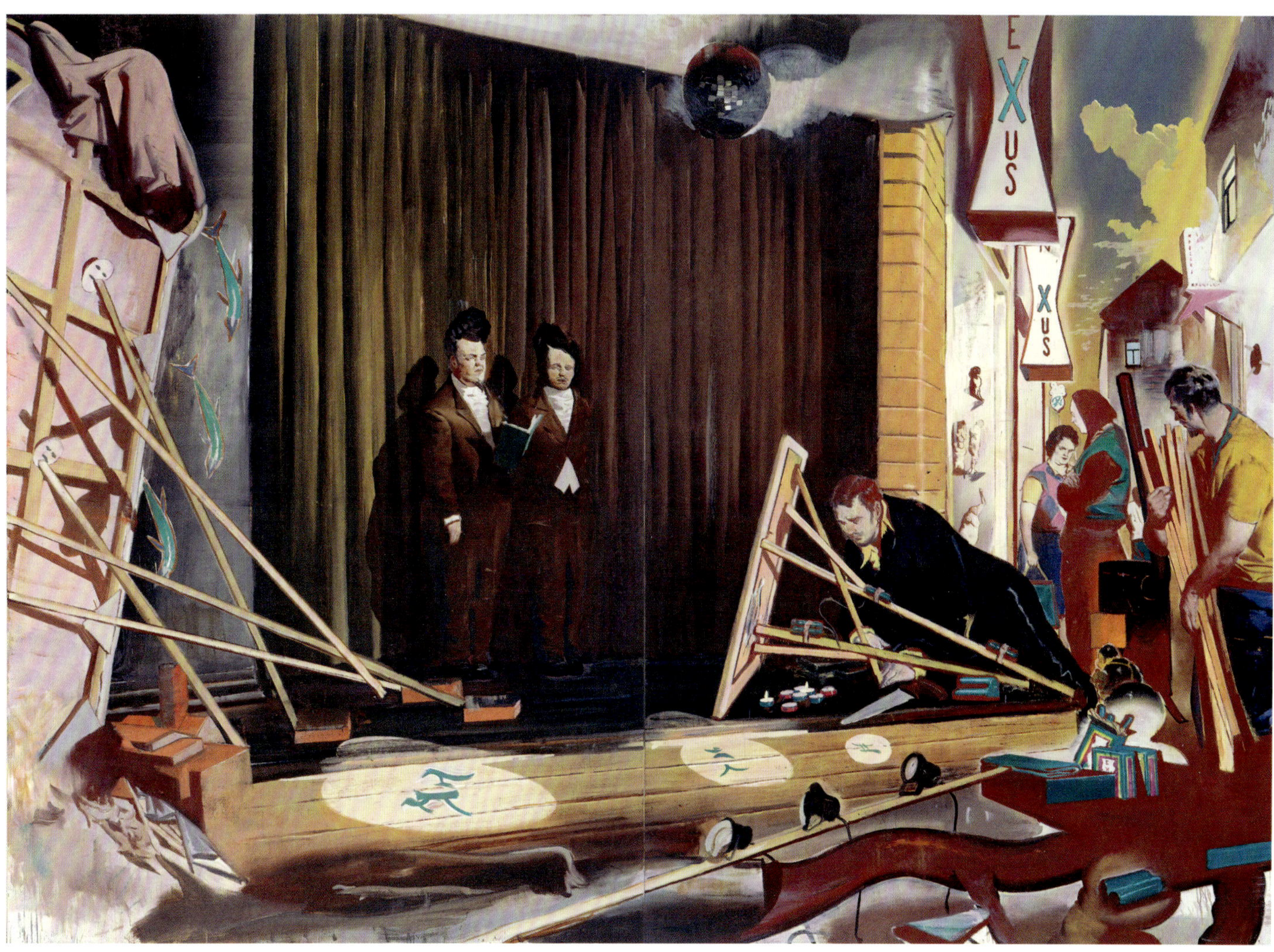

47. Nexus 2006

Oil on canvas
300 × 420 cm (118¼ × 165½ in)
Ovitz Family Collection, Los Angeles

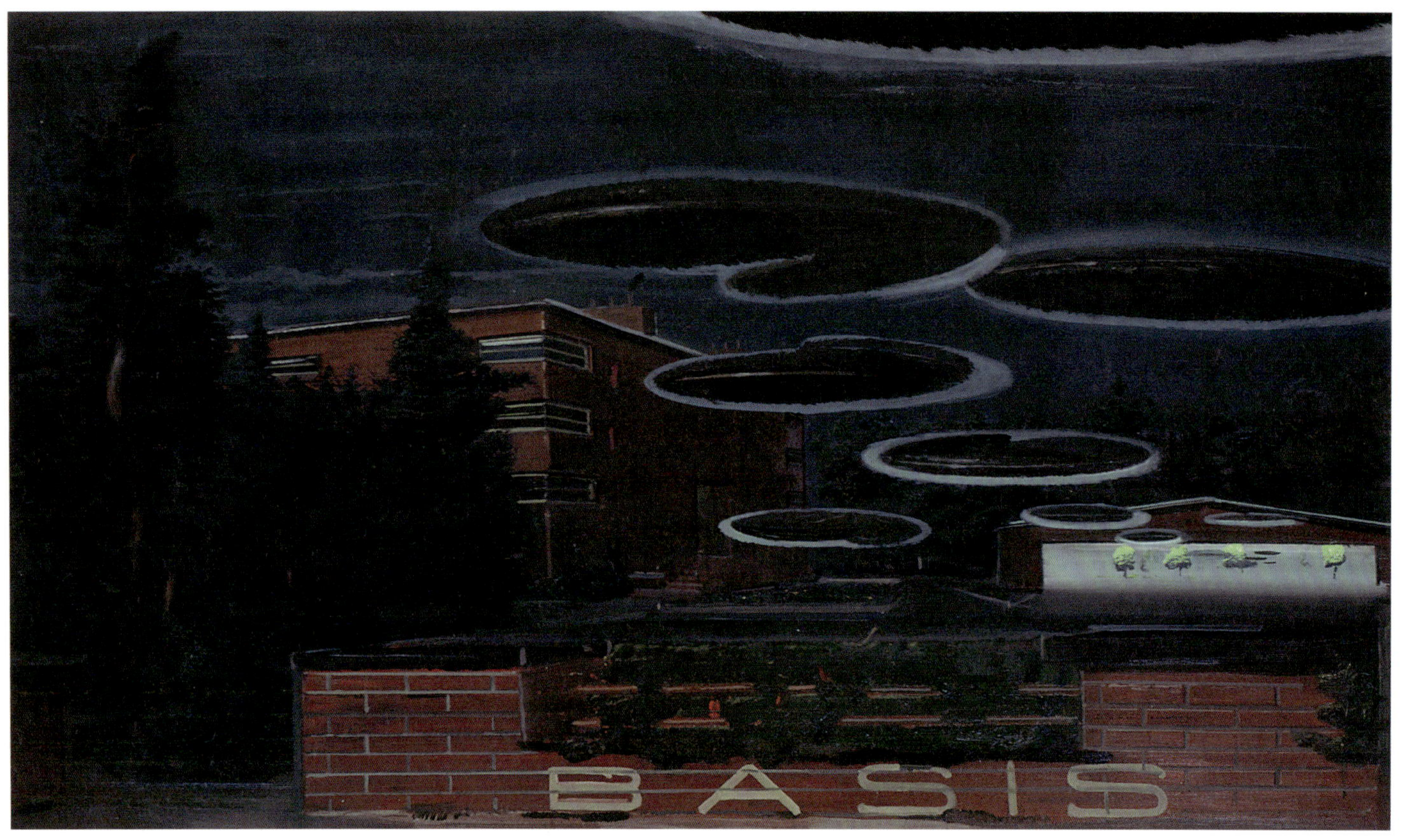

48. Basis 2000

Oil on canvas
120 × 210 cm (47¼ × 82⅝ in)
Collection Family Scharpf

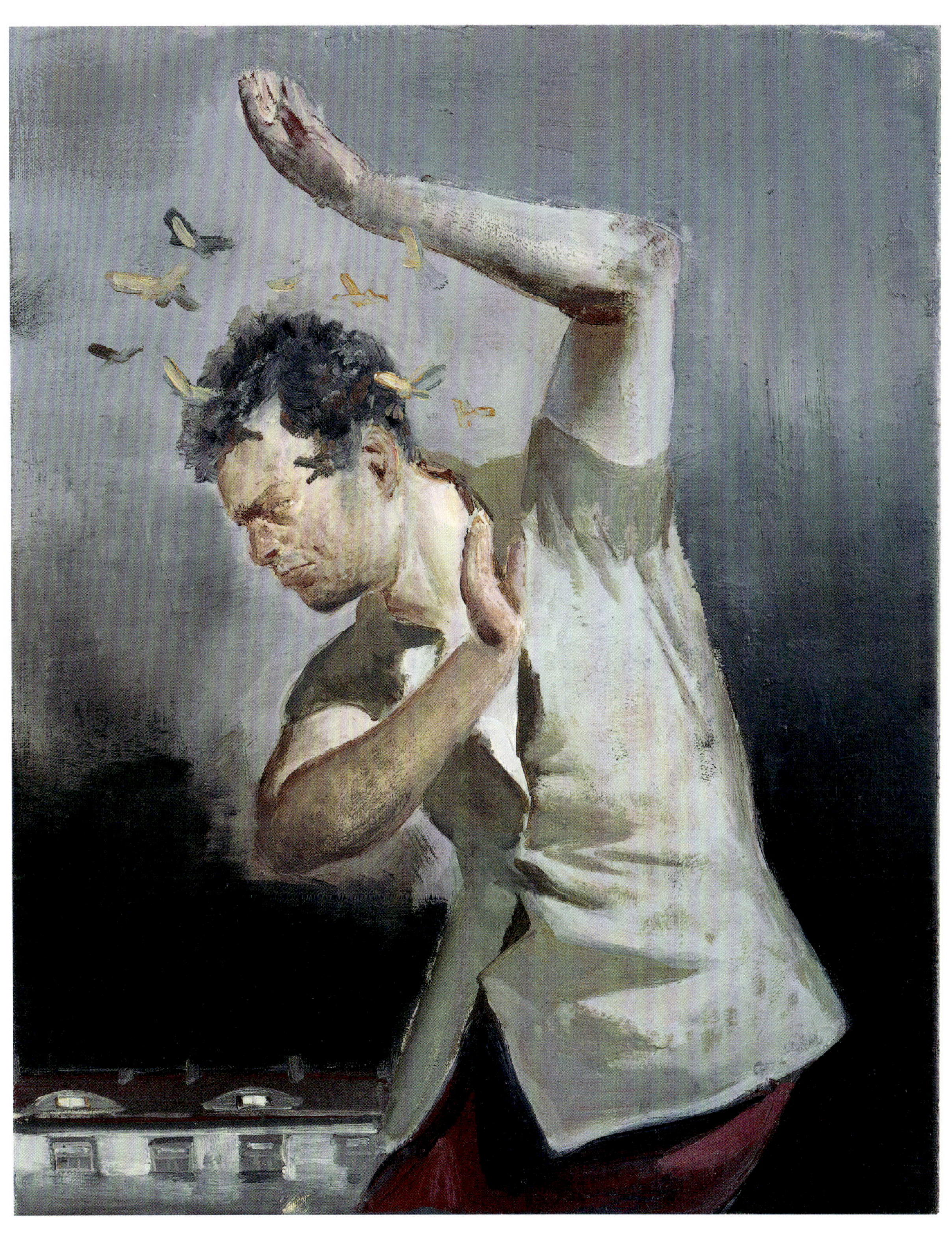

49. Ungeheuer 2006

Oil on canvas
50 × 40 cm (19¾ × 15¾ in)
Private collection, North Yorkshire

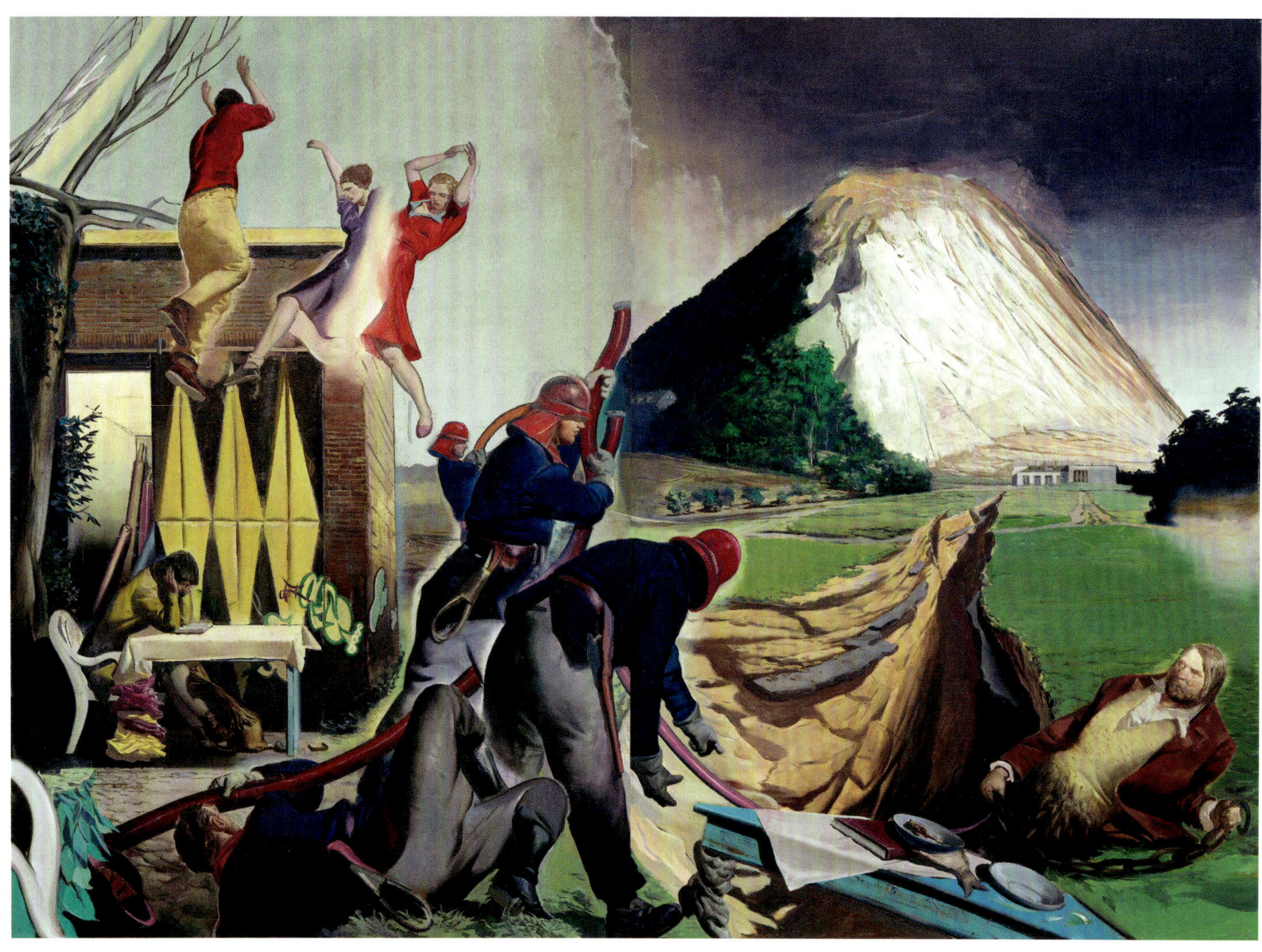

50. Die Fuge 2007

Oil on canvas
300 × 420 cm (118¼ × 165½ in)
Hamburger Kunsthalle

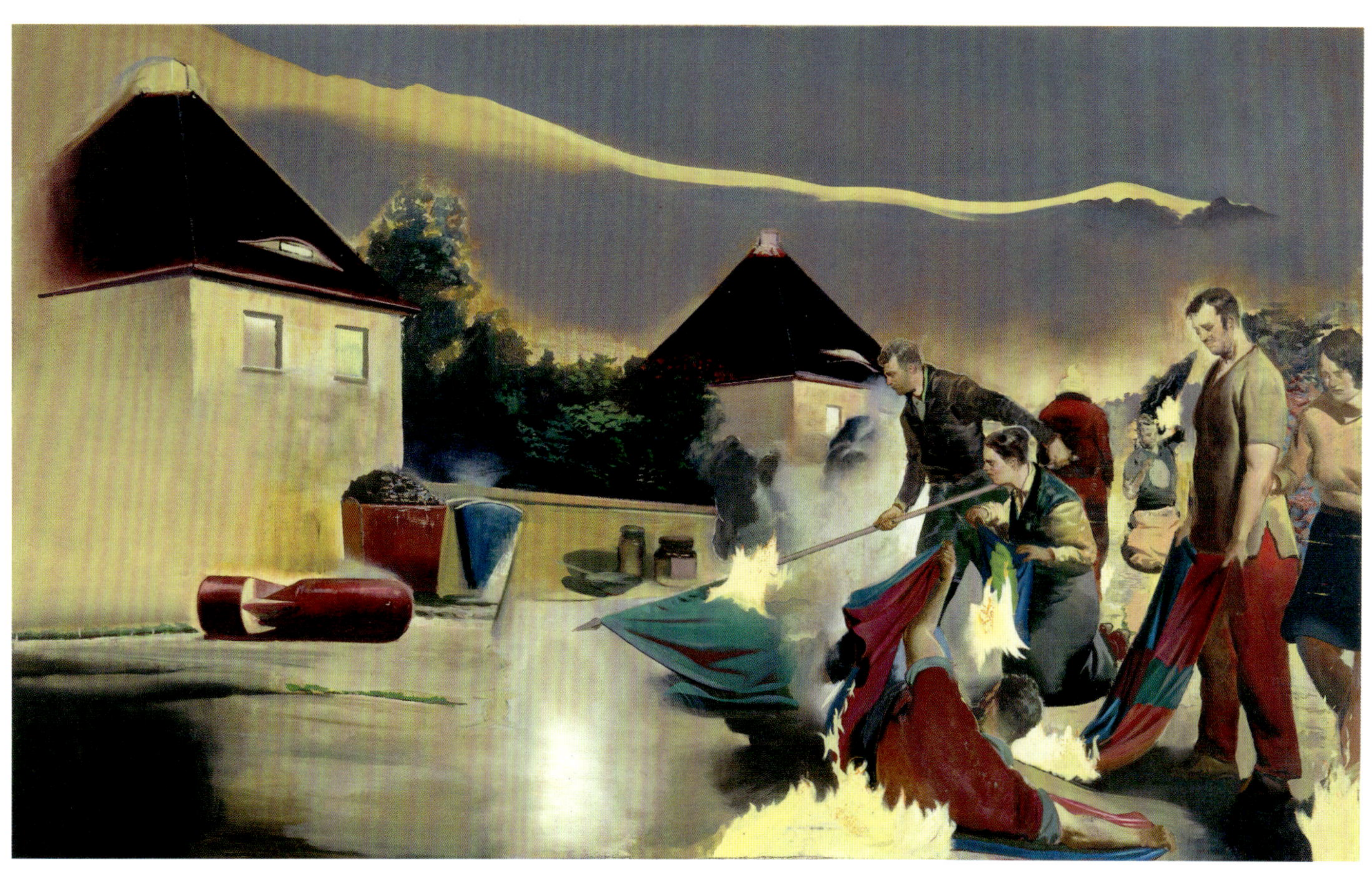

51. Vorort 2007

Oil on canvas
150 × 250 cm (59 × 98½ in)

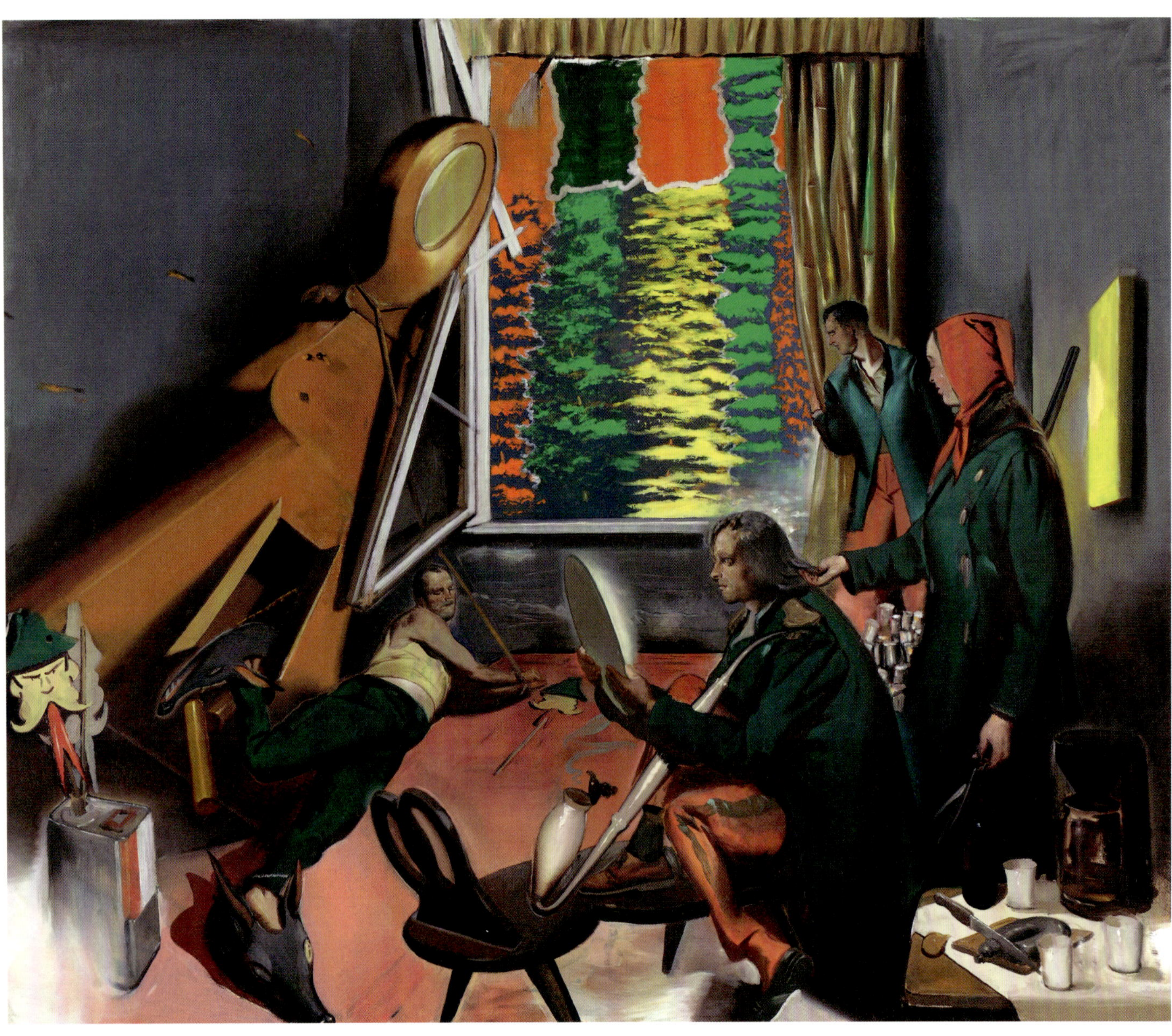

52. Unter Feuer 2010

Oil on canvas
250 × 300 cm (98½ × 118¼ in)
Museum der bildenden Künste, Leipzig

4 Back to the Future

There is to be lunch, on the stroke of noon, at Neo Rauch's third-floor studio in the Spinnerei, and we are minutes late.[1] We hurry up many flights of concrete stairs, past walls of painted brick whose bareness is interrupted only by the occasional, defiant shout of graffiti. Having passed through the giant metal door into the sanctum of the studio, we all sit down at an old wooden table which looks as if it has served Neo Rauch well for the almost quarter of a century that he has occupied this wonderfully cluttered and phantasmagoric space. Everything is here that he needs, and more: catalogues, books strewn across various impromptu surfaces that have fallen open to particularly interesting and pertinent illustrations from the 18th or 19th century. The cover story of a magazine propped against the windowsill interrogates the insoluble mystery of Jesus Christ.

There are soft toys flung around; tools; a pair of black boots; posters of exhibitions of the past on the walls; partially squeezed-out tubes of paint; besmirched painting gloves flung down at random; silver tins a-bristle with brushes; ladders; easels; and, here and there, propped or hanging or taped to the walls, many large paintings in the making. There is also much dried paint spattered about the floor itself, which occasionally feels alarmingly uneven. 'Images rise up from these encrustations on the floor. Paint me, they seem to be saying. You have summoned me to life right on this spot', Neo Rauch once remarked.[2]

There is also a long, leather punchball, hanging down from its chain, for working off creative frustration; a mesmerising silver mirror ball suspended directly in front of a tidal wave of plants, which seems to come surging forward from the windowsill; and a stage for stepping up onto when painting – this stage is a survivor of his 50th birthday party, which happened all of eight years ago. No fewer than 300 crowded in on that occasion. What a night that had been! It reminded him of those parties he so loved as a teenager. 'It also makes me feel that there is an audience in the background', says Neo. Music plays in the background, drifting jazz. There is always music on in the studio. Sometimes, it is very loud indeed.

Neo and his wife – the painter Rosa Loy, who has her own studio a little way along the corridor – bring the food in, dish by dish: sauerkraut; boiled potatoes, skinned and trimmed; and goose, floating in its rich and tasty juice. And, ah yes, some seasoning: pink Himalayan salt, offered in an old tin from the Camargue. There is also a jug of drinking water in which a giant stick of charcoal is suspended. A little later there will be dessert too: slices of wintery *Stollen* cake – from his native Saxony, as Neo reminds us – and thin, curved biscuits from Korea. We are here to contemplate the present –

and the future. When we sit down, Smylla the pug wedges himself between me and the back of my seat. He rumbles, contentedly, like a small motor, as we talk. He is always hungry, says Neo resignedly.

I ask Neo Rauch about his influences, and whether or not he has any sense of fellow-feeling with other German painters of the postwar era: Kiefer, Baselitz, Polke, Richter. He hesitates to suggest common ground. I mention that he once spoke approvingly of a single word used by Jörg Immendorf: insubordination. Was that not what he had been seeking too as a young painter? Yes, he nods in agreement. Otherwise, not. He tells me that he is not the sort of artist who moves around in a pack or belongs to a group of any kind. I don't want to be a leader, he tells me. I would rather be a lonely wolf. No, he has no collaborators. And, generally speaking, it is better to avoid having idols. He cannot think of a single living painter who might be one. He mentions some idols from the past though: Bacon and Velázquez, for example. Nor could he be the master painter of a studio like Rubens's, doing the important parts – face, hands, etc. – and leaving the rest to the assistants. In fact, he seems to despise those artists who use fabricators. His fabricators consist of his own two hands. He tries to be responsible for every square centimetre of his canvas.

I probe further, about other German painters, seeking out the names of those he might admire. There is one above all: that fellow Leipziger, Max Beckmann (fig.53). He has always revered Beckmann. What exactly does he revere him for though?

> I do feel very close to Beckmann, and the way he painted. He is very strong. It is very German way, and it became more so the older he became. It is something about the avoidance of easy beauty. He didn't care about harmony. Things are always a little disturbed or broken. Quite brutal and strict. He was always very connected with his own subconscious. He was in contact with the other side of reality. He would ask visitors to read his paintings, tell him what he had painted.'

He pauses. 'I have often been asked: why do you describe yourself as a German painter? The fact is not changeable. I am connected to German history.' But there are older and newer Germanies.

> My identity as a Saxon and my identity as a German, the two work together. The Saxons often fought with Napoleon. Then they fought against him. There is a certain Saxon mentality. They were more interested in the good life than, say, the Prussians, who were more strict. The Prussians liked order.
>
> My family has lived here for many generations, since the 16th century. I feel deeply connected with the tragedy of my country, with the destiny of the people here. I cannot cut that connection.

53. Max Beckmann
Bildnis eines Teppichhandlers 1946

Oil on canvas
194.5 × 94.5 cm (76¾ × 37¼ in)
Museum der bildenden Künste, Leipzig

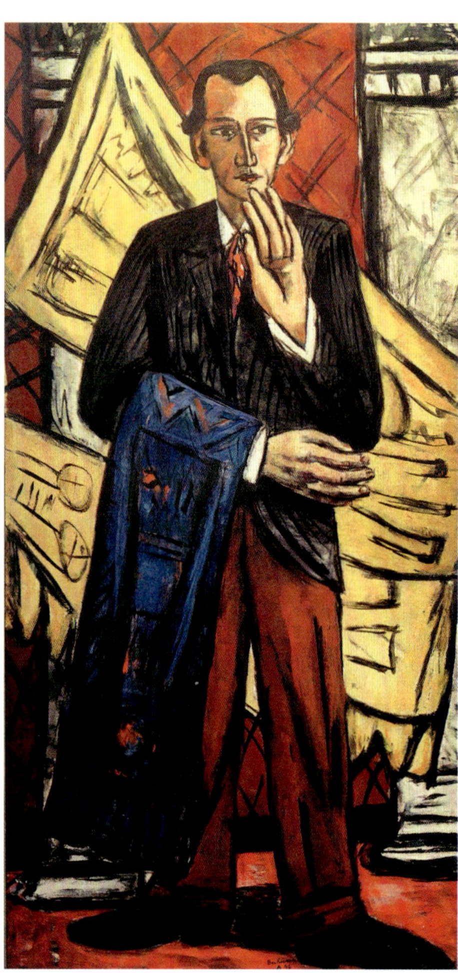

And yet, the idea of political art is anathema to him.

After lunch, we stand and walk around the studio. He introduces me to these new paintings of his in the making, one by one. There are seven of them, all very large figure groups with various elements of a hinterland – a snatch of landscape, the backdrop of buildings, a clustering of trees. There are often seven of them here at any one time, he tells me, as if that is a particularly pleasing number. He moves from one to another, pointing out this and that. Oil paint dries slowly; you have to be patient. He gradually coaxes them all into being. He brings them along together. It gets more and more difficult, he says. He is forever seeking out virgin territory, needing to surprise himself: 'I need to stay awake in front of my own canvas.' That is why he could never take to Abstraction, although he tried once, because when he was very young, he was striving, above all things else, to be a modern painter. It was just too boring in the end; he missed the figures:

> I came close to abstract art in the late 1980s, but then I came to the conclusion that by producing non-figurative stuff, I would be turning myself into one of the thousands of Sunday painters. It was at that point that I was in real danger of losing myself. It was a dream that saved me. I had to concentrate, throw out the colours, concentrate on the stuff I had left over. It has been a very gradual evolution. There has been no revolutionary moment.
>
> You see, there seemed to be no other way back then, at the end of the 1980s. I wanted to be part of the narrative of modern art. I had to behave like a modern painter, and abstraction was the hottest thing. How could I enter this stream of modernity? Finally I concluded that it was not only impossible, it was not even necessary. I had to tell things, and for me the only way was by painting figures. That striving, that yearning to enter the mainstream of modernity, now strikes me as both ridiculous and embarrassing. And anyway, it would not even have been possible for me to be amongst the wildest of the wild because we didn't have drugs! We lived in very different circumstances . . .

He speaks very fondly of these latest paintings in the studio, I notice. He talks of the figures – many of them are life-size, so it would be all the easier to step across and into their imaginative worlds just as Alice stepped through into her looking-glass world in Lewis Carroll's *Alice Through the Looking Glass* – as if he is their guardian, and it is his duty to protect them from that dangerous world beyond.

> I have to bring them in safely, out of the main problems of our time, under the roof of a house perhaps, or within the safe walls of a panic room. I must above all protect them from the disaster of politics. They should not be usable for political purposes. I always try to avoid political statements, meanings. You have to keep them clean.

The worst art is political art then? I ask him. 'Yes, and as Picasso once said: I am not a messenger. On the other hand, political meanings do happen', he sighs.

That is true, of course. Some have given social and political interpretations to his work. He also recognises the problem of his own circumstances: where he grew up, what he was inevitably a part of, his particular historical predicament:

> The walls of my studio are semi-transparent, porous. I cannot avoid these influences that come to me from the outside. I have to take a shower when I come into the studio. There is always some left over. Art is not a clean area. On the other hand, if I tried to be directly connected to reality, I would produce propaganda – or those shows you see daily on TV . . .

And so, we return to the paintings themselves, the ones which are in the making, the ones that he is currently nurturing. They are his family, he says. They keep up with each other – like a growing family. They are his companions. They are also a haven; a sanctuary; and tools, in part, of his own survival – perhaps better than reality. 'I have to be able to live with them.' He walks me across to the least-finished painting of them all, the one he started after his recent return from Palma. He points out a rocky coastline, land abutting sea. That is the rocky coastline of Palma, he says. There are cliffs, and cliff dwellings – you can clearly see the small, window-like apertures. These people made their homes in the cliff itself, he says. There is also a large male figure in a long frock coat to the right of the painting, standing on a promontory, pointing in the direction of the sea. Is that not an image somewhat reminiscent of Caspar David Friedrich, I ask him, of Man alone, brooding upon the immensity of the Void? The past may have caught up with him, as it often seems to do. How exactly does it work though? How does he begin, with a canvas of this enormity?

'I put in the background first. I make that decision early. It is a grace to be able to discover things – like a birth from the darkness. I am trying to suggest the art of everyone's subconscious.' The struggle is always the same. The interest is the same. The shapes change. 'I create things as if they existed many decades before. The gestures, the actions are ambiguous. There are many millions of possibilities. One or two are quite enough. It makes it so difficult. It makes me feel so insecure. It would be so much easier to use photographs.' But he would never work from photographs.

We move on to another new painting in the making. Such is its state of completeness that you could readily say that this one has been surging ahead, though it is far from finished. So far, it has been eight months in the fabrication. At this point in time it is a landscape with figures – and much else. A group of men with flags is climbing a hillside. 'I began it in June of last year, when the leaves were fresh green on the trees.' He points to that vivid greenness. And now it is winter, though summer clings on in that painting. 'I wanted to paint a landscape – but then these figures appeared, one after the other.

After that, I put in a big figure on the right.' There are often large figures on the right in your paintings, I mention. Little by little, that early summer landscape found itself challenged, if not almost overwhelmed, by other kinds of activity – a group of buildings from perhaps the early 19th century, the era of the Napoleonic Wars for example, has also interposed itself. And so, the painting continues to emerge.

I ask him about dreams as the source of his work. Yes, he has used them from time to time, but not so much. He does not paint what he saw last night. He is trying to simulate the way dreams work, to evoke their suggestive power. He depends most of all on inspiration. He concentrates most of all on the white canvas. He is trying to see inside that wall of fog. 'I don't know what will happen next. I have no idea.' He regards himself as a kind of medium, the bearer of a message from above:

> There is a lot of pressure, to be gifted in this way. It is a little like playing chess against yourself. You put a piece down on the board. You make the first move. And then perhaps you change position. You play from the other side. You also have to be a player who doesn't think, just reacts. You have to balance things. I am perhaps a juggler, a *jongleur*. I have to decide what elements I am juggling with.

Neither of these paintings has been named yet. Sometimes he is quite helpless to find a title for a new painting. His wife helps. Every title has to have a good, suggestive sound. 'West Wind', he mentions, giving me an example in English. That wouldn't do though, because 'Ode to the West Wind' is a celebrated poem written by the great English Romantic poet Percy Bysshe Shelley. He agrees. 'I'm too vain to take a title from a poem.' He weaves everything out of himself. That is how it must be.

When Rauch has spoken about his paintings in the past, he has often sounded as if he believes their making to be a kind of sacred mystery.[3] And yet he himself is a declared atheist. Religious references – glancing or otherwise – are abundant. There are many gestures, moments, which look and feel biblical – see how the female figure dandles her scissors in *Unter Feuer* (Under Fire, 2010) (fig.52). Is this not Delilah in all but name, threatening the potency of the male? In *Der Altar* (The Altar, 2008) (fig.54), a pious-seeming ancient reaches up to touch the tip of a sacred flame. Will the cowering child in this scene be sacrificed? *Goldgrube* (Gold Mines, 'Goldmine'/Jackpot, 2007) (fig.55) – in which two workers stuff bones (or limbs) into a wheelbarrow, illuminated by the uncanny glow of gold – seems to hover on the brink of a parable thirsting for explication. In *Späte Heimkehr* (Late Return, Late Homecoming, 2013) (fig.56), a matronly woman clutches a red bird in a lantern-lit doorway. An act of ritualistic foot-cleansing seems to recall Jesus's behaviour on Maundy Thursday in *Nach der Schicht* (After the Layers, 2011) (fig.57).

How does Rauch square those two things? Is he an atheistical pantheist, by any chance? 'Sometimes I feel guided in a certain sense. There is something behind the reality, something that protects me. I cannot explain this by referring to any particular religion. It is a kind of energy, sometimes present, at other times absent. It is always

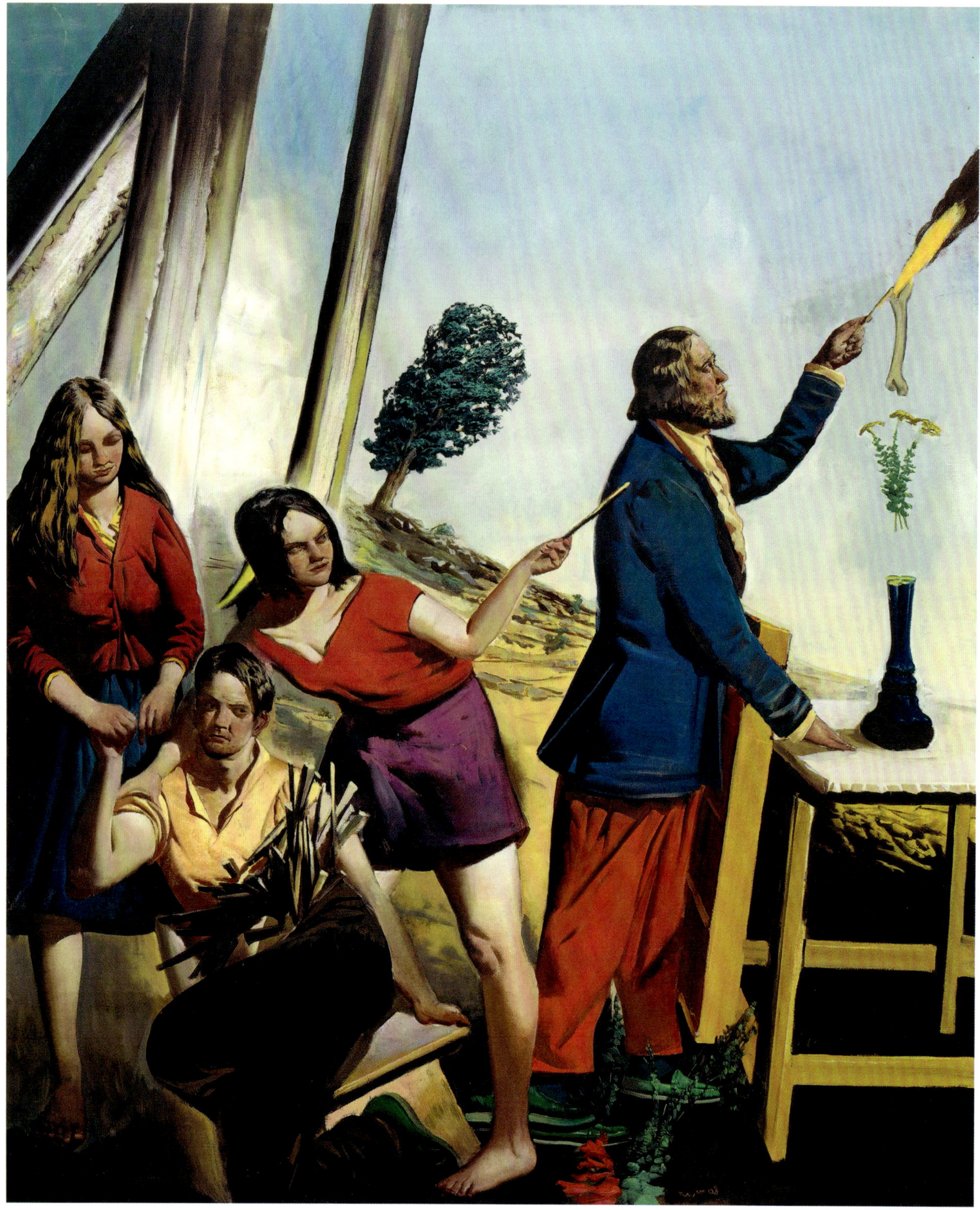

54. Der Altar 2008

Oil on canvas
250 × 210 cm (98½ × 82¾ in)
Private collection, Artvest Ltd

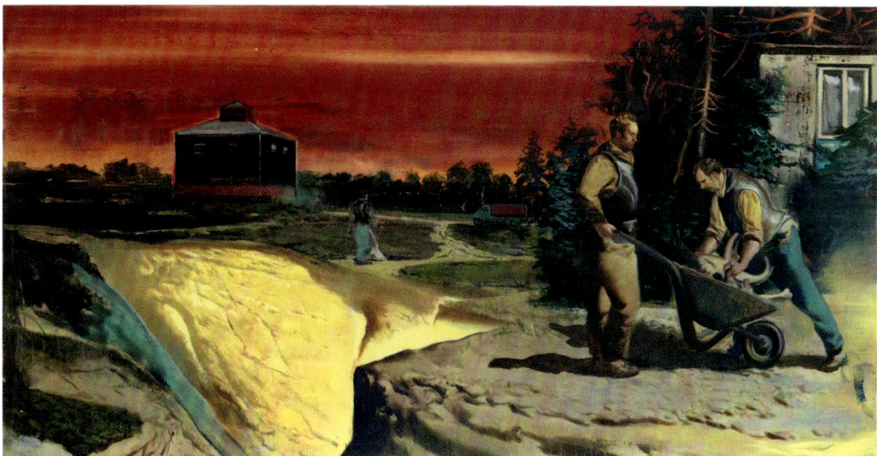

55. Goldgrube 2007

Oil on canvas
80 × 160 cm (31½ × 63 in)
Private collection

good – energy, nature, cosmic reality . . .' The current challenge – the new challenge of every working day – is what counts (he puts in five days' work a week, about eight hours a day, and he has the weekend off), to coax this new family of paintings into life. And that challenge, that burden, is quite sufficient unto the day. The weekend means an escape from the chaos within. Understood.

In 2003, the artist Frank Stella said, 'Figuration has already done so much. It has had its moment. There are so many different possibilities open to abstraction, not just geometric abstraction.'[4] Yet in the 1990s, even the abstract artist Stella felt marginalised, almost made irrelevant, by what was then fashionably described as the New Media – video art, installation art. Neo Rauch came to quite a different conclusion about Abstraction and the New Media. They held no appeal and no meaning for him. Abstract art bored him – even though he has also recognised why it was perhaps necessary for it to exist after Hiroshima and Auschwitz. 'Man had forfeited the privileges of being depicted as a result of these atrocities – no more representational painting.'[5]

Why would abstract art do when representational art would not? Abstract art, you could argue, is apolitical, unbesmirched by images that can be interpreted – or perhaps misinterpreted – for political ends. Is this not why abstract art sits so comfortably in offices, and why an abstract artist such as Sean Scully is such a hit in China? And yet, it was Neo Rauch's experience that only by discovering a new relationship with the art of the human figure was he able to find meaning as an artist. And now the wheel has turned full circle. Figurative art has made a powerful comeback across the globe. It is regarded as legitimate once again. Think of such important, young-to-mid-career painters as Ryan Mosley, Lynette Yiadom-Boakye, Nina Chanel Abney, Chantal Joffe, Toyin Ojih Odutola and Robin F. Williams . . . And so, you could argue that Neo Rauch, once regarded as hopelessly anachronistic,

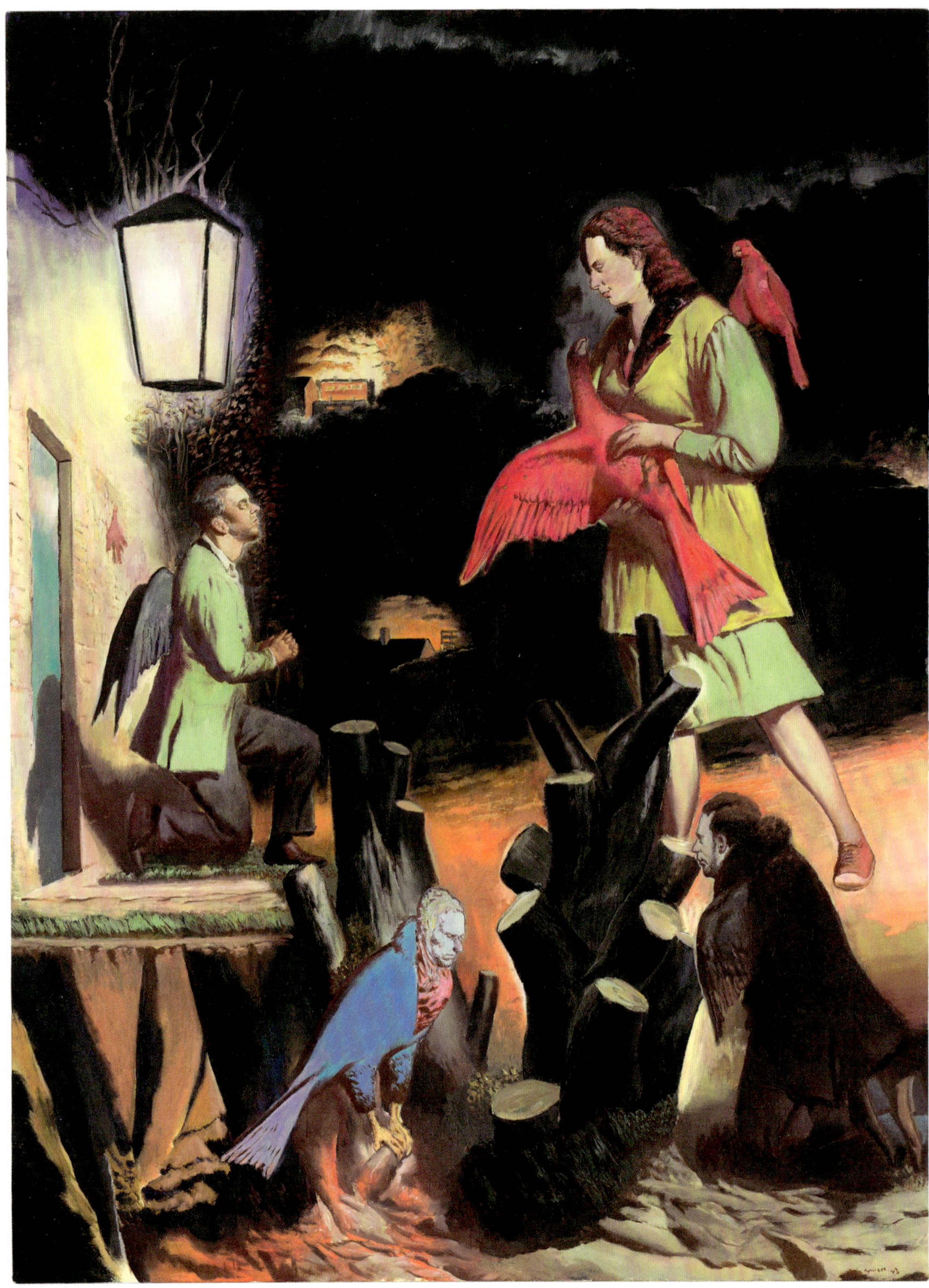

56. Späte Heimkehr 2013

Oil on canvas
280 × 210 cm (110¼ × 82¾ in)
Collectie De Heus-Zomer

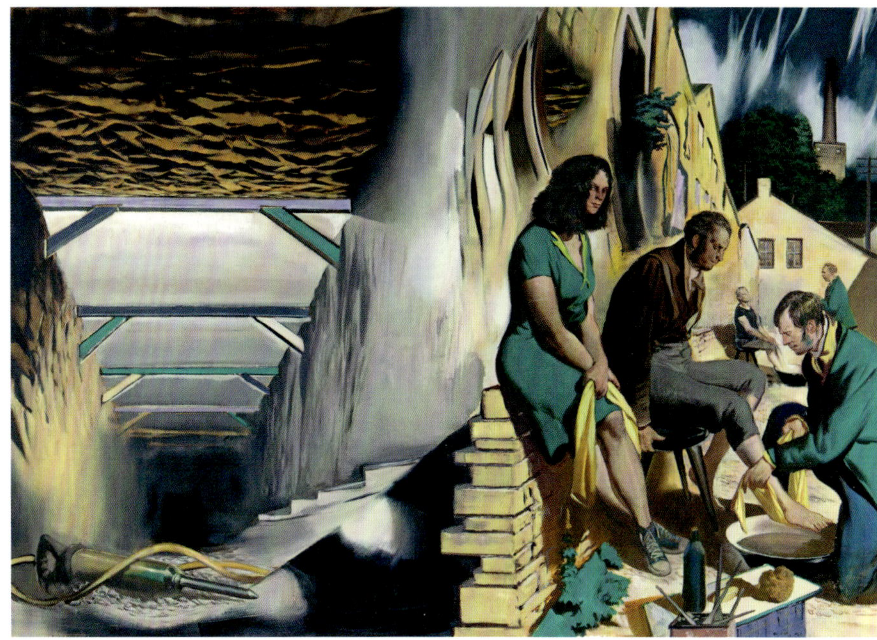

57. Nach der Schicht 2011

Oil on canvas
210 × 300 cm (82¾ × 118¼ in)
Private collection

finds himself in the vanguard of the return of figuration. I put this to him as we stand beside one of his giant figure groups in the studio. Is he in the vanguard? No! No! He looks horrified, if not a little sullied by such an idea – and the thought of being, perhaps, not quite so alone any more.

No painter can be said to know his own work perfectly. It can wrest itself from his grip. Neo Rauch's is not a self-enclosed world at all, subject only to the strange vicissitudes of the subconscious. European history, politics, the ever-enduring presence of human conflict – everything is here for the seeing if you wish to look hard enough, and with a sufficiently super-subtle eye.

Nor does it necessarily consist of happy families. These are not safe or biddable creatures at all. They may not even be likeable or desirable. They can be the stuff of nightmare. Exactly how loveable can any enslaved dog-man of the kind that we see in *Randgebiet* (Periphery, 2000) (fig.58) ever hope to be? This is pure gothic. It frightens and unnerves even as it purports to create an atmosphere of an unusually settled normality. The clashings, the shriekings of colours in *Die Kontrolle* (The Check, 2010) (fig.59) set our teeth on edge. And so they might because this absurdly extravagant and near-chaotic scene of the oppression of the human spirit by two malignant officials in shrill green caps – what is it, exactly, that is being checked or accounted for? – which includes a mighty gladiatorial battle between two dog-men, one of them bespectacled, represents everything that Neo Rauch may also find abhorrent.

The fact is that Rauch's creatures are as unruly as the subconscious itself. They outwit us even as we endeavour to tame them, speak well of them, or even lend them

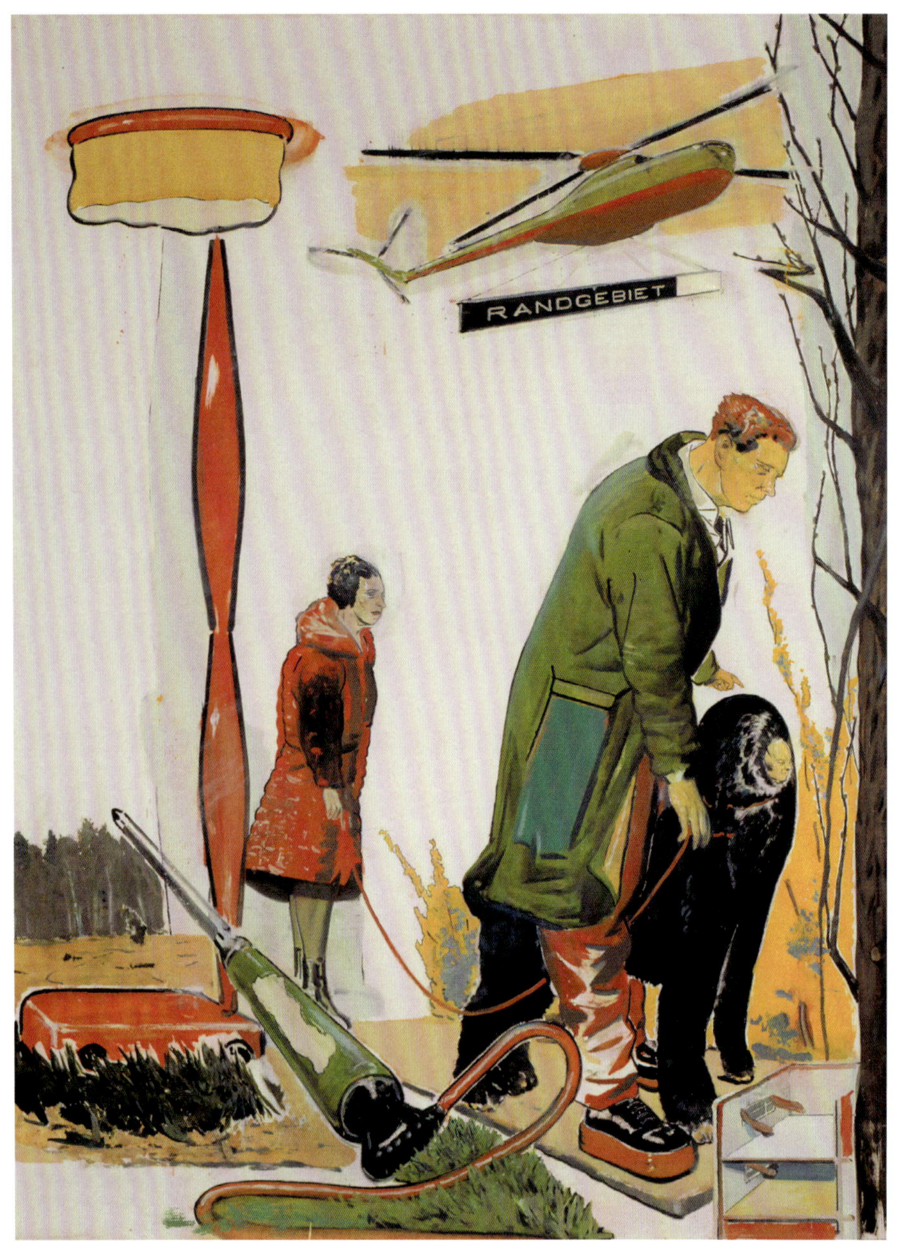

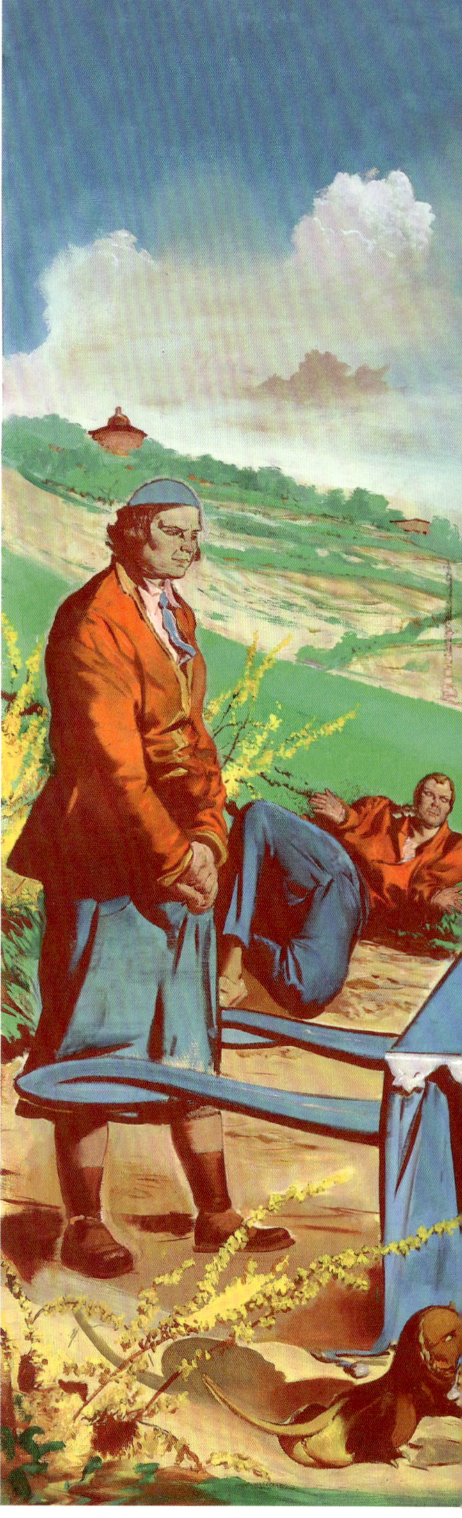

58. Randgebiet 2000

Oil on paper
265 × 200 cm (104½ × 78¾ in)
Sammlung Droege

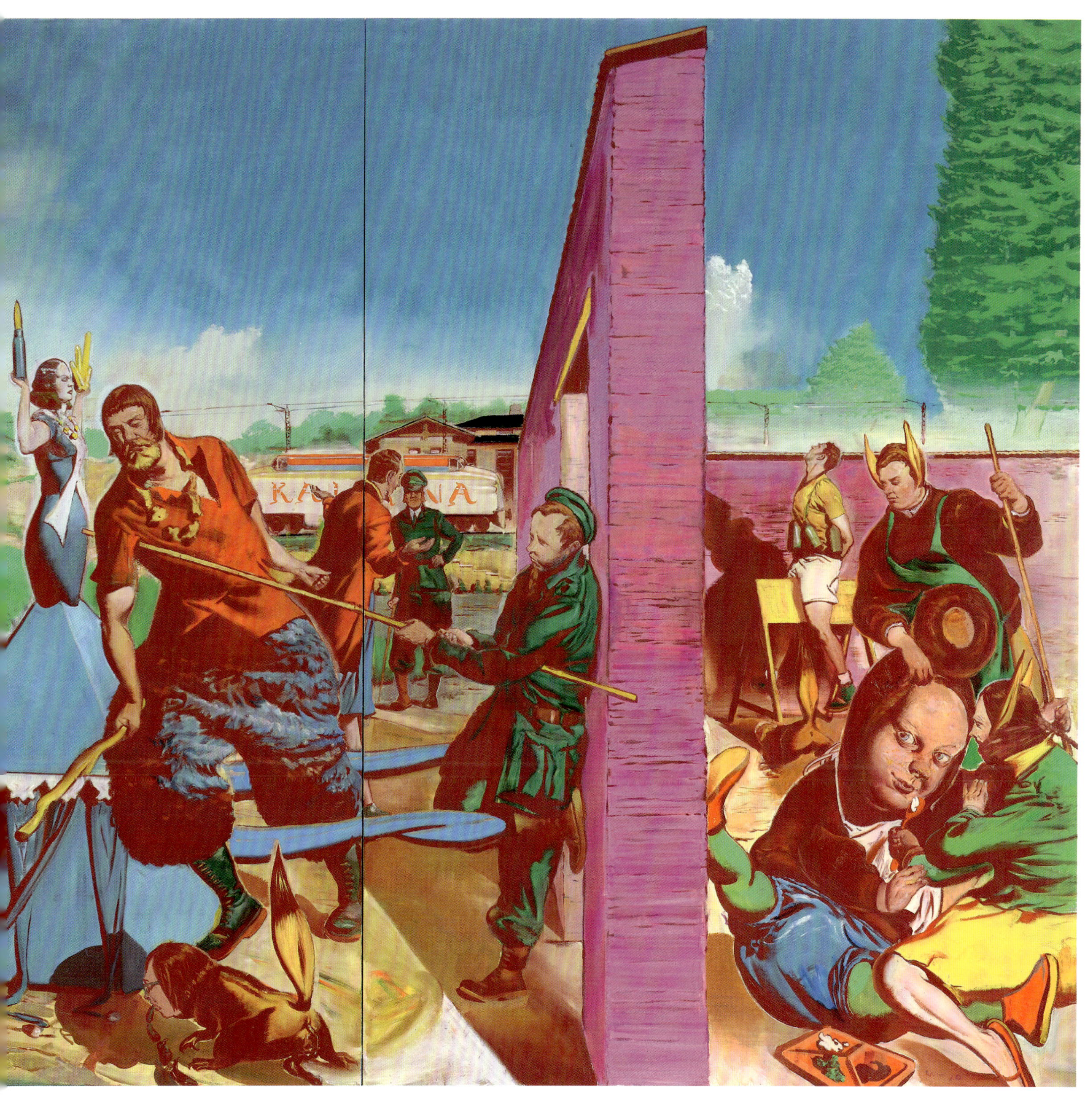

59. Die Kontrolle 2010

Oil on canvas
300 × 420 cm (118¼ × 165½ in)
Private collection, Basel

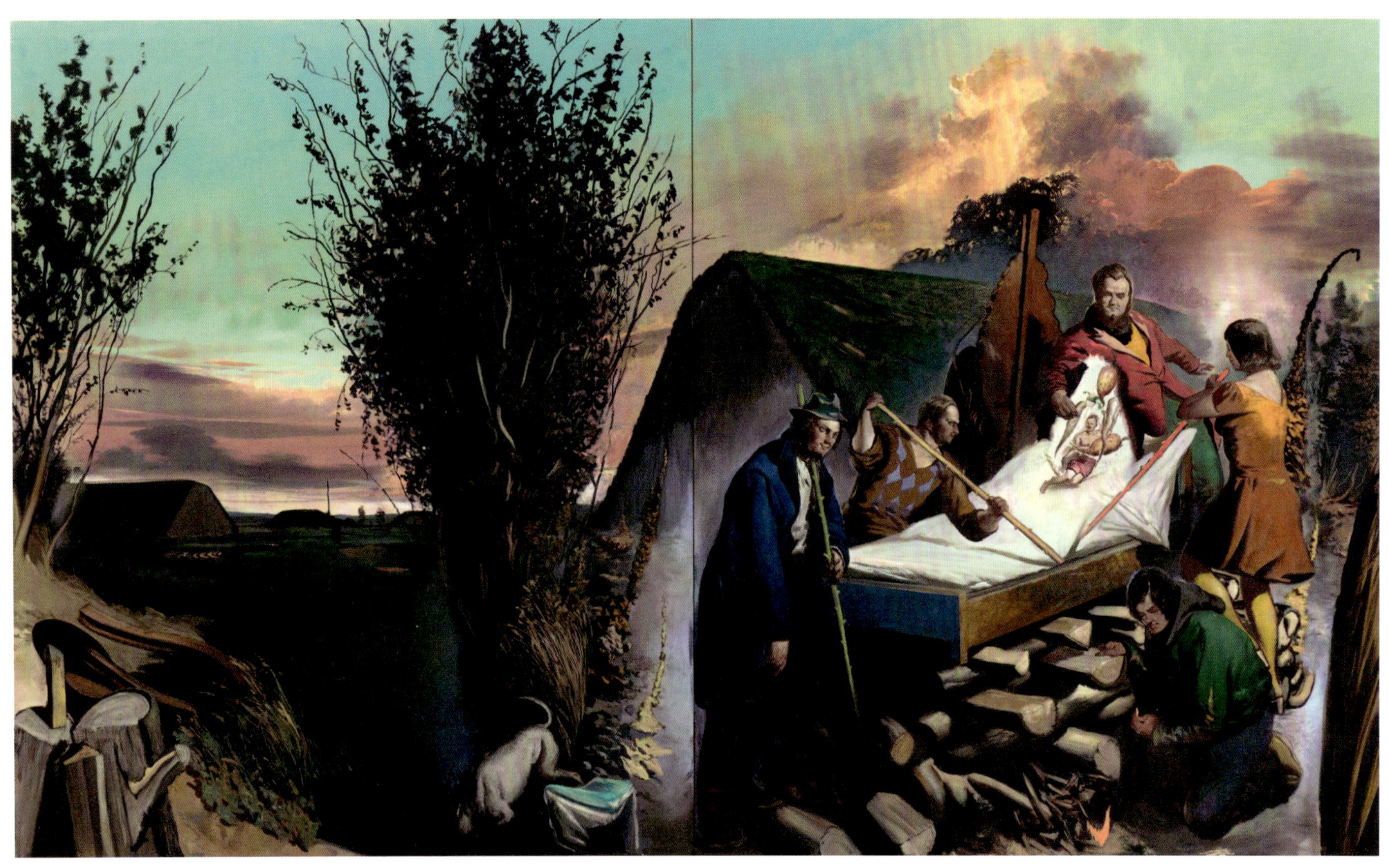

60. Der böse Kranke 2012

Oil on canvas
300 × 500 cm (118¼ × 197 in)
Private collection

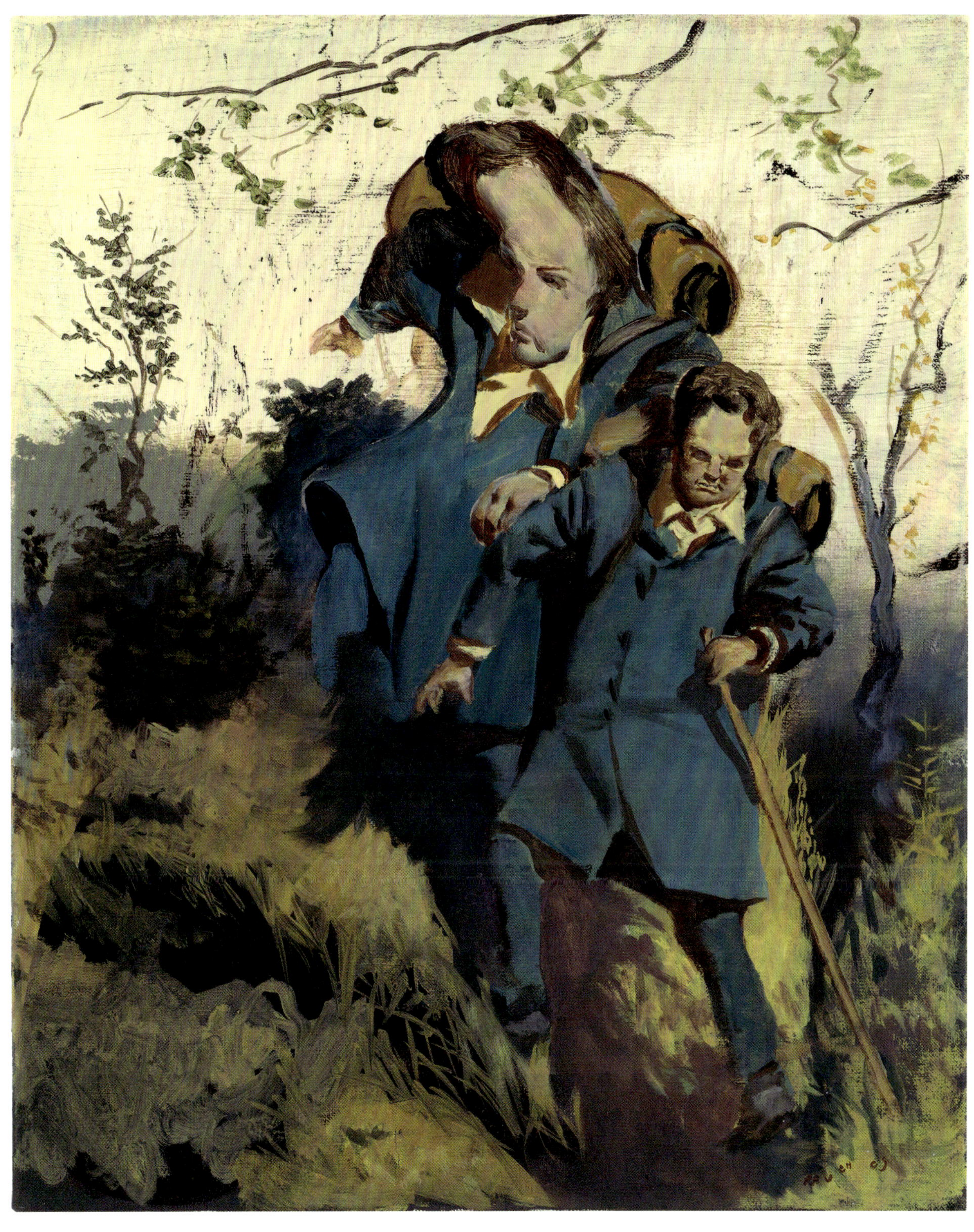

61. Abstieg 2009

Oil on canvas
60 × 50 cm (23¾ × 19¾ in)
Private collection

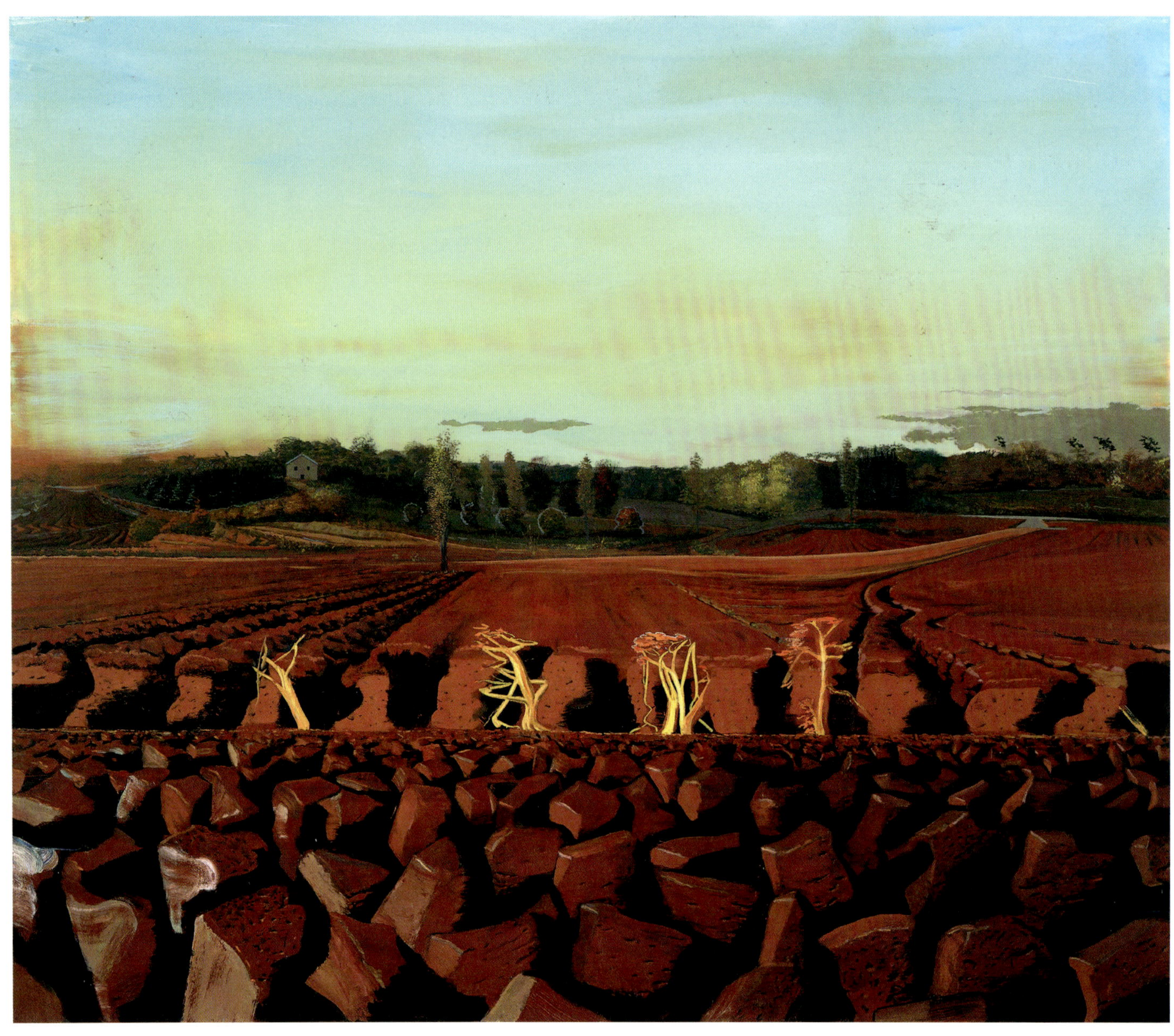

63. Acker 2002

Oil on canvas
210 × 250 cm (82¾ × 98½ in)
Private collection, Connecticut

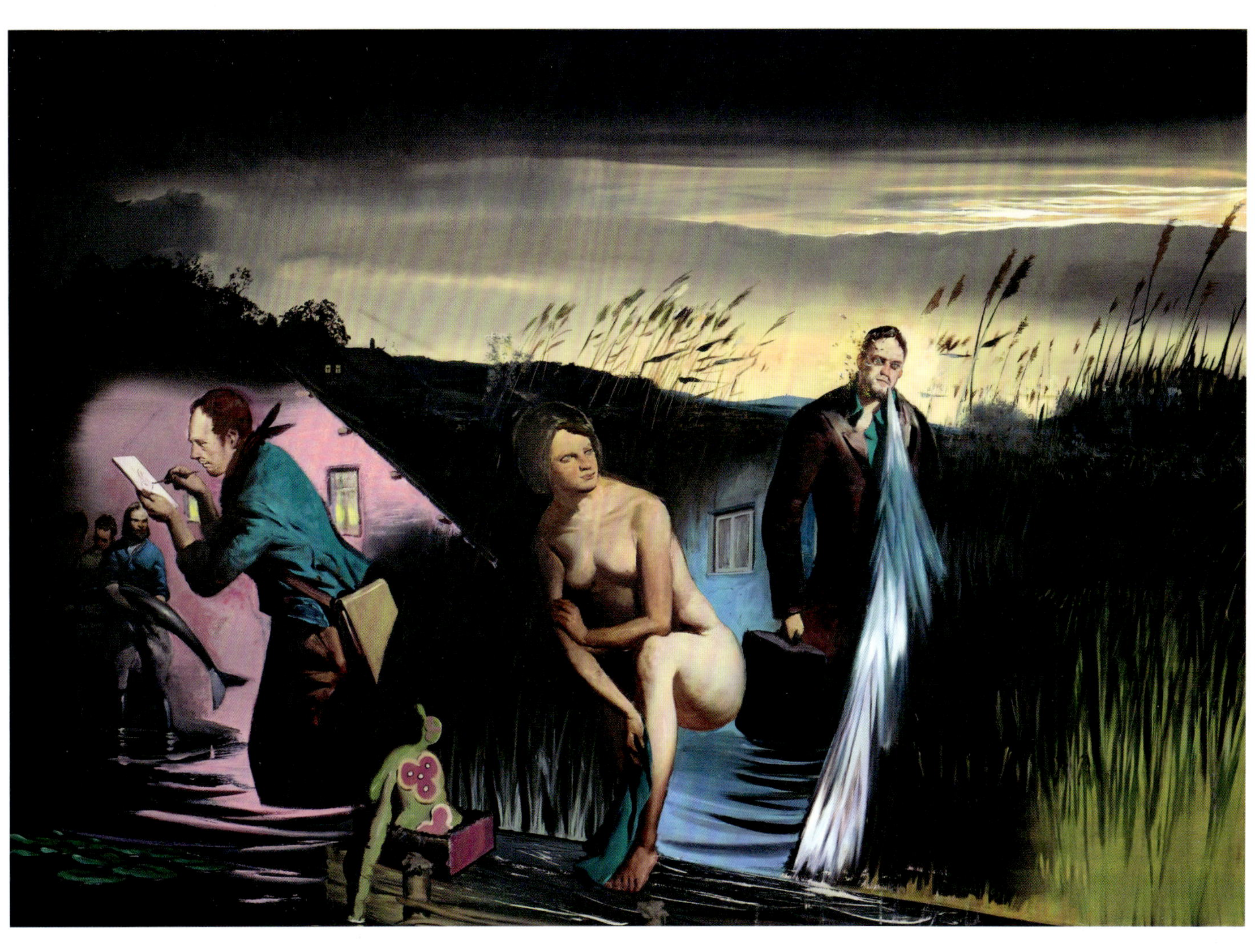

64. Schilfland 2009

Oil on canvas
210 × 300 cm (82⅝ × 118¼ in)
Private collection

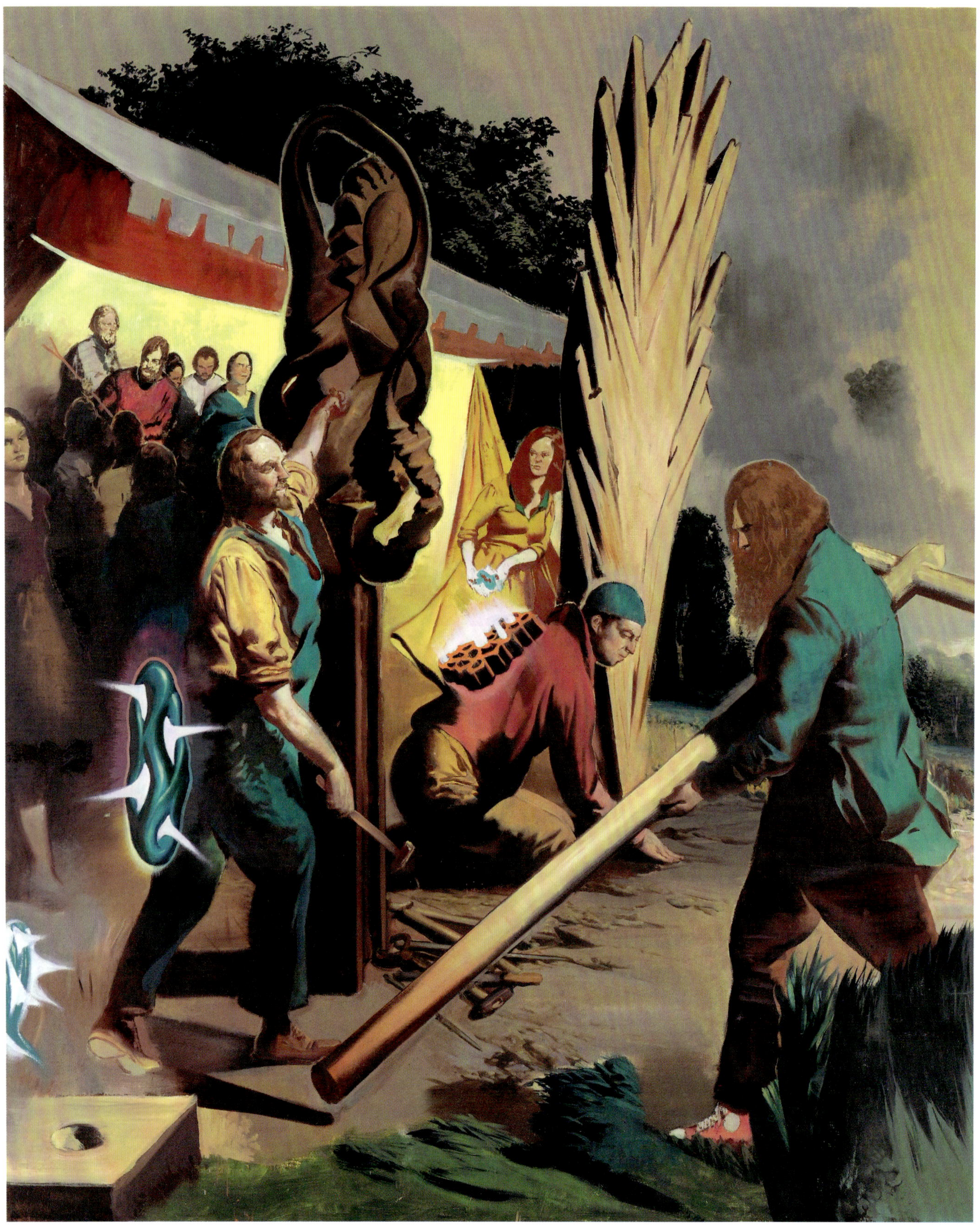

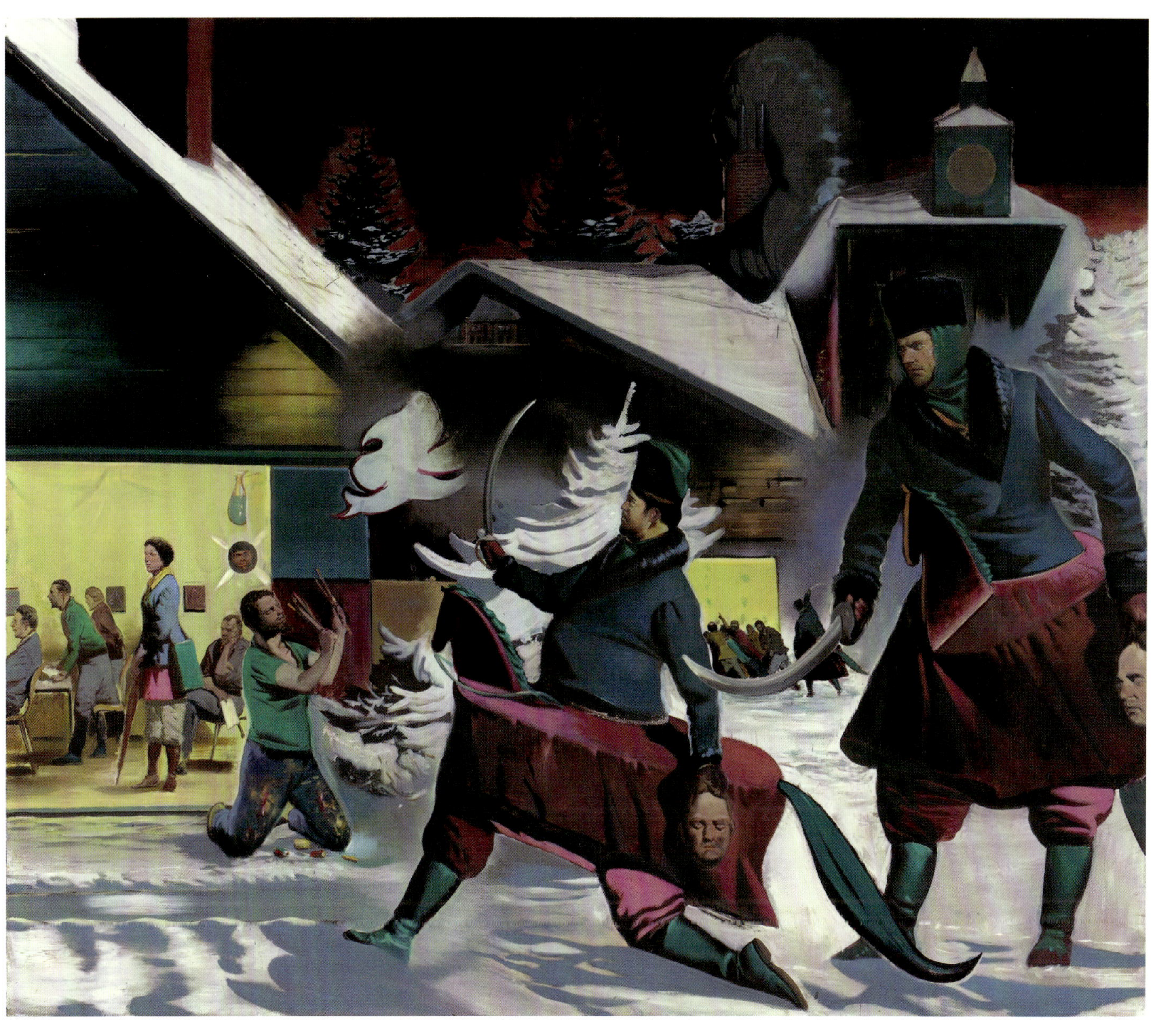

65. Bergfest 2010

Oil on canvas
300 × 250 cm (118¼ × 98½ in)
Private collection

66. Fastnacht 2010

Oil on canvas
250 × 300 cm (98½ × 118¼ in)

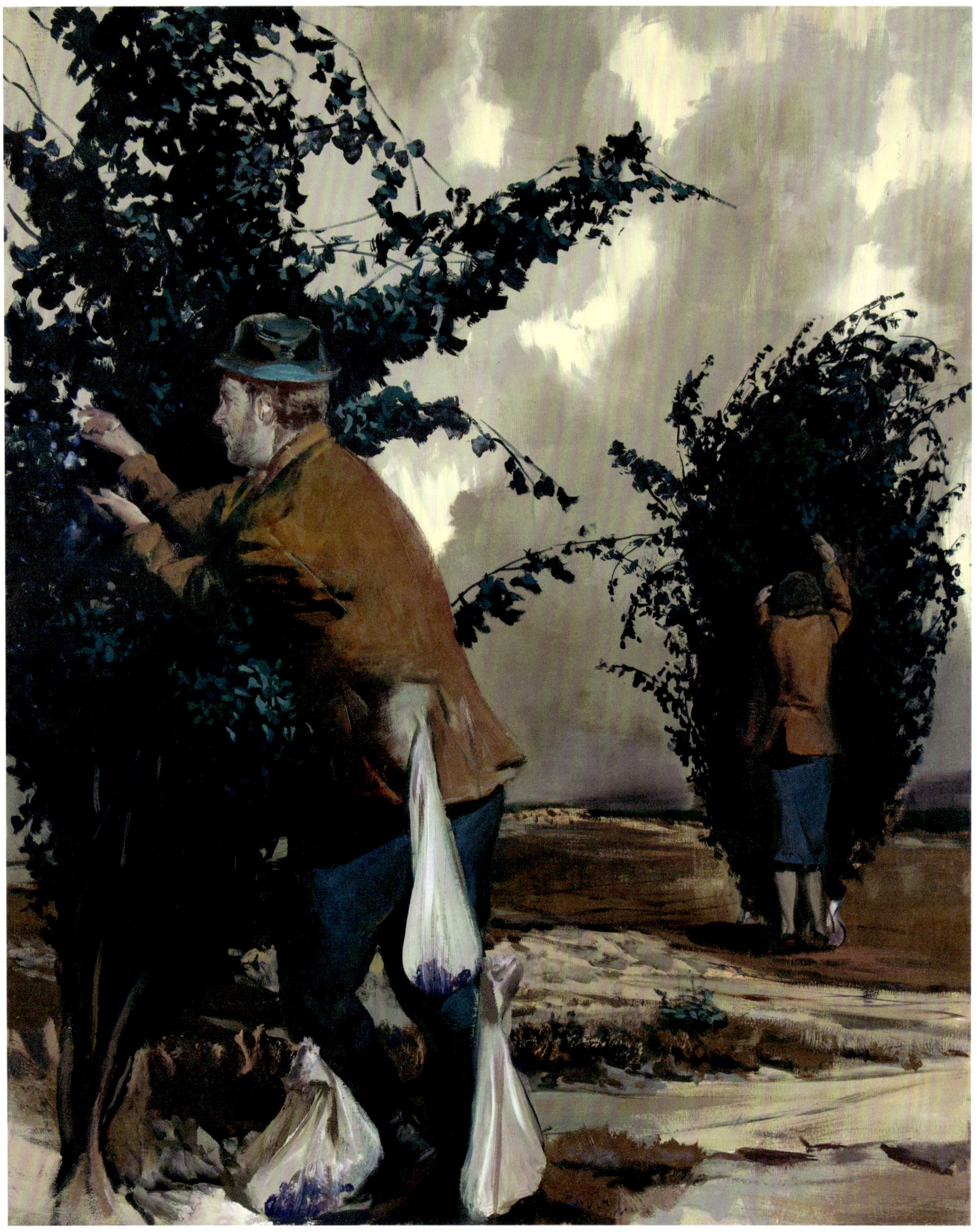

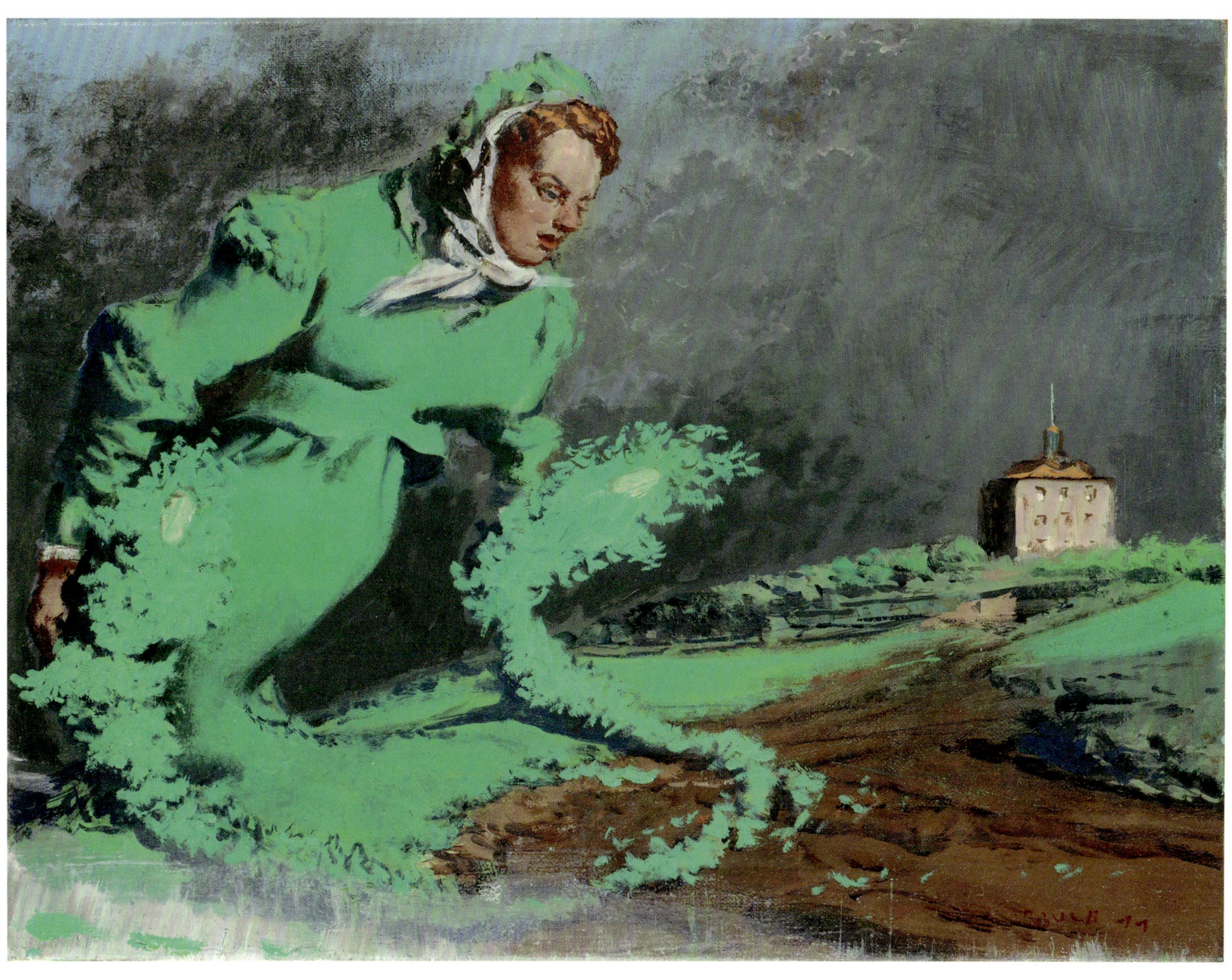

67. Beerenpflücker 2011

Oil on canvas
120 × 100 cm (49¼ × 39⅜ in)
Private collection

68. Die Warte 2011

Oil on canvas
30 × 40 cm (11¾ × 15¾ in)
Private collection

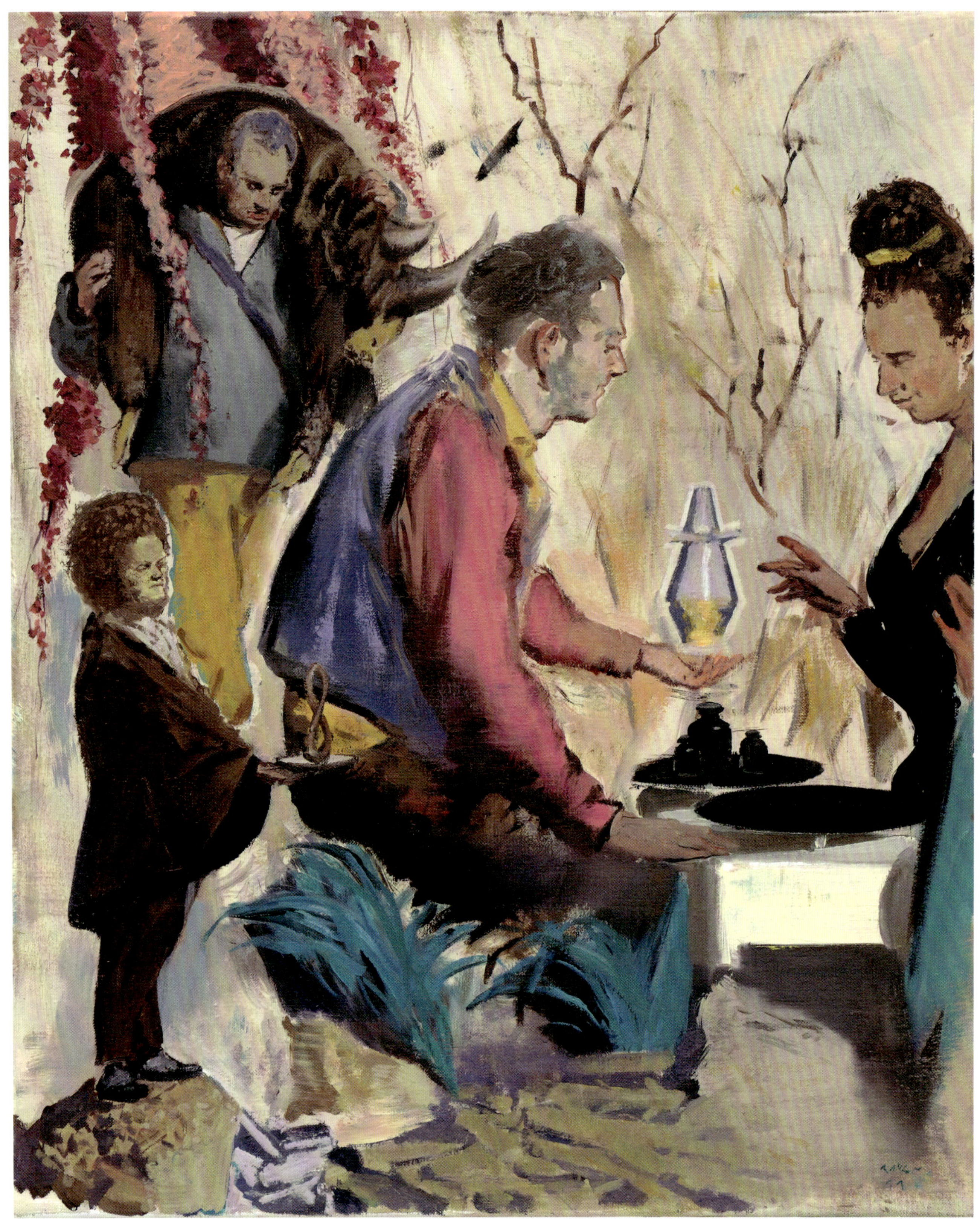

69. Feldwaage 2011

Oil on canvas
60 × 50 cm (23¾ × 19¾ in)
Collectie De Heus-Zomer

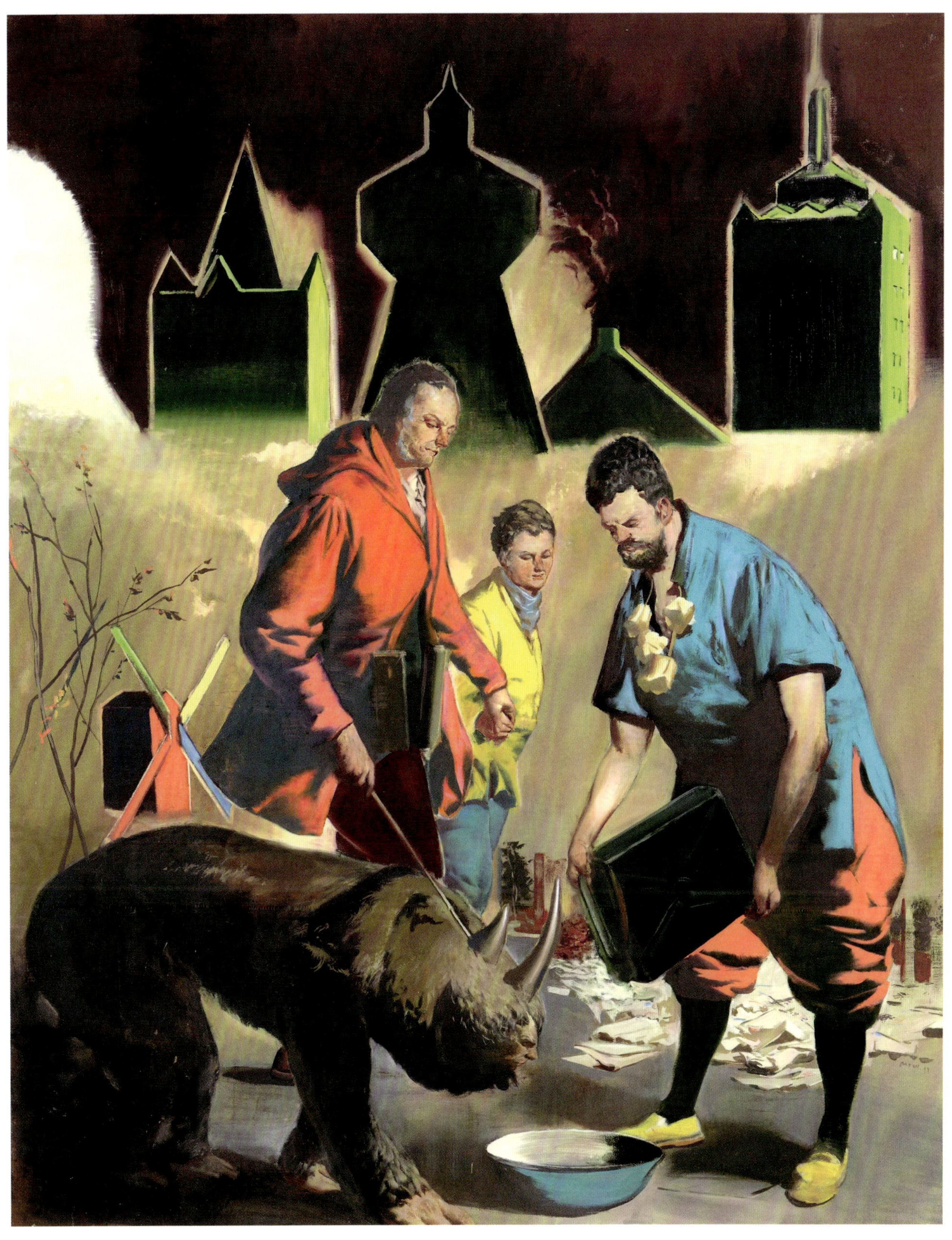

70. Türme 2011

Oil on canvas
250 × 200 cm (98½ × 78¾ in)
Private collection

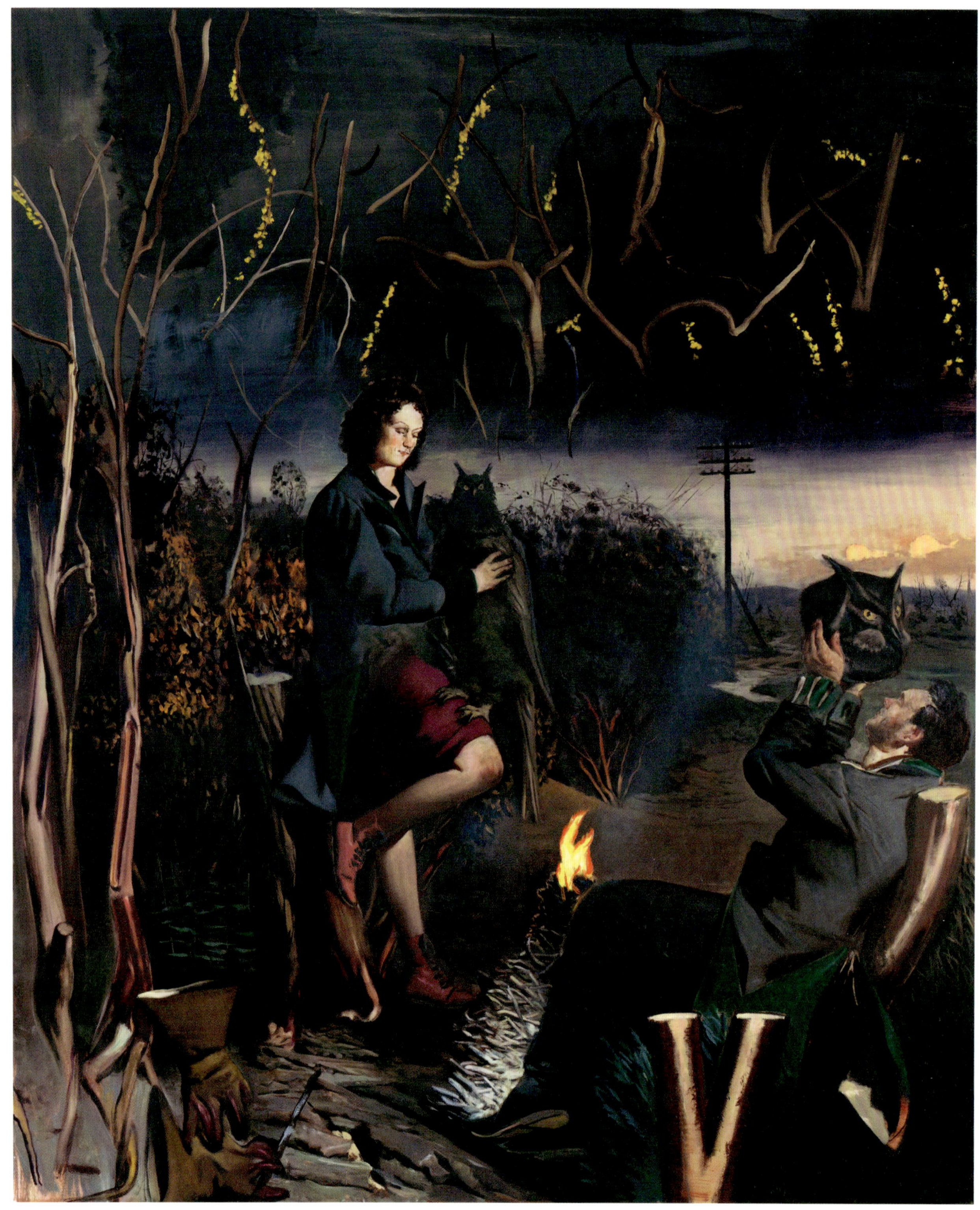

71. Aprilnacht 2011

Oil on canvas
300 × 250 cm (118¼ × 98½ in)
Private collection, courtesy David Zwirner

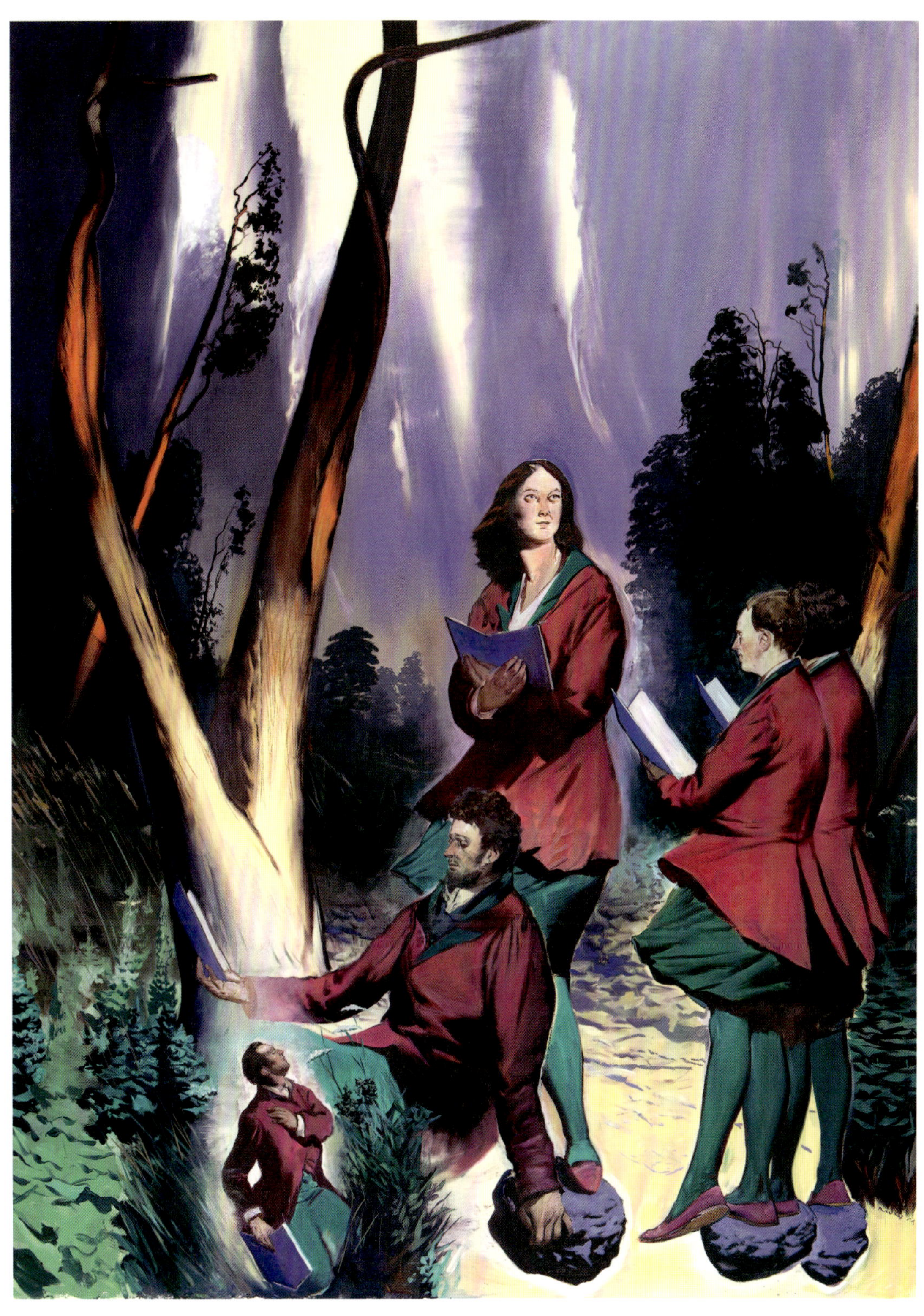

72. Chor 2011

Oil on canvas
300 × 220 cm (118¼ × 86¾ in)
Sammlung HGN

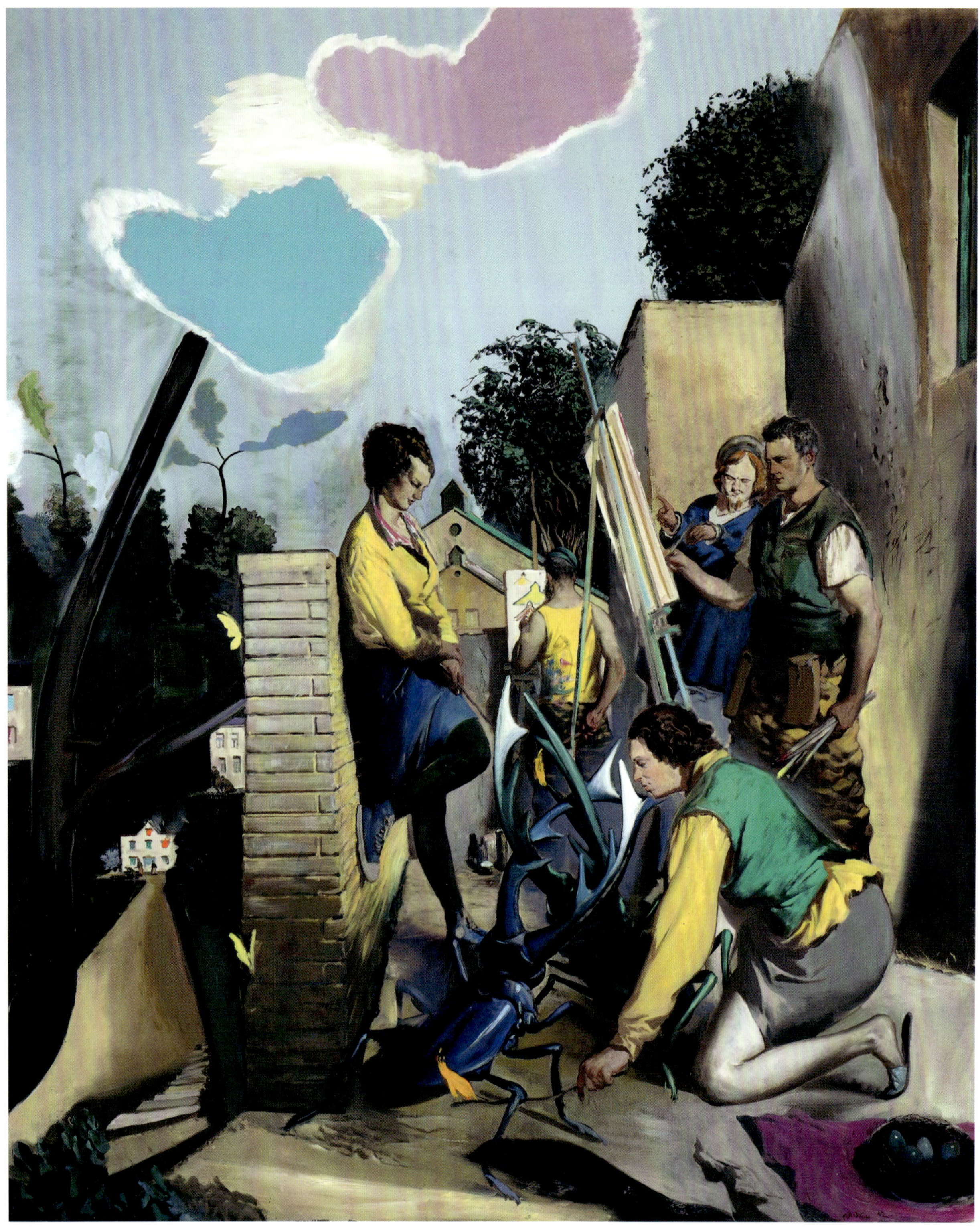

73. Nest 2012

Oil on canvas
300 × 250 cm (118¼ × 98½ in)
Collectie De Heus-Zomer

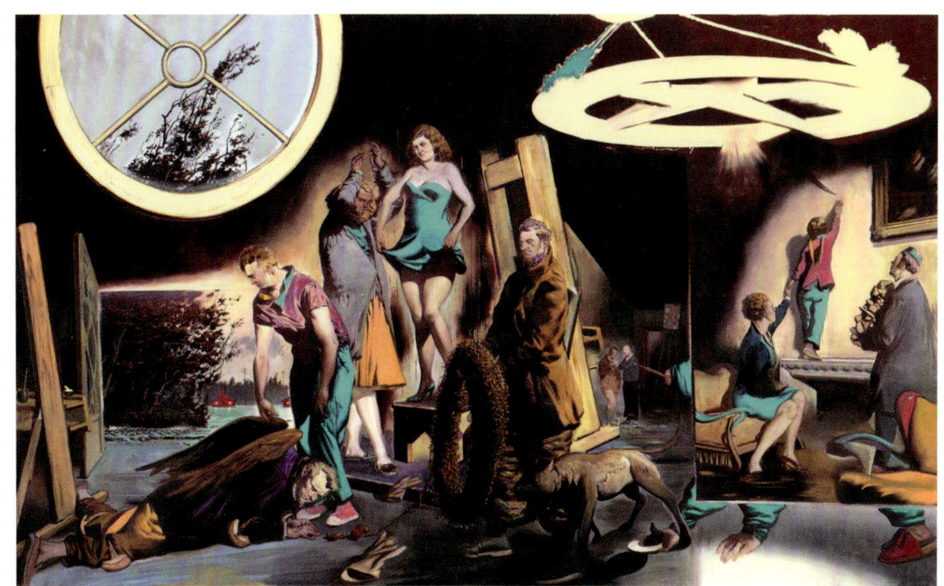

74. Das Kreisen 2011

Oil on canvas
300 × 500 cm (118¼ × 197 in)
Private collection

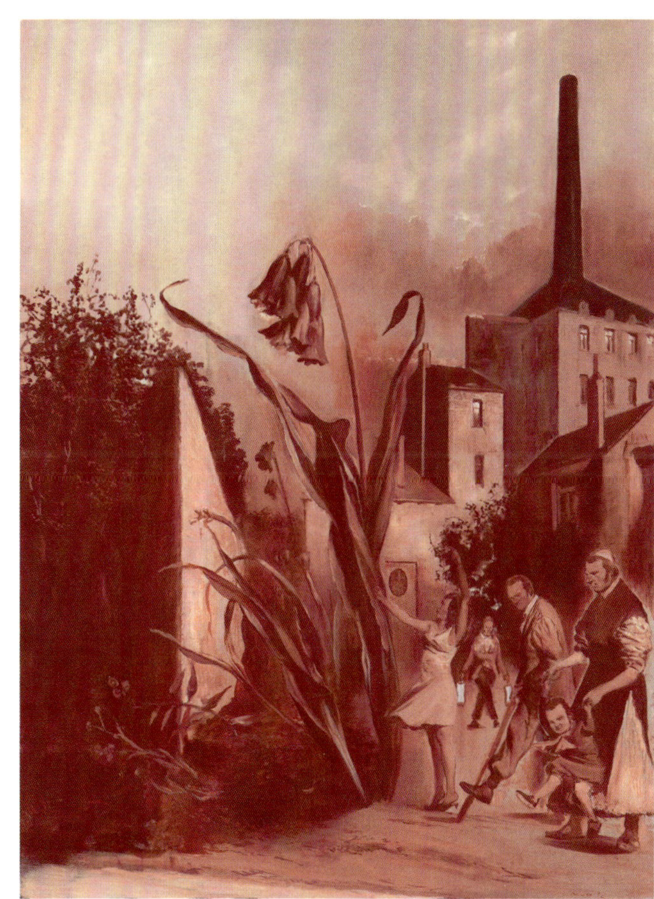

75. Blumenhof 2012

Oil on canvas
200 × 150 cm (78¾ × 59 in)
Private collection

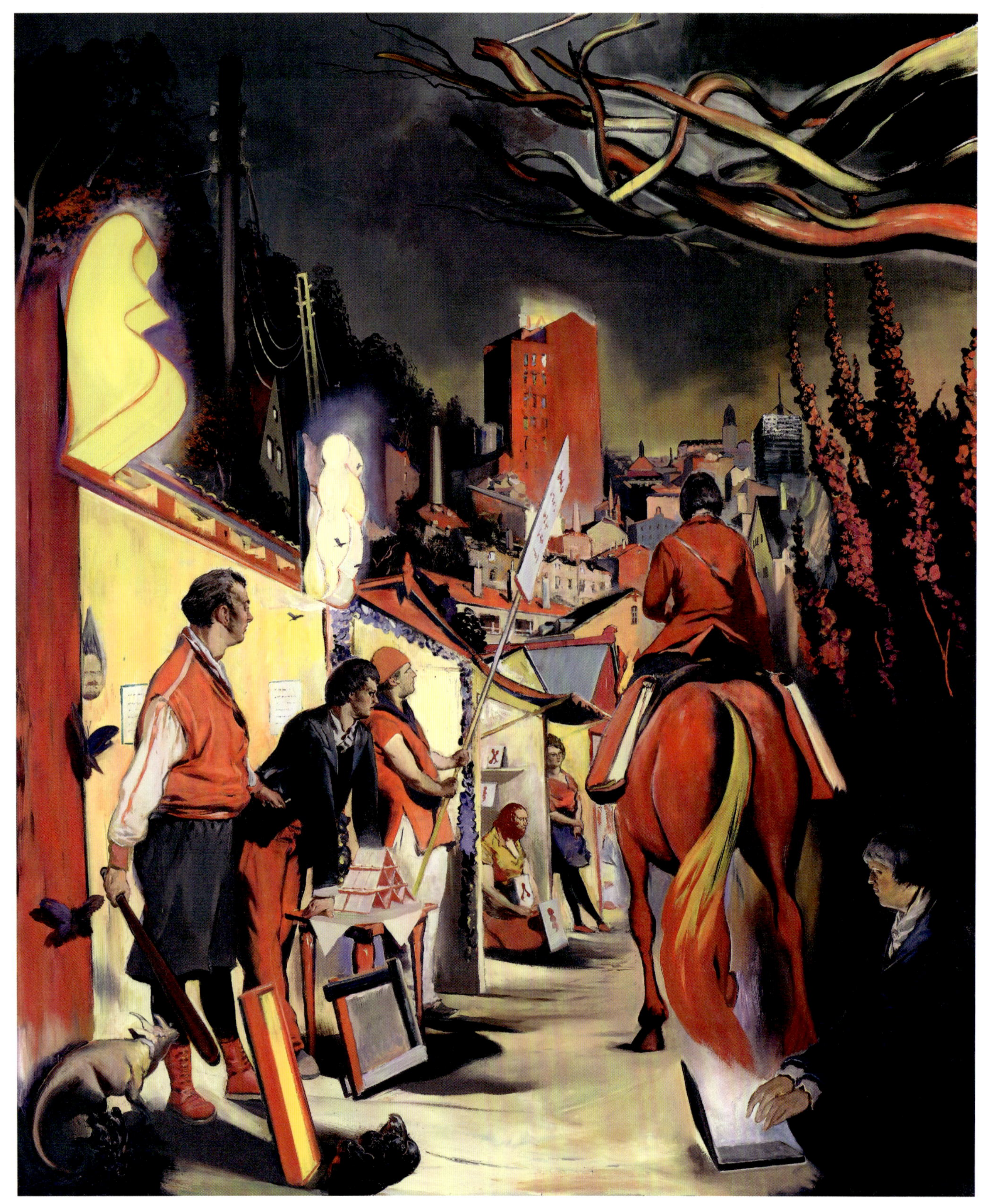

76. Abendmesse 2012

Oil on canvas
300 × 250 cm (118¼ × 98½ in)
Private collection

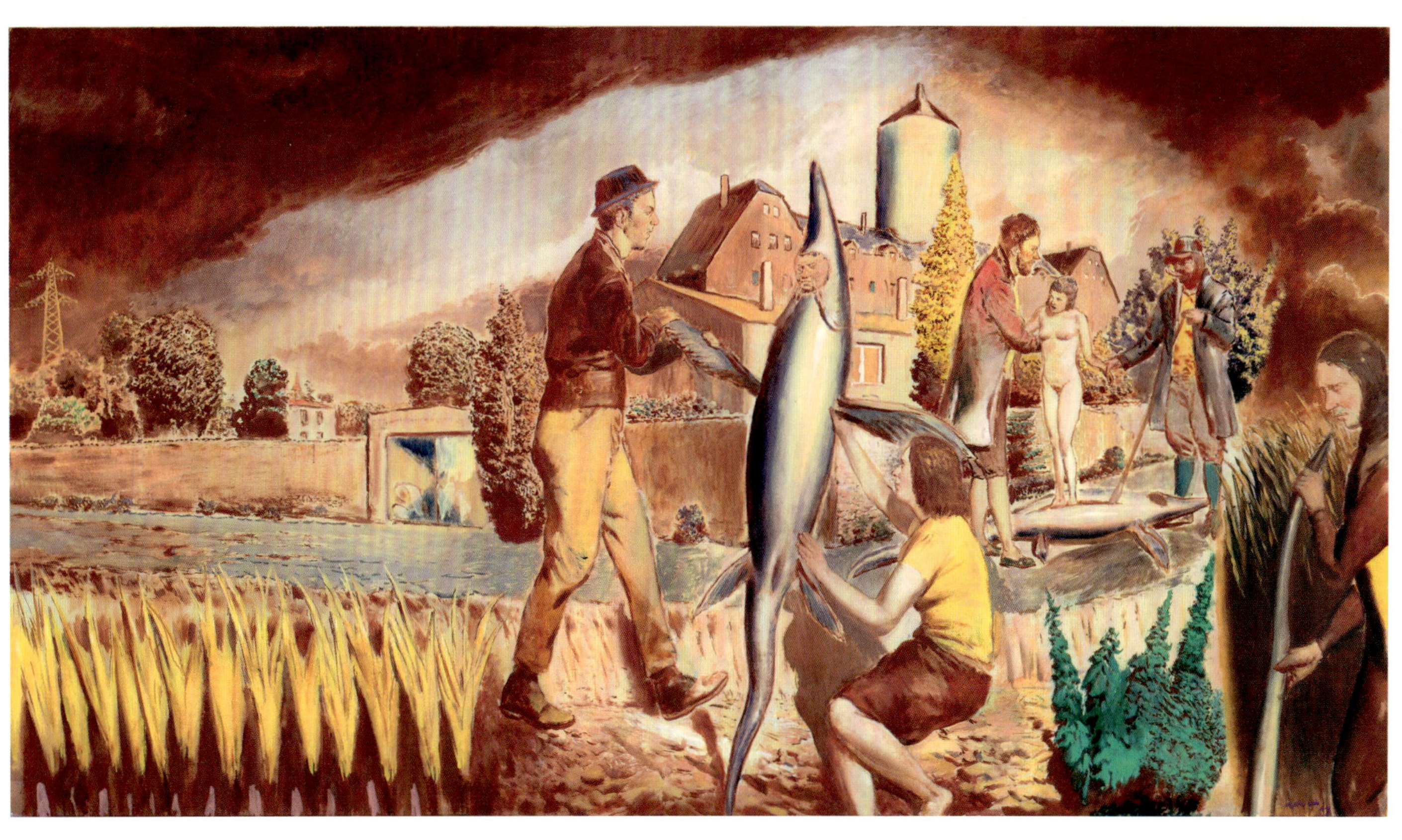

77. Geborgen 2013

Oil on canvas
120 × 220 cm (47¼ × 86¾ in)
Collectie De Heus-Zomer

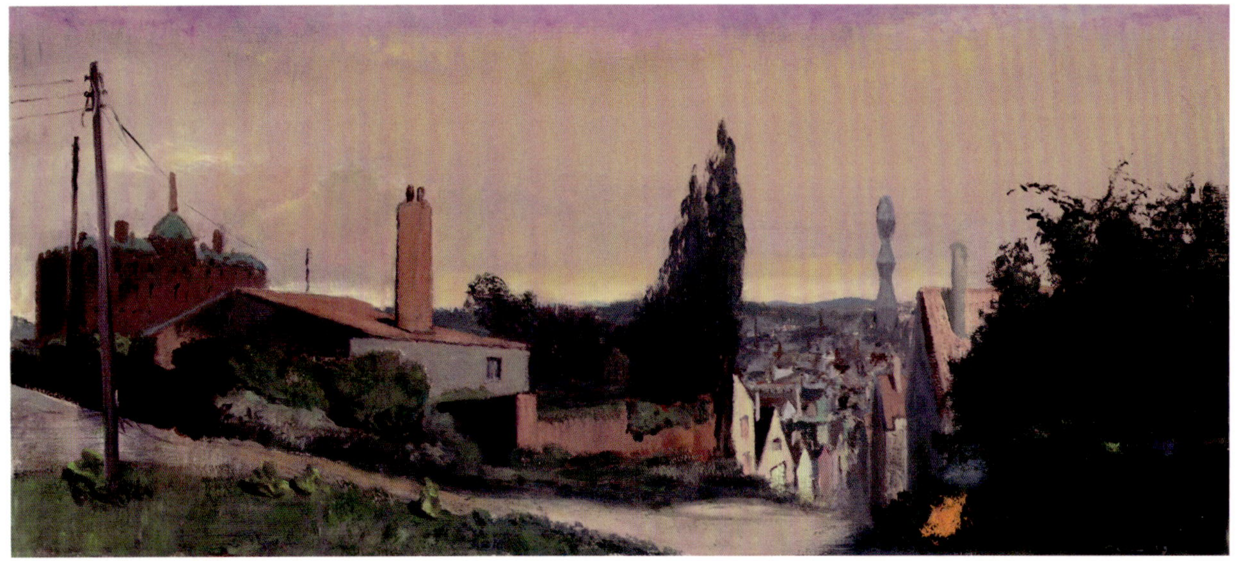

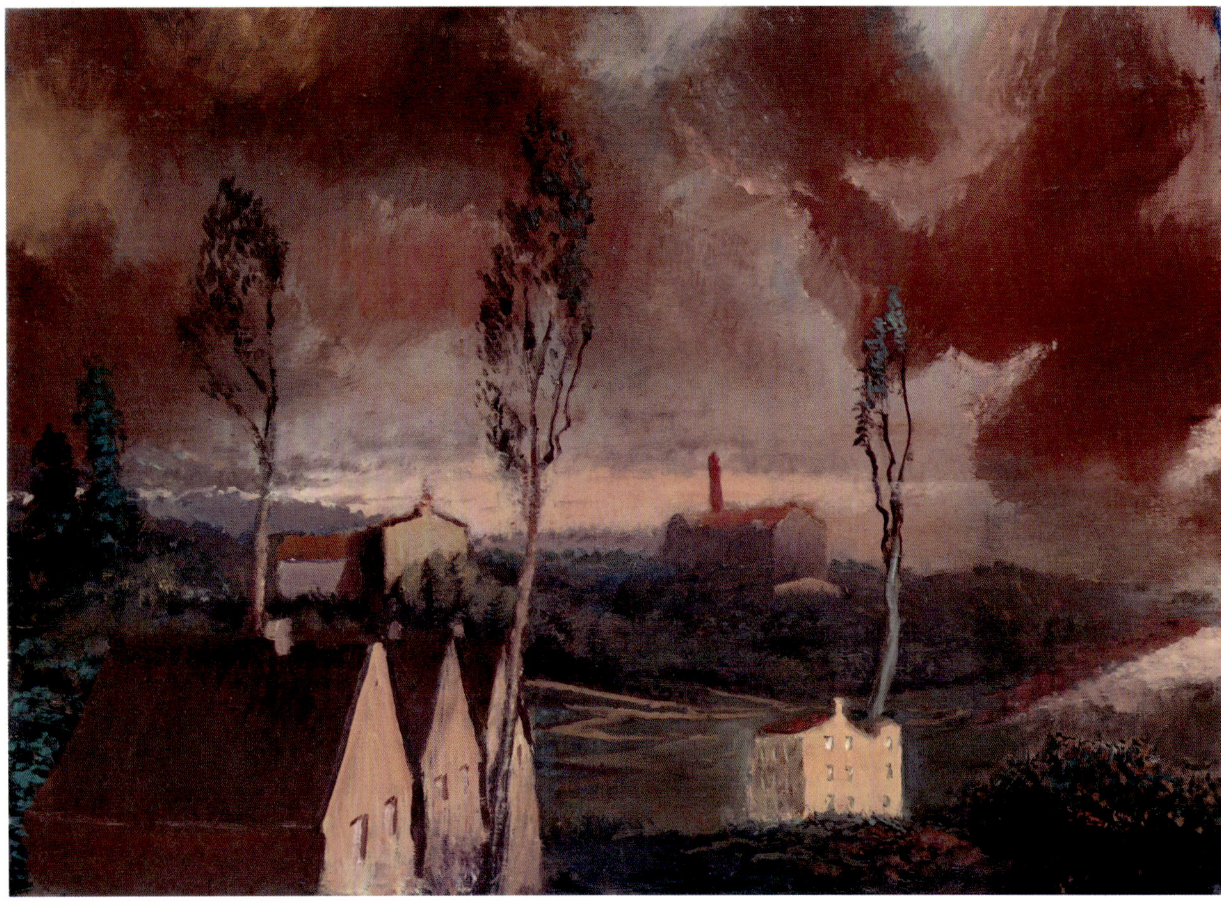

78. Ankunft 2013

Oil on canvas
40 × 94.6 cm (15¾ × 37¼ in)
Private collection

79. September 2013

Oil on canvas
35 × 50 cm (13¾ × 19¾ in)
Private collection

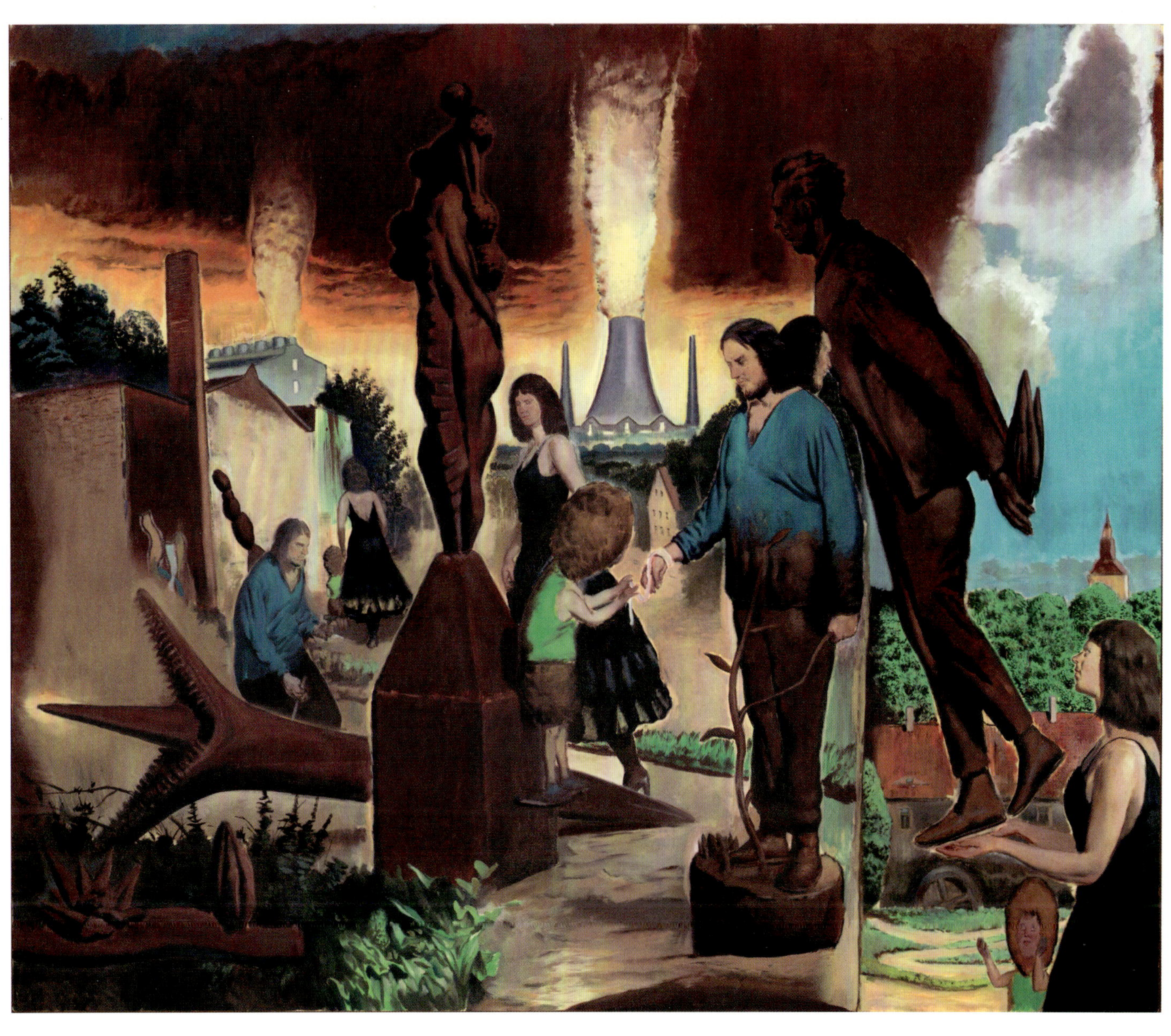

80. Rost 2013

Oil on canvas
250 × 300 cm ($98\frac{1}{2}$ × $118\frac{1}{4}$ in)
Private collection

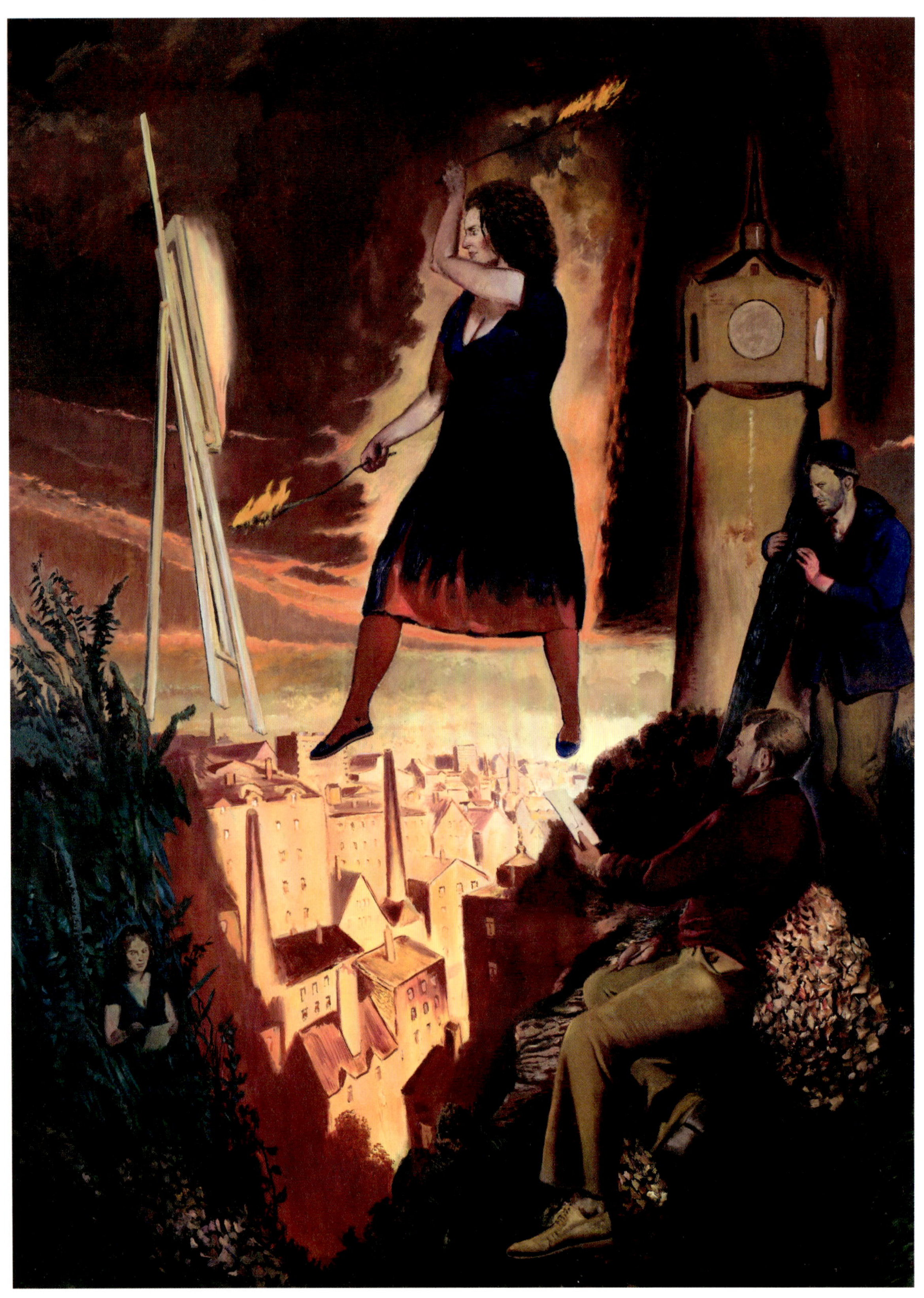

81. Die Stadt im Tal 2013

Oil on canvas
300 × 220 cm (118¼ × 86¾ in)
Private collection

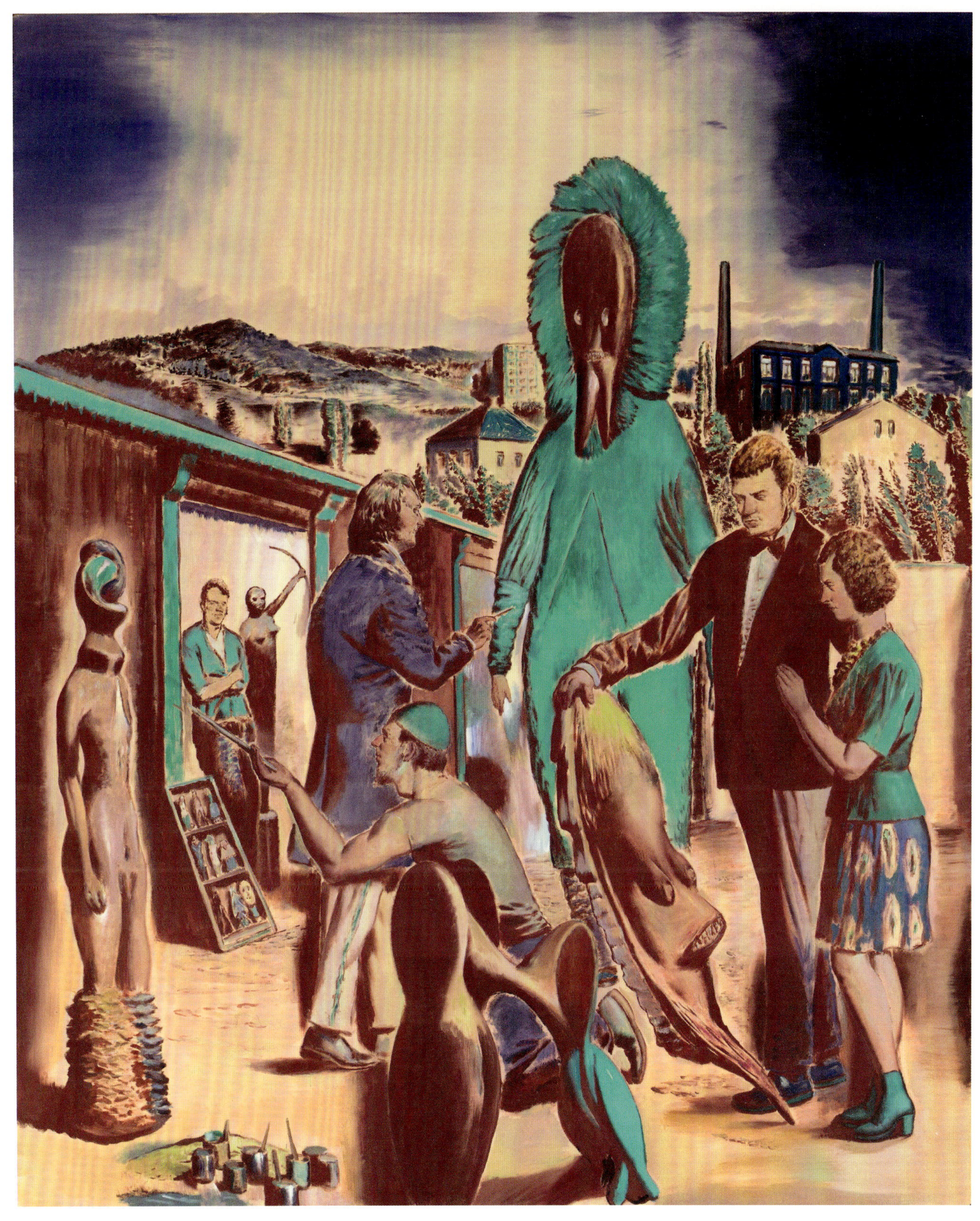

82. Das Bannende 2013

Oil on canvas
300 × 250 cm (118¼ × 98½ in)
Sammlung HGN

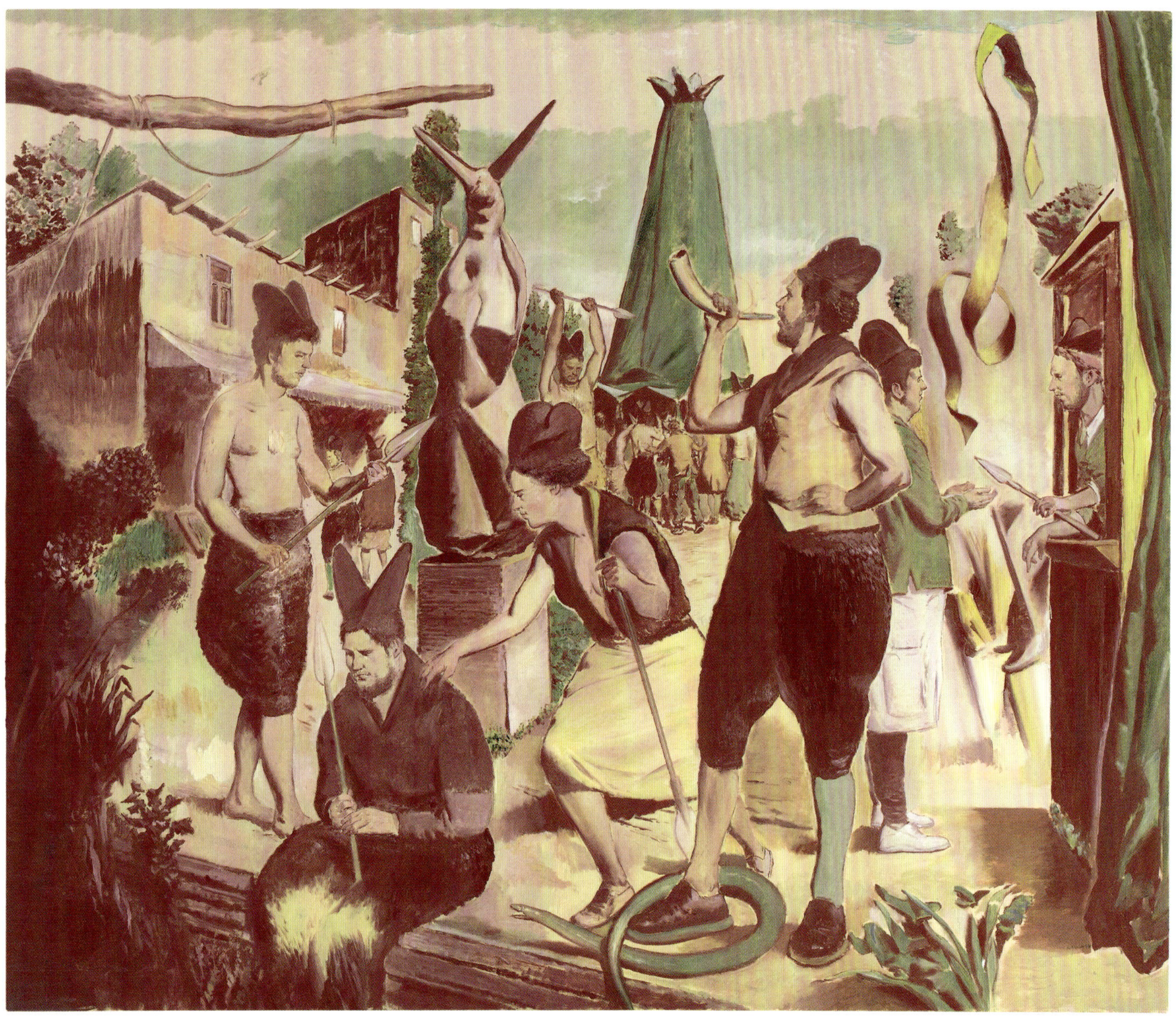

83. Das Horn 2014

Oil on canvas
250 × 300 cm (98½ × 118¼ in)
Private collection

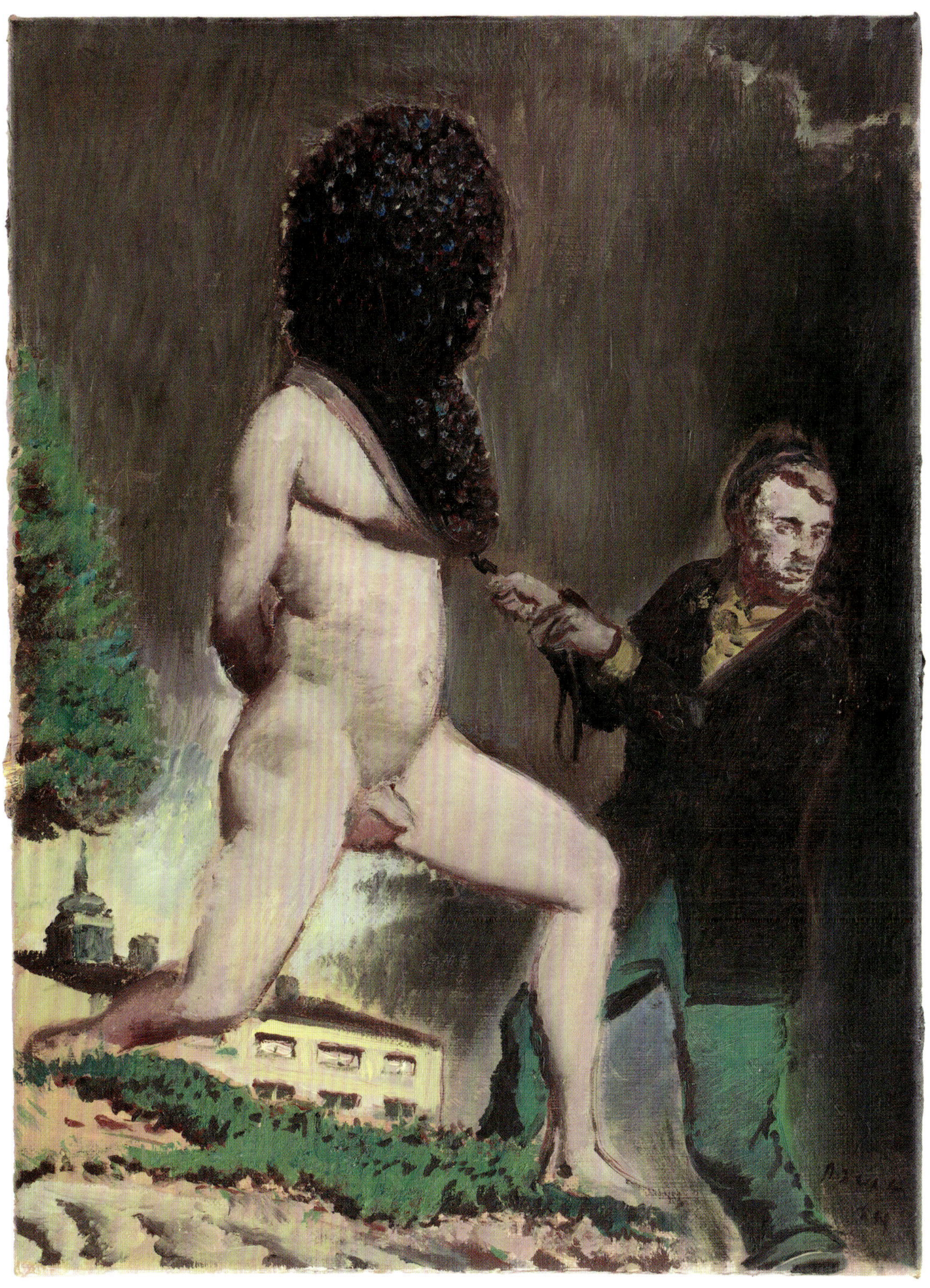

84. Am Rand 2014

Oil on canvas
40 × 30 cm (15¾ × 11¾ in)
Private collection

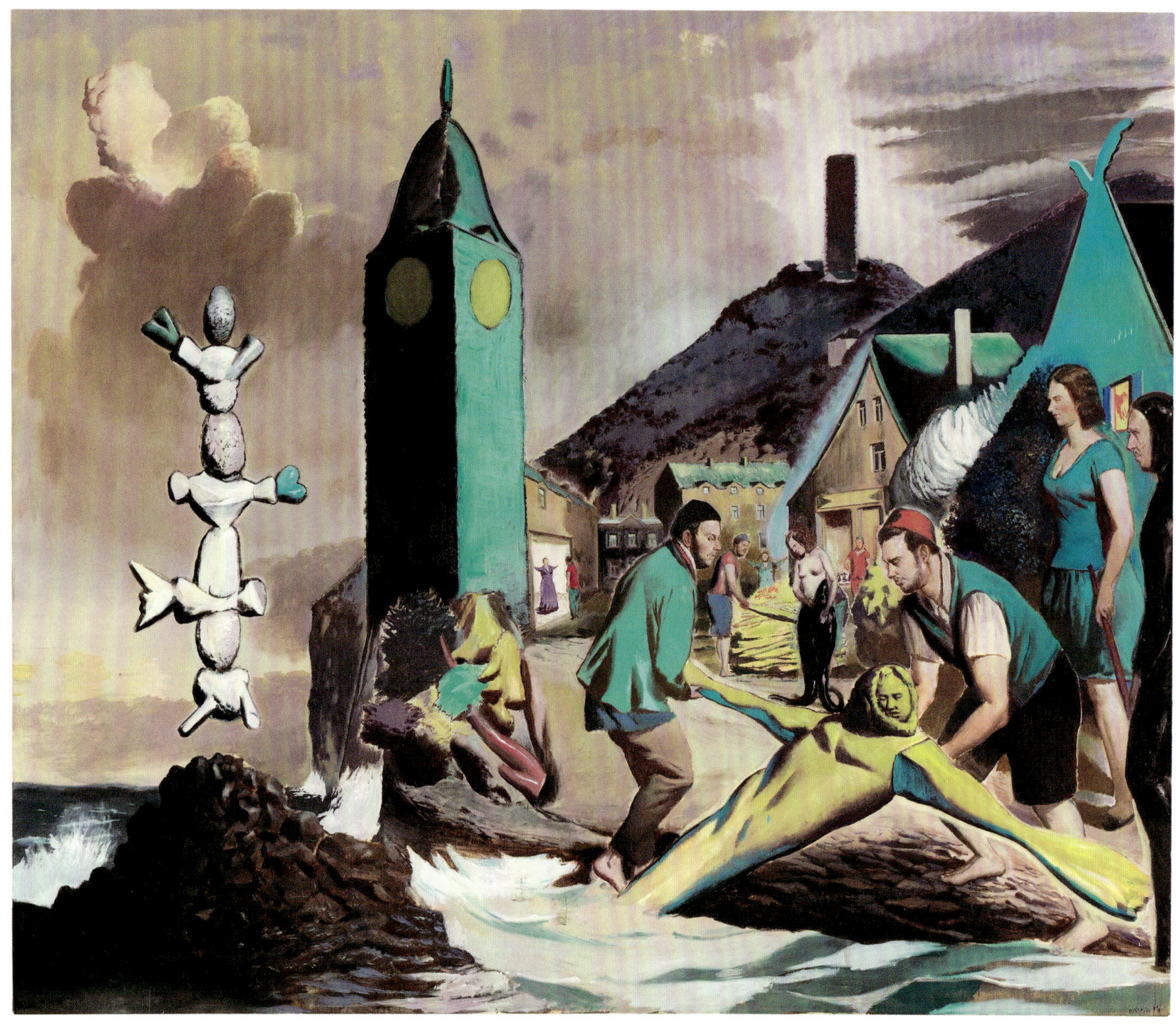

85. Marina 2014

Oil on canvas
250 × 300 cm (98½ × 118¼ in)
Private collection, Los Angeles

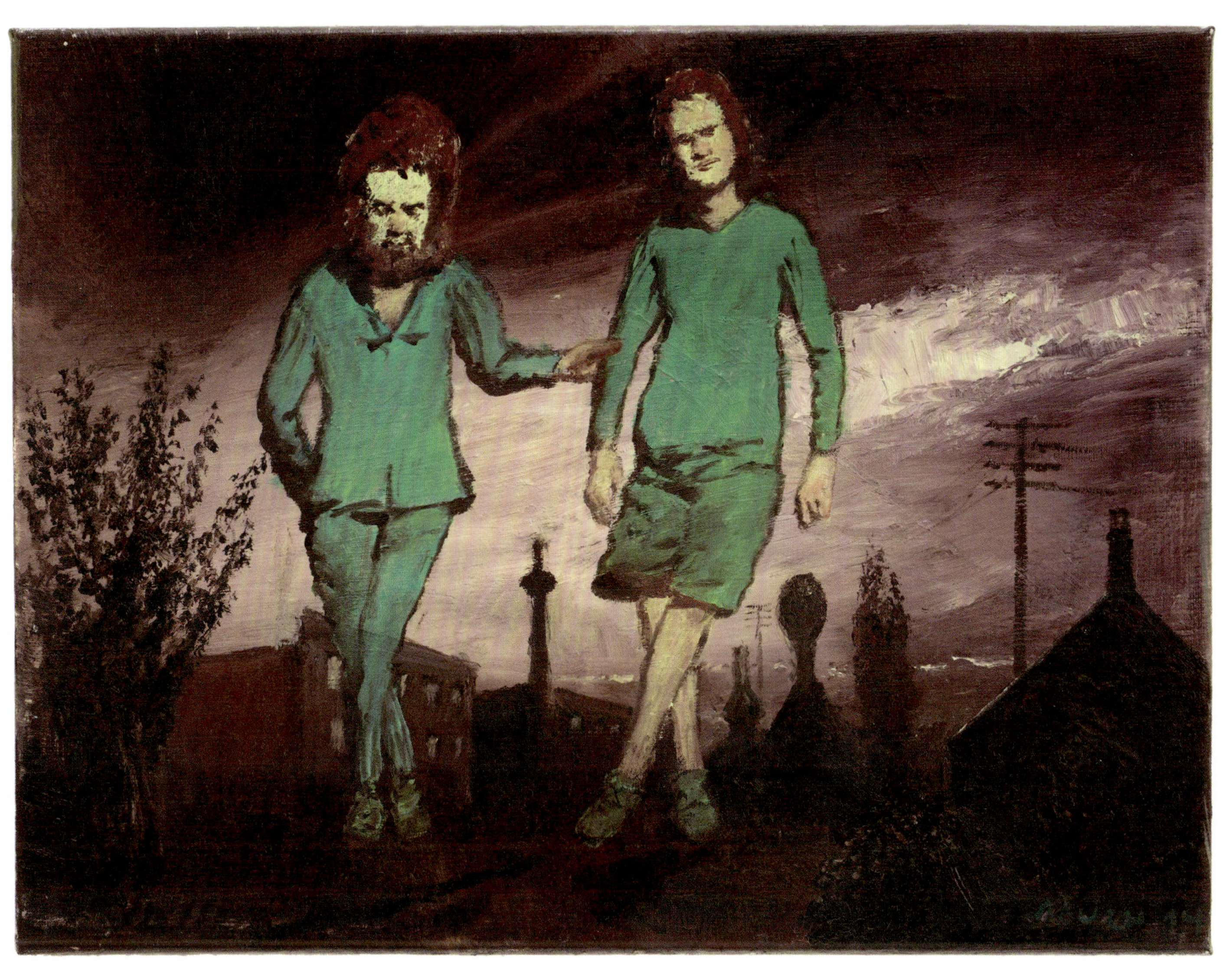

86. Duo 2014

Oil on canvas
30 × 40 cm (11¾ × 15¾ in)
Edward Nicoll and Helen Kent-Nicoll

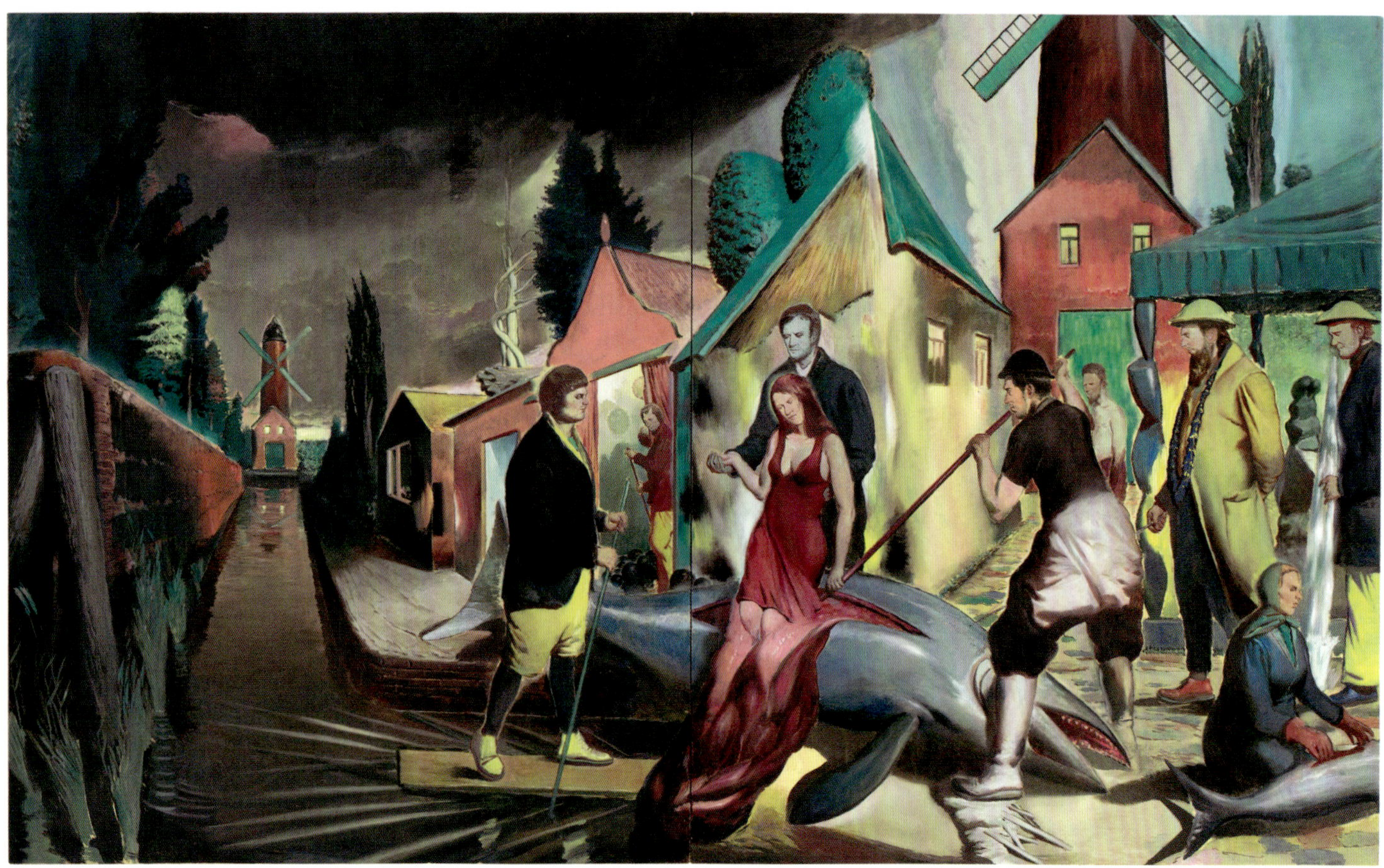

87. Der Blaue Fisch 2014

Oil on canvas, diptych
300 × 500 cm (118¼ × 197 in)
National Gallery of Canada, Ottawa

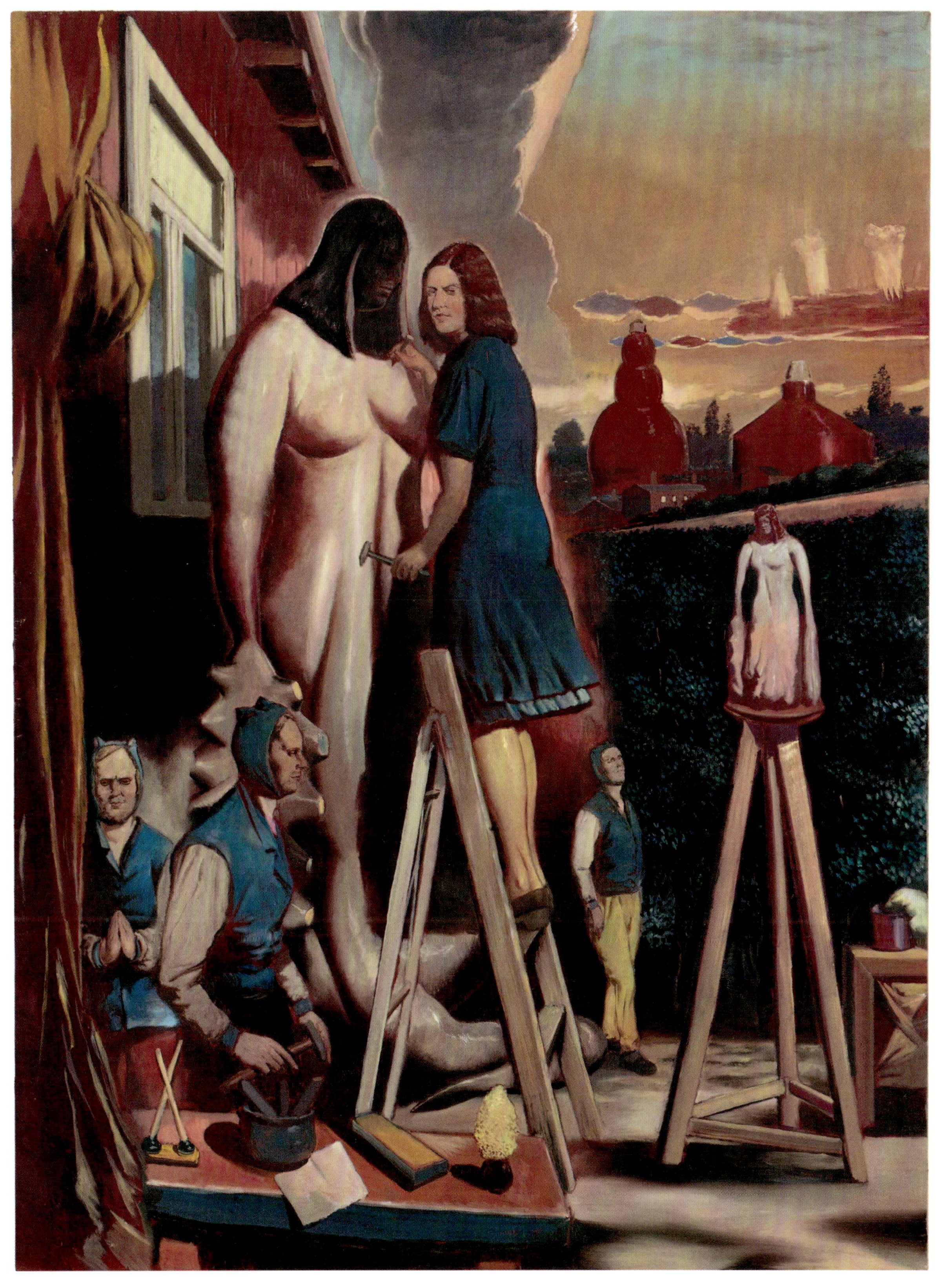

88. (Die) Skulpteurin 2014

Oil on canvas
280 × 210 cm (110¼ × 82⅝ in)
Courtesy of Gome Art Foundation

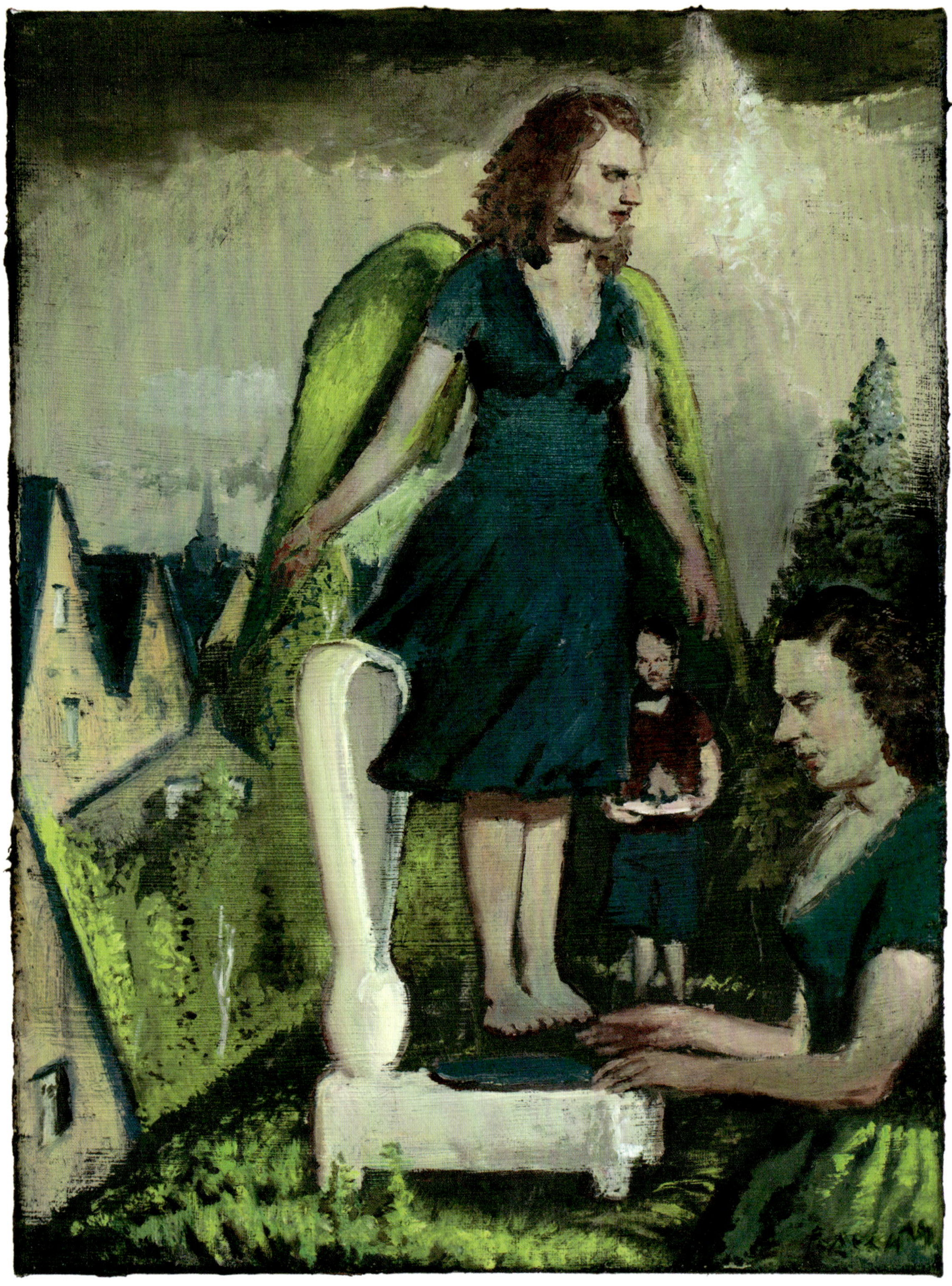

89. Die Engelswaage 2014

Oil on canvas
40 × 30 cm (15¾ × 11¾ in)
Sammlung Hildebrand, Leipzig

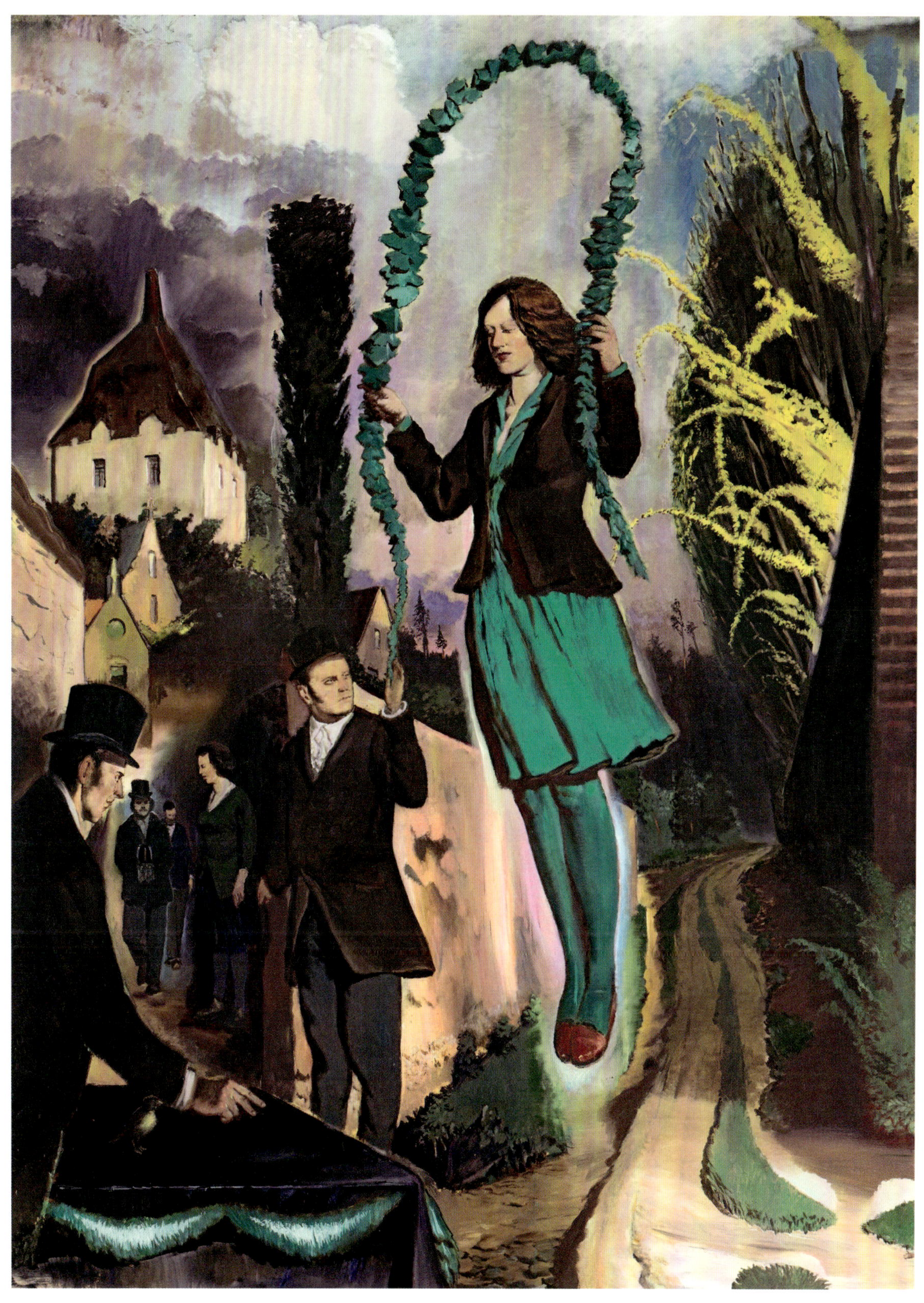

90. Die Erste 2015

Oil on canvas
270 × 200 cm (106½ × 78¾ in)
ACT Art Collection, Berlin

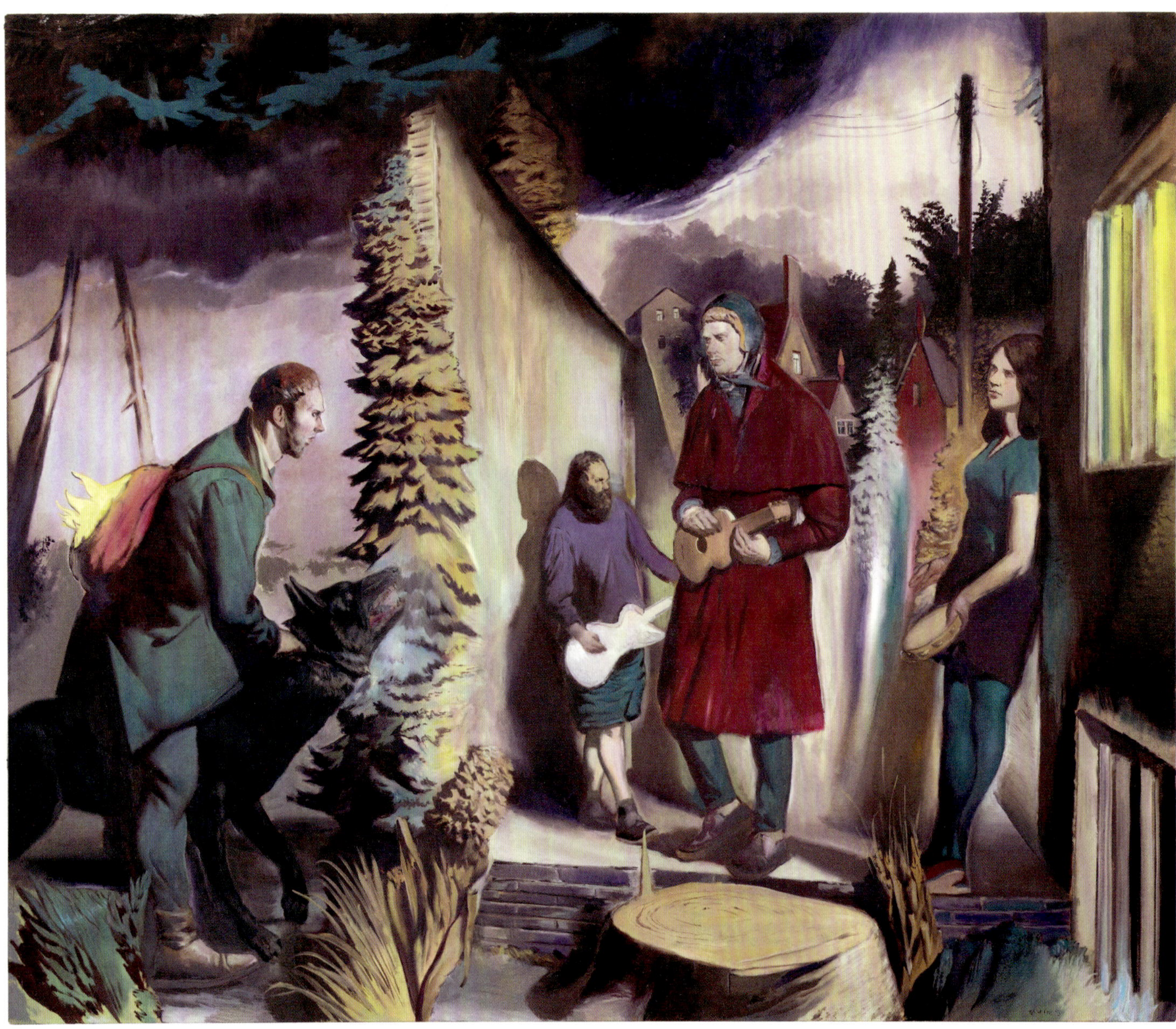

91. Die Fremde 2015

Oil on canvas
250 × 300 cm (98½ × 118¼ in)

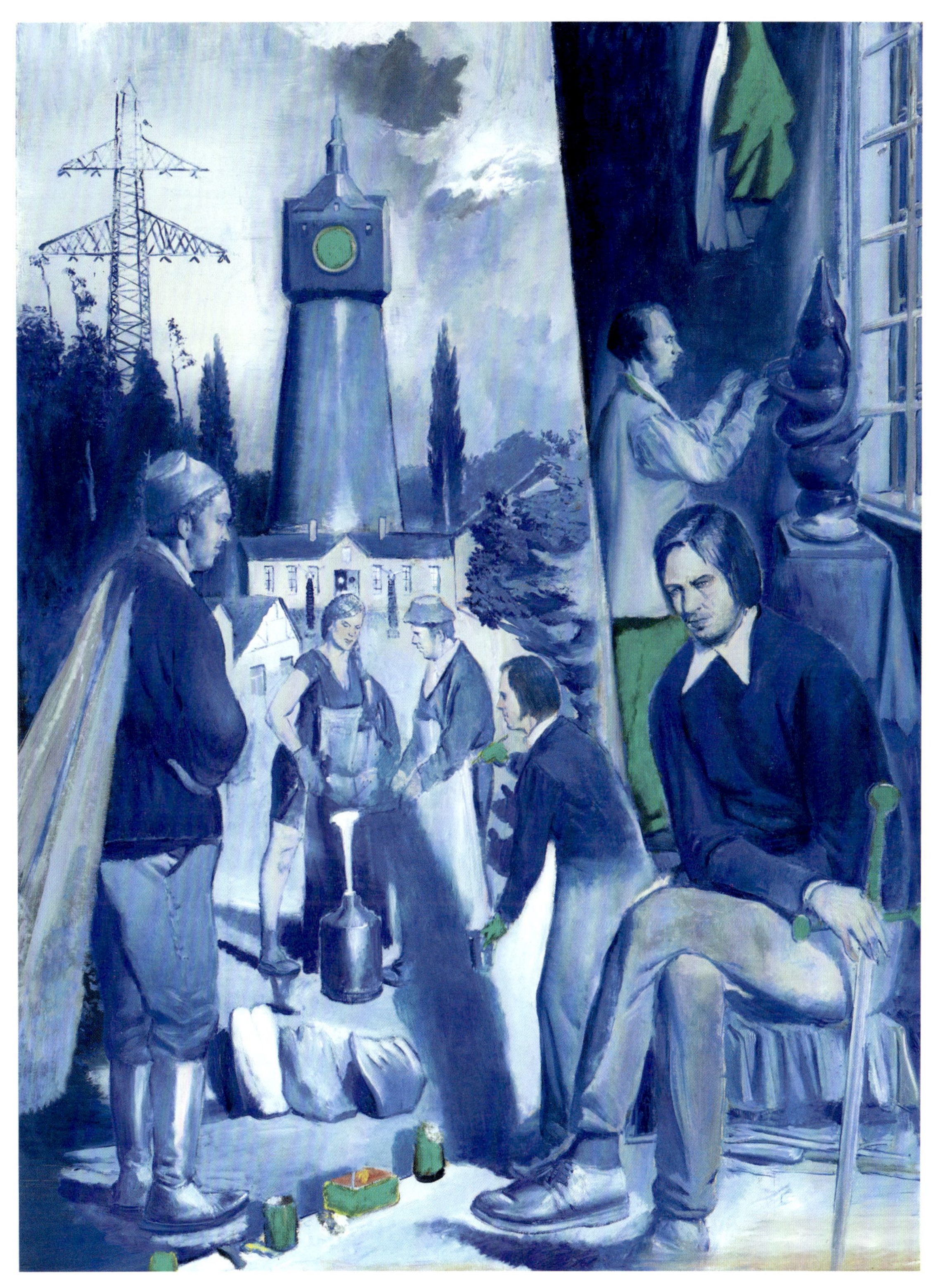

92. Der Former 2016

Oil on canvas
200 × 150 cm (78¾ × 59 in)
ACT Art Collection, Berlin

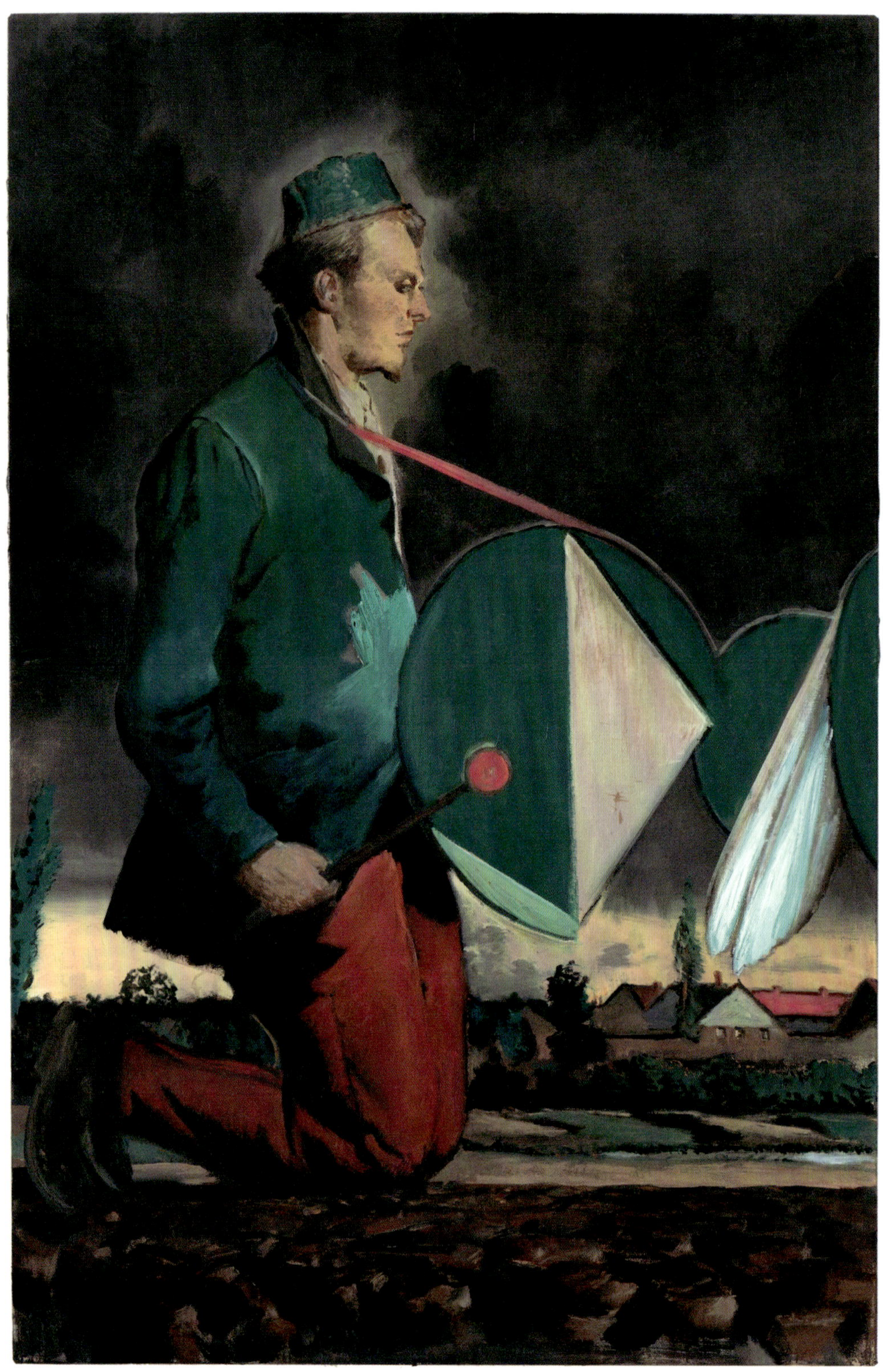

93. Gewitterfront 2016

Oil on canvas
150 × 100 cm (59 × 39½ in)
Collectie Museum de Fundatie, Zwolle

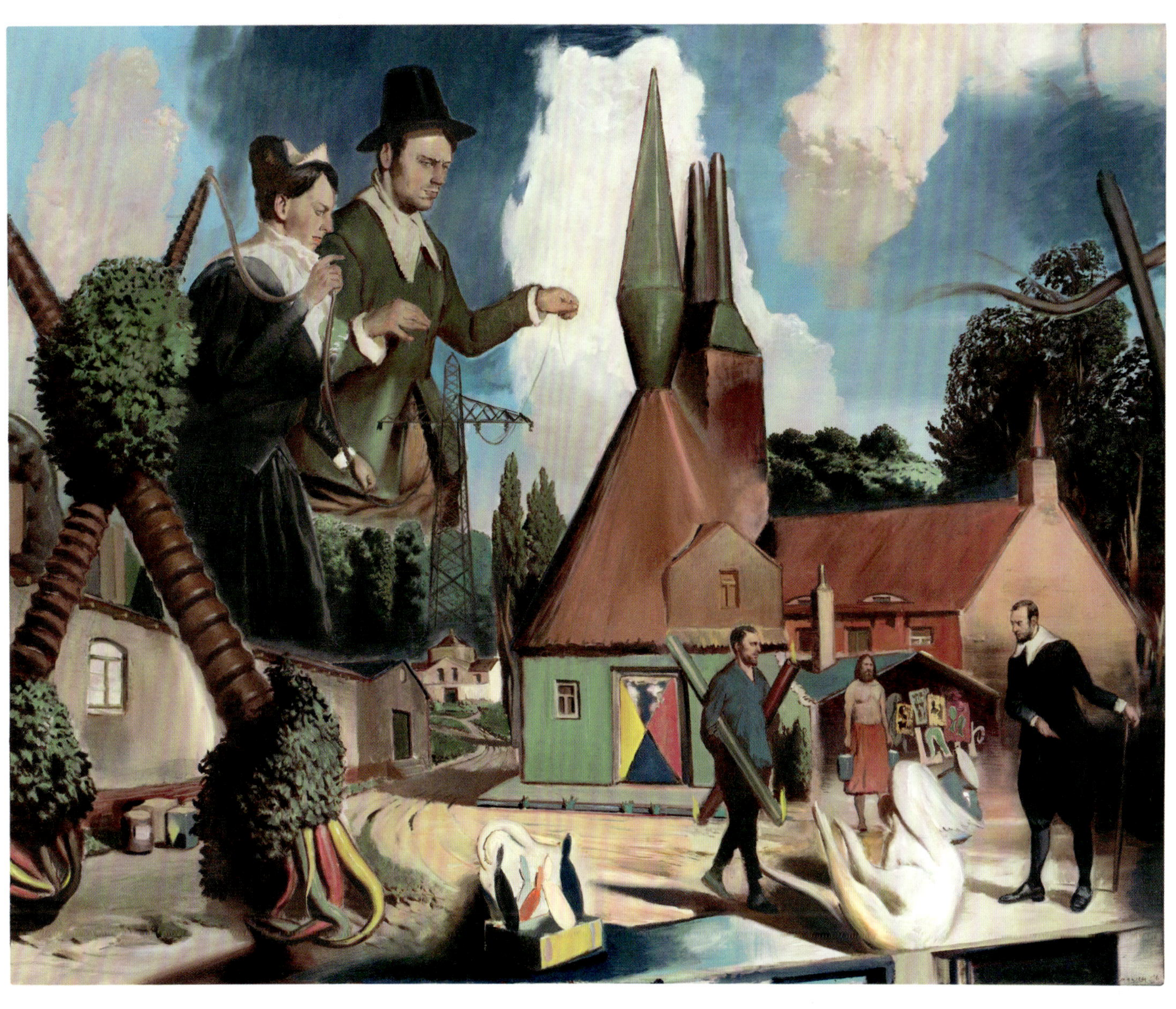

94. Zustrom 2016

Oil on canvas
200 × 250 cm (78¾ × 98½ in)
Private collection

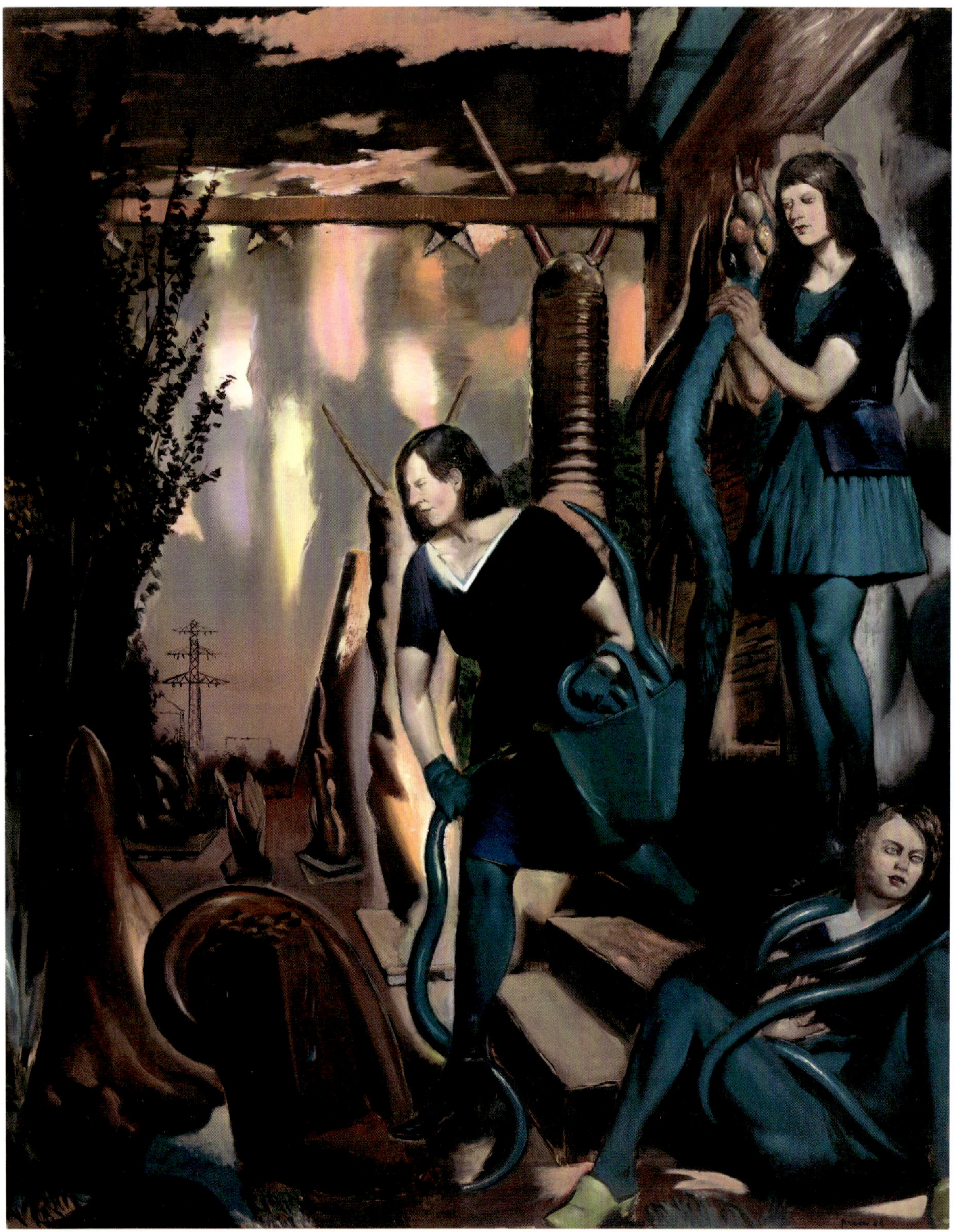

95. Spannung 2016

Oil on canvas
250 × 200 cm (98½ × 78¾ in)
Private collection

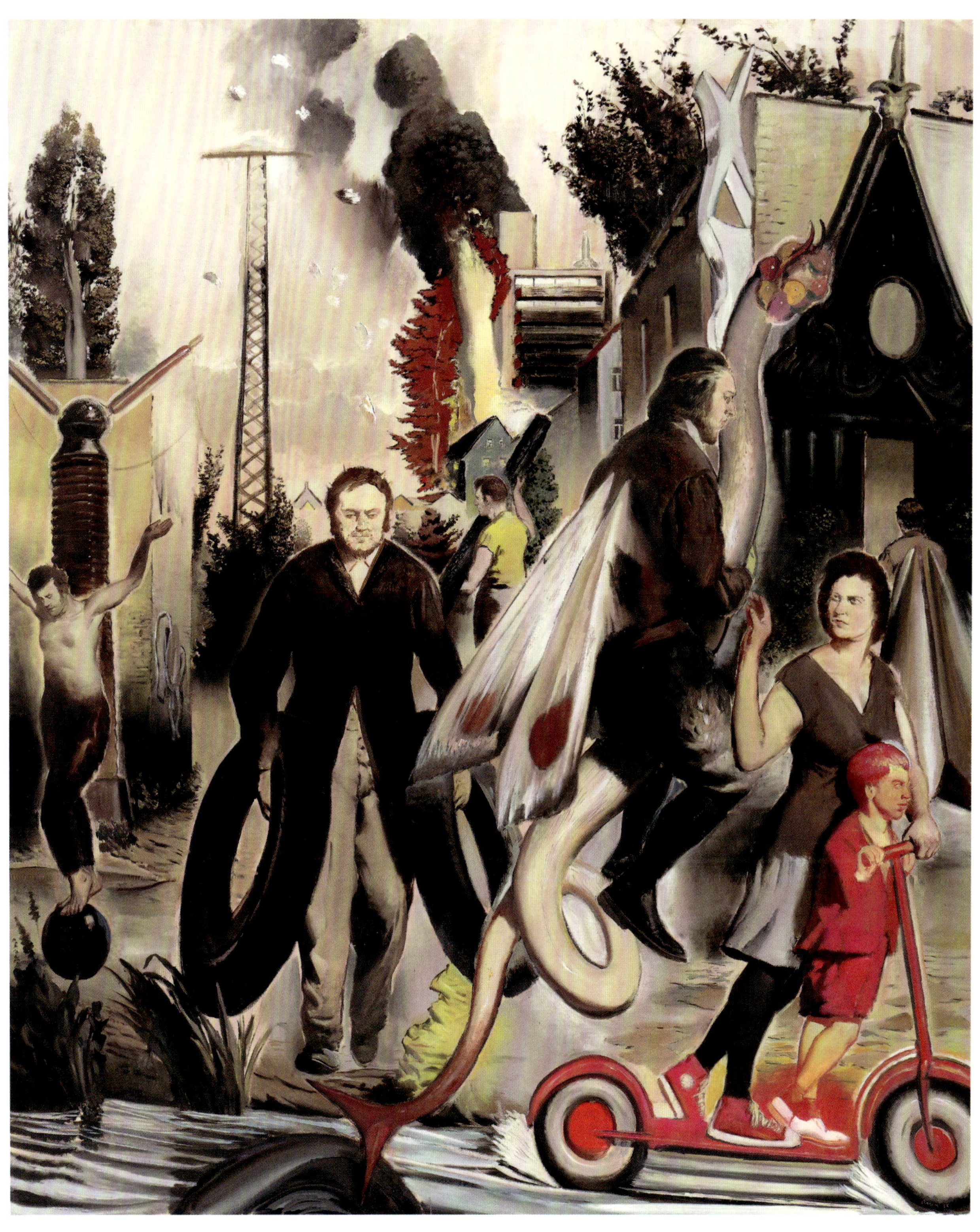

96. Gummiland 2016

Oil on canvas
300 × 250 cm (118¼ × 98½ in)
Private collection, Basel

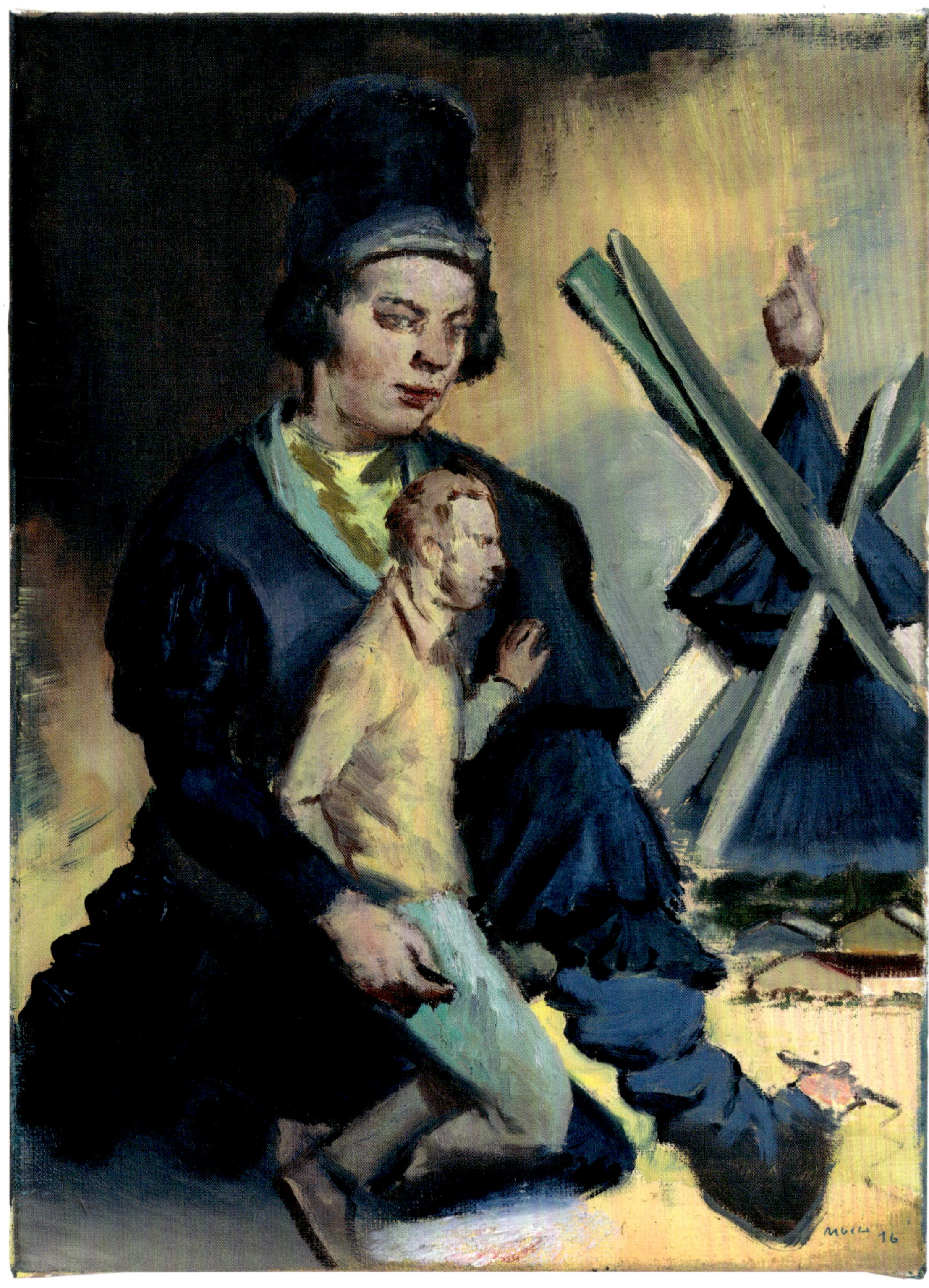

97. Müllers Frau 2016

Oil on canvas
40 × 30 cm (15¾ × 11¾ in)
Private collection, Leipzig

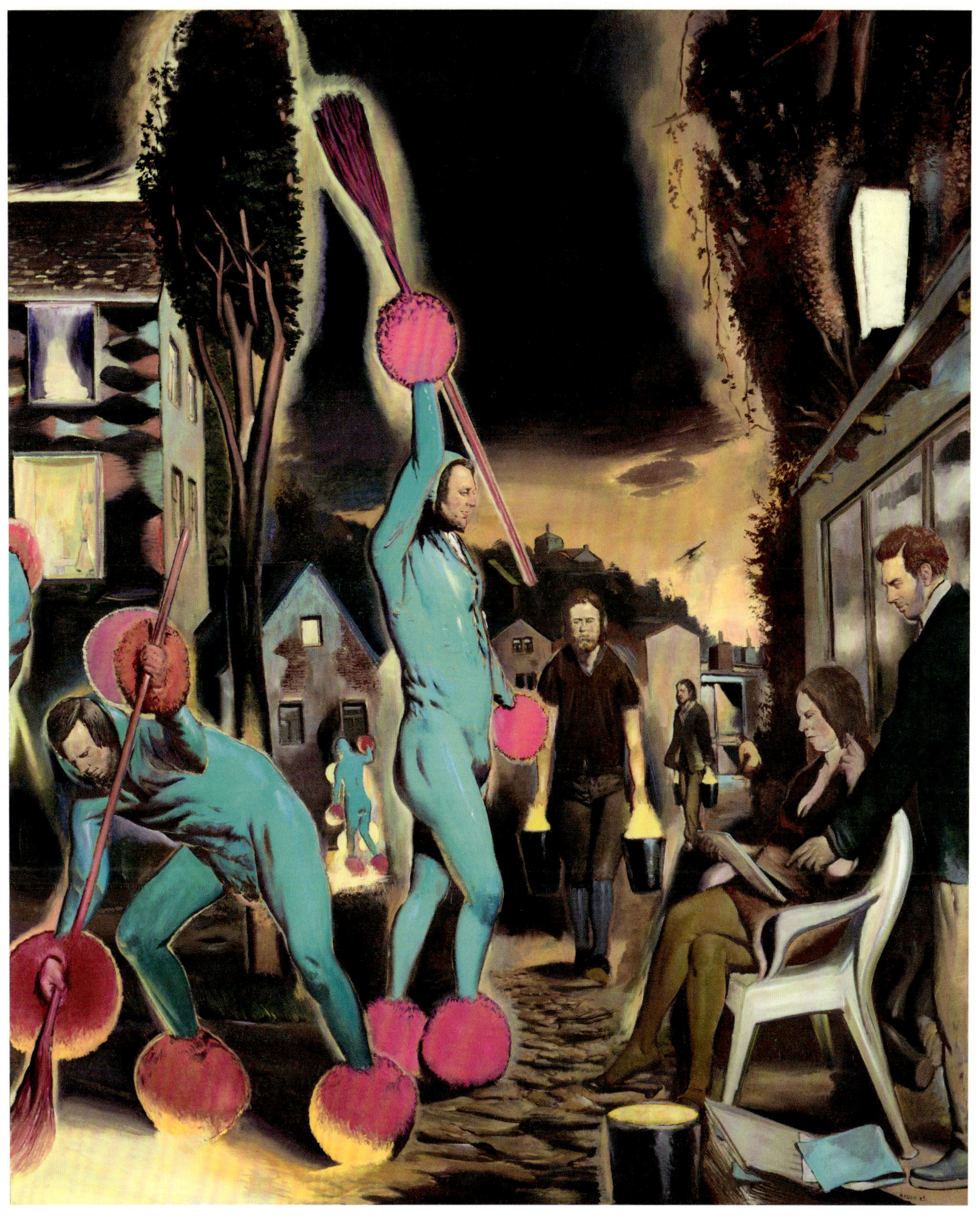

98. Der Lehrling 2015

Oil on canvas
300 × 250 cm (118¼ × 98½ in)
Arthaus

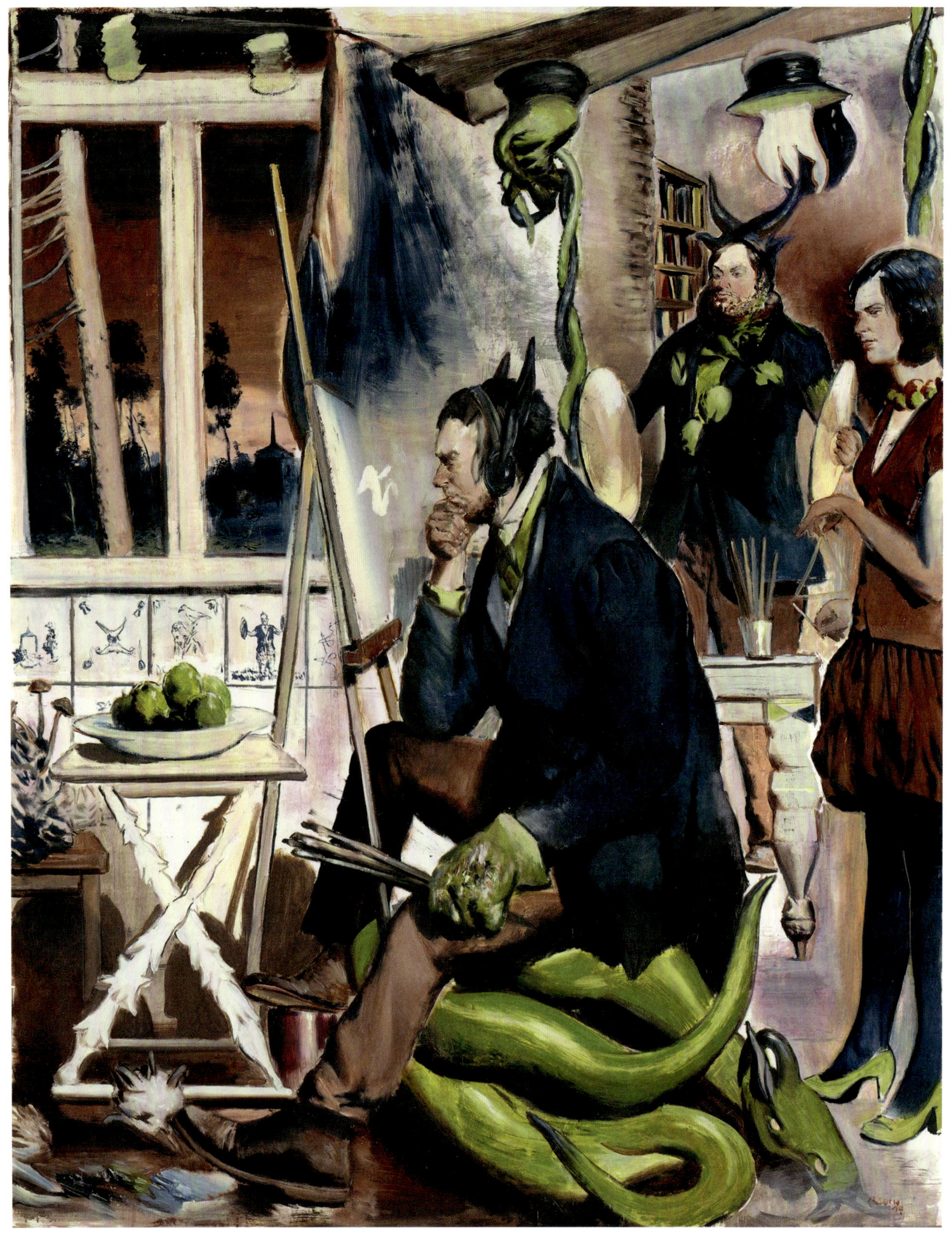

99. Die Erwartung 2017

Oil on paper
205.9 × 163.7 cm (81 × 64½ in)
Private collection

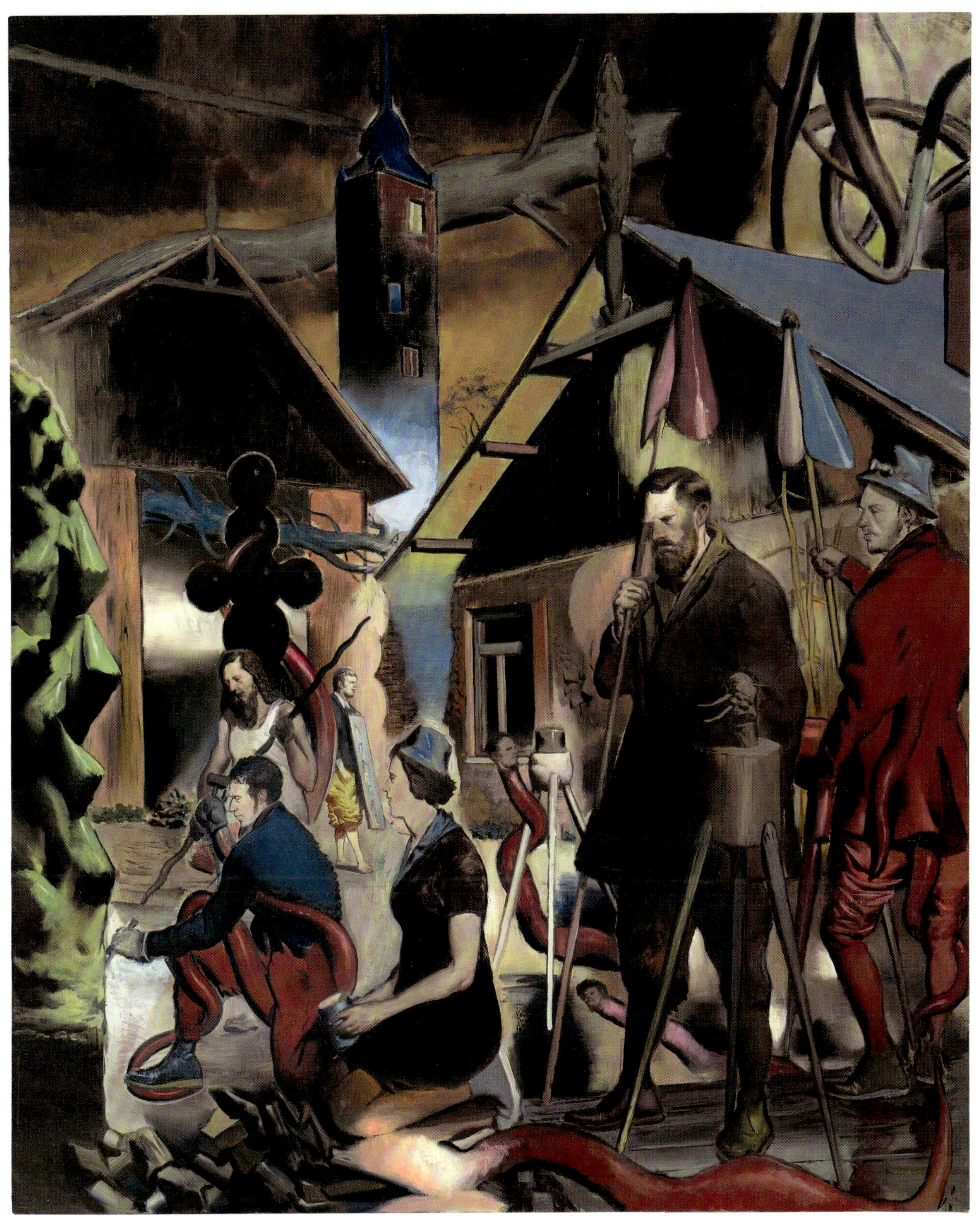

100. Der Durchstich 2017

Oil on canvas
300 × 250 cm (118¼ × 98½ in)
Sammlung HGN

Notes

1: In the Studio

This chapter owes a large debt of gratitude to Nicola Graef and Weltkino Filmverleih GmbH for allowing me to quote from and refer to her documentary on Neo Rauch and his practice, *Neo Rauch: Gefährten und Begleiter*, which was released in 2017.

1. From a conversation with Günther Oberhollenzer, *Hinter den Garten*, exh.cat., Essl Museum, Klosterneuburg bei Wien, 2011, p.215.
2. ibid, p.223.
3. From an interview with the *Huffington Post*, 12 August 2016.
4. From a conversation with Michael Glover at Neo Rauch's studio in the Spinnerei, Leipzig, 5 January 2018.
5. Nicola Graef, *Neo Rauch: Gefährten und Begleiter* (film), Weltkino Filmverleih GmbH, 2017.
6. ibid.
7. Neo Rauch in conversation with Ralph Keuning at a press conference to mark the opening of *Dromos* at the Museum de Fundatie, Zwolle, Netherlands, on 19 January 2018.
8. ibid.
9. ibid.
10. Friedrich Nietzsche, *Untimely Meditations*, trans. R.J. Hollingdale, Cambridge University Press, 1983, p.74.
11. From a conversation with Michael Glover at Neo Rauch's studio in the Spinnerei, Leipzig, 5 January 2018.
12. Graef, *Gefährten und Begleiter*.
13. ibid.
14. *Para*, exh.cat., Metropolitan Museum of Art, New York, 2007, p.64.
15. From an interview with the *Huffington Post*, 12 August 2016.
16. ibid.
17. ibid.
18. ibid.
19. From a conversation with Michael Glover at Neo Rauch's studio in the Spinnerie, Leipzig, 5 January 2018.

2: Emerginng from the GDR

1. Interview in *Elephant*, issue 30, spring 2017, p. 137.
2. Conversation between Michael Glover and Dr Alfred Weidinger at the Museum der bildenden Künste, Leipzig, 4 January 2018.
3. Interview in *Elephant*, issue 30, spring 2017, p.137.
4. ibid.
5. '. . . the centre cannot hold; / Mere anarchy is loosed upon the world . . .' from 'The Second Coming', W.B. Yeats, first published 1919.

3: Towards a Fabricated Credibility

1. Ernst Jünger, *In Stahlgewittern* (*Storm of Steel*), 1920, English trans. Michael Hofmann, Penguin/Allen Lane, London, 2003.
2. From a conversation with Michael Glover at Neo Rauch's studio in the Spinnerei, Leipzig, 5 January 2018.
3. See, for example, Noga Stiassny's account of Ingeborg Bachmann's influence upon Kiefer in: ef.huji.ac.il/sites/default/files/europe/files/noga_stiassny_for_web.pdf
4. From a conversation between Michael Glover and Anselm Kiefer at White Cube, Hoxton Square, on the occasion of the presentation of *Des Meeres und der Liebe Wellen*, 11 March–8 April 2011.
5. From a conversation with Michael Glover at Neo Rauch's studio in the Spinnerei, Leipzig, 5 January 2018.
6. From an interview with the *Huffington Post*, 12 August 2016
7. T.S. Eliot, 'The Three Voices of Poetry', 1953, delivered as the eleventh annual lecture of the National Book League in 1953, published for the NBL by Cambridge University Press and later collected in *On Poetry and Poets*, Faber & Faber, London, 1957.
8. From a conversation with Michael Glover at Neo Rauch's studio in the Spinnerei, Leipzig, 5 January 2018.
9. *Para* was exhibited at the Metropolitan Museum of Art, New York from 22 May to 23 September 2007, and then at the Max Ernst Museum Brühl/LVR from 28 October 2007 to 30 March 2008.
10. *Neo Rauch*, exh.cat., Museum der bildenden Künste, Leipzig, Bayerische Staatsgemäldesammlungen, Munich, 2011, p.97.
11. *Hanno Rauch & Neo Rauch: Vater und Sohn* was exhibited at the Grafikstiftung Neo Rauch in Aschersleben in 2016.
12. From a conversation with Michael Glover at Neo Rauch's studio in the Spinnerei, Leipzig, 5 January 2018.
13. My discussion of these two paintings and their impact upon visitors to the foundation owes a large debt of gratitude to a conversation with its director, Anka Ziefer, on 8 January 2018.

4: Back to the Future

1. All quotations from Neo Rauch in this chapter are extracted from our conversation at his studio on 5 January 2018 unless indicated otherwise.
2. Quoted in *Neo Rauch – Ein deutscher Maler*, 2007, a documentary by Rudij Bergmann, Zweitausendeins Edition, produced by Südwestrundfunks.
3. 'Painting . . . puts a spell on something, transfixes it by capturing it on canvas . . . The painting triumphs over the subject it addresses . . .' Quoted from a conversation with Günther Oberhollenzer, *Hinter den Garten*, exh.cat., Essl Museum, Klosterneuburg bei Wien, 2011, p.214.
4. Michael Glover in conversation with Frank Stella, *Independent*, 20 May 2003.
5. Quoted from a conversation between Neo Rauch and Wolfgang Büscher in Wolfgang Büscher, *Neo Rauch: Schilfland/Works on Paper*, Prestel, Munich, 2003, p.103.
6. Quoted from a conversation between Neo Rauch and Wolfgang Büscher on the evening of 26 November 2011 at the Villa Westerberge, in *Neo Rauch: Das grafische Werk / the Graphic Work, 1993–2012*, Hatje Cantz, Ostfildern, 2012, p.49.

Bibliography

Begegnung: An Encounter, Karl Blossfeldt & Neo Rauch, exh.cat., texts by Kerstin Wahala, Ann and Jürgen Wilde, Neo Rauch and Bernhart Schwenk, Grafikstiftung Neo Rauch, Aschersleben, 2015

Büscher, Wolfgang, *Neo Rauch: Schilfland/Works on Paper*, Prestel Verlag, Munich, Berlin, London, New York, 2009

"Dear Painter, paint me . . ." – painting the figure since late Picabia, exh.cat., with various texts, Centre Pompidou, Kunsthalle Wien, Schirn Kunsthalle Frankfurt, 2002

Gespenster Neo Rauch, exh.cat., EIGEN+ART, Leipzig, 2013

Hanno Rauch & Neo Rauch, Vater und Sohn, exh. cat., with texts by Kerstin Wahala, Hartwig Ebersbach and Neo Rauch, Grafikstiftung Neo Rauch, Aschersleben, 2016

Holzwarth, Hans Werner (ed.), *Rauch*, texts by Wolfgang Büscher, Harald Kunde and Gary Tinterow, Taschen, Cologne, 2010

Lauter, Rolf, *Neo Rauch*, exh.cat., Dresdner Bank AG, Frankfurt am Main, 1993

Little, Stephen, *Neo Rauch: Works 1994–2002*, exh.cat., Leipziger Volkszeitung Collection at Honolulu Academy of Arts, Berlin, 2005

Loy, Rosa and Neo Rauch, *Hinter den Garten*, exh.cat., texts by Prof. Karlheinz Essl, Bernhart Schwenk, Tilo Baumgärtel, and Neo Rauch and Rosa Loy in conversation with Günther Oberhollenzer, Essl Museum, Klosterneuburg bei Wien, 2011

Mössinger, Ingrid, *Neo Rauch: Abwägung*, Ein Gemälde für den Ratssaal im Neuen Rathaus in Chemnitz, Deutscher Kunstverlag, Berlin, 2013

Neo Rauch, exh.cat., text by Klaus Werner, Galerie Alvensleben, Munich, 1993

Neo Rauch, exh.cat., with texts by Martin Schick and Bazon Brock, Galerie der Stadt Backnang, 1998

Neo Rauch, exh.cat. on the occasion of Neo Rauch winning the Vincent Van Gogh Award for Contemporary Art, with texts by Harald Szeemann, Lynne Cooke and Daniel Birnbaum, Bonnefantenmuseum, Maastricht, 2002

Neo Rauch, exh.cat., with texts by Eduard Beaucamp, Philippe Dagen, Rose-Maria Gropp, Durs Grünbein, Andreas Platthaus, Peter-Klaus Schuster and Werner Spies, Museum Frieder Burda, Baden-Baden, 2011

Neo Rauch, exh.cat., Museum der bildenden Künste, Leipzig, Bayerische Staatsgemälde sammlungen, Munich, 2011

Neo Rauch: At the Well, exh.cat., texts by Norman Rosenthal and the Brothers Grimm, David Zwirner, New York, 2014

Neo Rauch auf Bötzow, exh.cat., with texts by Hans Georg Näder and Rudij Bergmann, Bötzow Berlin, 2015

Neo Rauch: Ausgewählte Werke/Selected Works 1993–2012, exh.cat., texts by Paul Dujardin, Etienne Davignon, Harald Kunde, BOZAR (Centre for Fine Arts), Brussels, 2013

Neo Rauch – Begleiter, exh.cat., forewords by Hans-Werner Schmidt and Bernhart Schwenk and various texts, Pinakothek der Moderne, Munich and Museum der bildenden Künste, Leipzig, 2010

Neo Rauch: Das grafische Werk/The Graphic Work (1993–2012), texts by Kerstin Wahala, Rudij Bergmann, Neo Rauch and Wolfgang Büscher, Hatje Cantz Verlag, Ostfildern, 2012

Neo Rauch Dromos Paintings 1993–2017, exh.cat., with texts by Ralph Keuning, Klaus Werner, Harald Kunde, Ulf Küster and Norman Rosenthal, Museum de Fundatie, Zwolle, Ostfildern, 2018

Neo Rauch »Manöver«, exh.cat., with texts by Harald Kunde, Neo Rauch and Klaus Werner, EIGEN+ART, Berlin, 1997

Neo Rauch – Neue Rollen. Bilder 1993–2006, exh. cat., with texts by Gottfried Boehm, Gernot Bohme, Holger Broeker, Markus Bruderlin, Wolfgang Büscher, Harald Kunde and Donald Kuspit, Kunstmuseum Wolfsburg, 2006

Neo Rauch: Renegaten, exh.cat., with a text by Christine Mehring, David Zwirner, New York, 2005

Neo Rauch: Der Zeitraum, exh.cat., with a text by Rudji Bergmann, EIGEN+ART, Leipzig, 2006

New Smoke: an anthology of poetry inspired by Neo Rauch paintings, introduction by John Yau, Off the Park Press, New York, 2009

Para, exh.cat., texts by Gary Tinterow, Werner Spies and other selected texts, Metropolitan Museum of Art, New York, and Max Ernst Museum Brühl/LVR, 2007

Peters, Olaf, *New Objectivity: Modern German Art in the Weimar Republic, 1919–1933*, Delmonico Books/Prestel, Munich, 2015

Rink, Arno, *Malerei und Zeichnung*, exh.cat., texts by Ulrich Ptak, Neo Rauch and Michael Triegel, Kunsthalle Rostock and Museum für Aktuelle Kunst – Sammlung Hurrle Durbach, 2015

Tuymans, Luc, *The Reality of the Lowest Rank – a vision of Central Europe*, Lannoo, Tielt, Belgium, 2006, pp 169–71

Biography

Born 1960 in Leipzig. Lives and works in Leipzig.

Education and Teaching

2009–2014
Honorary Professor, Hochschule für Grafik und Buchkunst, Leipzig

2005–2009
Professor, Hochschule für Grafik und Buchkunst, Leipzig

1993–1998
Assistant, Hochschule für Grafik und Buchkunst, Leipzig

1986–1990
Master Student, with Professor Bernhard Heisig, Hochschule für Grafik und Buchkunst, Leipzig

1981–1986
Student, with Arno Rink, Hochschule für Grafik und Buchkunst, Leipzig

Exhibitions

2018
Neo Rauch: Aus dem Boden, Des Moines Art Center, Iowa, USA (itinerary: The Drawing Center, New York)
Neo Rauch, Dromos Schilderijen 1993–2017, Museum de Fundatie, Zwolle, the Netherlands (catalogue)
Neo Rauch & Rosa Loy, Grafikstiftung Neo Rauch, Aschersleben, Germany (joint exhibition)

2017
Arno Rink & Neo Rauch, Grafikstiftung Neo Rauch, Aschersleben, Germany (joint exhibition)
Hanno & Neo Rauch Vater und Sohn, Grafikstiftung Neo Rauch, Aschersleben, Germany

2016
Neo Rauch: Rondo, David Zwirner, London, UK
Hanno & Neo Rauch: Vater und Sohn/Father and Son, Grafikstiftung Neo Rauch, Aschersleben, Germany (joint exhibition)
Neo Rauch auf Bötzow Berlin, Bötzow Berlin, Germany
Neo Rauch, Galerie EIGEN+ART, Berlin, Germany

2015
Begegnung/An Encounter: Karl Blossfeldt & Neo Rauch, Grafikstiftung Neo Rauch, Aschersleben, Germany (catalogue) (joint exhibition)
Rosa Loy – Neo Rauch: Perlmutt. Eigene Arbeiten aus der Sammlung beider Künstler, Fotofoyer, Zwickau, Germany (organised by Freunde Aktueller Kunst, Zwickau, Germany) (joint exhibition)

2014
Neo Rauch: At the Well, David Zwirner, New York, USA (catalogue)
Neo Rauch: The Graphic Work/Das grafische Werk – Part 3, Grafikstiftung Neo Rauch, Aschersleben, Germany
Neo Rauch: The Graphic Work/Das grafische Werk – Picture & Book, Grafikstiftung Neo Rauch, Aschersleben, Germany

2013
Neo Rauch: Gespenster, Galerie EIGEN+ART, Leipzig, Germany (catalogue)
Neo Rauch: The Graphic Work/Das grafische Werk – Part 2, Grafikstiftung Neo Rauch, Aschersleben, Germany
Neo Rauch: The Obsession of the Demiurge. Selected Works 1993–2012, BOZAR – Centre for Fine Arts, Brussels, Belgium (catalogue)

2012
Neo Rauch: The Graphic Work/Das grafische Werk – Part 1, Grafikstiftung Neo Rauch, Aschersleben, Germany (catalogue)
Neo Rauch: Abwägung / Rosa Loy" Gravitation, Kunstsammlungen Chemnitz, Germany (catalogue and exhibition publication) (joint exhibition)

2011
Neo Rauch: Begleiter. The Myth of Realism, Zachęta National Gallery of Art, Warsaw, Poland (catalogue)
Neo Rauch: Heilstätten, David Zwirner, New York, USA
Neo Rauch, Museum Frieder Burda, Baden-Baden, Germany (catalogue and exhibition publication)
Neo Rauch and Rosa Loy: Hinter den Garten, Essl Museum, Klosterneuburg bei Wien, Austria (catalogue) (joint exhibition)

2010
Neo Rauch: Begleiter, Museum der bildenden Künste, Leipzig, Germany, and Pinakothek der Moderne, Munich, Germany (catalogue)
Neo Rauch, German Ambassador's Residence, Palais Beauharnais, Paris, France

2009
City of Heroes: London Leipzig Week. Neo Rauch, German Ambassador's Residence,London, UK
Neo Rauch: Schilfland, Galerie EIGEN+ART, Berlin, Germany (catalogue)

2008
Neo Rauch, David Zwirner, New York, USA (catalogue)

2007
Neo Rauch: para, Metropolitan Museum of Art, New York, USA (itinerary: Max Ernst Museum, Brühl, Germany) (catalogue)

2006
Neo Rauch: Der Zeitraum, Galerie EIGEN+ART, Leipzig, Germany (catalogue)
Neo Rauch, Musée d'art contemporain de Montréal, Canada (catalogue)
Neo Rauch: Neue Rollen, Kunstmuseum Wolfsburg, Germany (itinerary: Galerie Rudolfinum, Prague) (catalogue)

2005
Neo Rauch, Centro de Arte Contemporáneo de Málaga, Spain (catalogue)
Neo Rauch: Renegaten, David Zwirner, New York, USA (catalogue)
Neo Rauch: Works 1994–2002: The Leipziger Volkszeitung Collection, Honolulu Academy of Arts, Hawaii, USA (catalogue)

2004
Neo Rauch: Arbeiten auf Papier/Works on Paper 2003–2004, Albertina, Vienna, Austria (catalogue)

2003
Currents 90: Neo Rauch, St Louis Art Museum, Missouri, USA (exhibition brochure)

2002
Neo Rauch, Bonnefantenmuseum, Maastricht, Netherlands (catalogue)
Neo Rauch, David Zwirner, New York, USA
Neo Rauch, Galerie EIGEN+ART, Berlin, Germany

2001
Neo Rauch: Zeichnungen und Gemälde aus der Sammlung Deutsche Bank, Mannheimer Kunstverein, Mannheim, Germany (itinerary: Neues Museum Weserburg, Bremen, Germany; Deutsche Guggenheim Museum, Berlin, Germany; Douglas Hyde Gallery, Dublin, Ireland; International Cultural Centre, Kraków, Poland) (catalogue published in 2000)

2000
Neo Rauch, David Zwirner, New York, USA
Neo Rauch, Galerie EIGEN+ART, Leipzig, Germany
Neo Rauch: Randgebiet, Galerie für Zeitgenössische Kunst Leipzig, Germany (itinerary: Haus der Kunst, Munich, Germany; Kunsthalle Zürich, Switzerland) (catalogue)

1998
Neo Rauch, Galerie der Stadt Backnang, Germany (catalogue)
Neo Rauch, Galerie EIGEN+ART, Berlin, Germany

1997
Neo Rauch: Kunstpreis der Leipziger Volkszeitung 1997, Museum der bildenden Künste, Leipzig, Germany (catalogue)
Neo Rauch: Manöver, Galerie EIGEN+ART, Leipzig, Germany (catalogue)

1995
Maren Roloff and Neo Rauch: Echoes, Goethe House, New York, USA (catalogue) (joint exhibition)
Neo Rauch: Marineschule, Overbeck-Gesellschaft, Lübeck, Germany (catalogue)
Neo Rauch, Dresdner Bank, Leipzig, Germany
Neo Rauch, Galerie EIGEN+ART, Leipzig, Germany

1994
Neo Rauch, Projekt Galerie, Kunstverein Elsterpark e.V., Leipzig, Germany

1993
Neo Rauch, Dresdner Bank, Frankfurt am Main, Germany
Neo Rauch, Galerie Alvensleben, Munich, Germany (catalogue)
Neo Rauch, Galerie EIGEN+ART, Leipzig, Germany
Neo Rauch, Galerie VOXXX, Chemnitz, Germany
Neo Rauch, Imkabinett Galerie, Berlin, Germany

1991
Neo Rauch, Galerie Schwind, Frankfurt am Main, Germany (catalogue)
Neo Rauch and Klaus Killich. Das Gewitter, Galerie am Kraftwerk, Leipzig, Germany (joint exhibition)

1989

Neo Rauch, Galerie am Thomaskirchhof, Leipzig, Germany (catalogue)

Selected Public Collections

Albertinum, Dresden
The Broad, Los Angeles
Carnegie Museum of Art, Pittsburgh
De La Cruz Collection Contemporary Art Space, Miami
Denver Art Museum, Denver, Colorado
Essl Museum, Klosterneuburg bei Wien, Austria
Fondation Beyeler, Riehen, Switzerland
Friedrich Christian Flick Collection, Hamburger Bahnhof – Museum für Gegenwart, Berlin
Galerie für Zeitgenössische Kunst Leipzig
Gemeentemuseum, The Hague
Hall Art Foundation, Reading, Vermont
Hamburger Kunsthalle, Hamburg
Kunsthalle HGN, Duderstadt, Germany
Kunsthalle zu Kiel, Germany
Kunstmuseum Walter im Glaspalast, Augsburg, Germany
Kunstmuseum Wolfsburg, Germany
Kunstsammlung Deutscher Bundestag, Bonn
Kunstsammlungen Chemnitz, Germany
Lindenau-Museum Altenburg, Germany
Ludwig Forum für Internationale Kunst, Aachen, Germany
The Metropolitan Museum of Art, New York
Museum der bildenden Künste, Leipzig
Museum of Contemporary Art, Los Angeles
Museum Frieder Burda, Baden-Baden, Germany
Museum Ludwig, Cologne
The Museum of Modern Art, New York
National Gallery of Canada, Ontario
Neuberger Neuman Collection, New York
Pinakothek der Moderne, Munich
Rubell Family Collection, Miami
Sammlung der Deutsche Bank, Frankfurt am Main
Sammlung Goetz, Munich
Sammlung der Landesbank Hessen-Thüringen, Frankfurt am Main
Sammlung der Landesbank Sachsen, Leipzig
Sammlung Zeitgenössischer Kunst der Bundesrepublik Deutschland, Bonn
San Francisco Museum of Modern Art, San Francisco
Solomon R. Guggenheim Museum, New York
Stedelijk Museum, Amsterdam
UBS Art Collection

Acknowledgements

This book could not have been written without the unstinting support and generosity of many people: Neo Rauch, Rosa Loy and Sylvia Meinel at the Spinnerei studio in Leipzig; Gerd 'Judy' Lybke, Elke Hannemann, and all at EIGEN+ ART in Leipzig and Berlin; Nicola Graef; Doro Globus, James Green and the research team at David Zwirner gallery in London and New York; John Yau; Barry Schwabsky; Anka Ziefer; Anne-Kathrin Sturm; Dr Alfred Weidinger; Max Hollein – who first brought me face to face with Neo's work at the Schirn Kunsthalle, Frankfurt; Ralph Keuning; Hilary Davies; Cathy Johns at the Royal College of Art in London; Ryan Mosley; and Ruth Dupré.

The publisher gratefully acknowledges the generous support of David Zwirner gallery.

Image Credits

Index

Page numbers in *italics* refer to illustrations
Titles of paintings are for works by Rauch unless followed by the name of the artist in brackets.

First published in 2019 by Lund Humphries

Lund Humphries
Office 3, Book House
261A City Road
London
EC1V 1JX
www.lundhumphries.com

ISBN: 978-1-84822-293-9

A Cataloguing-in-Publication record for this book is available from the British Library.

Copy-edited by Ian MacDonald
Designed by Oliver Keen
Set in Custodia (Fred Smeijers)
Printed in Italy

Frontispiece: Neo Rauch in his studio, photograph by Uwe Walter
Cover: *Blutsbrüder*, 2017, oil on canvas, 300 × 250 cm (118¼ × 98½ in), Collection of Michael Wilkinson, New Orleans.